TONI MORRISON'S FICTION

CRITICAL STUDIES IN BLACK LIFE AND CULTURE
VOLUME 30
GARLAND REFERENCE LIBRARY OF THE HUMANITIES
VOLUME 1602

CRITICAL STUDIES IN BLACK LIFE AND CULTURE

C. JAMES TROTMAN, *General Editor*

Toni Morrison's Fiction
Contemporary Criticism

Edited by
David L. Middleton

Garland Publishing, Inc.
New York and London
1997

Library of Congress Cataloging-in-Publication Data

Toni Morrison's fiction : contemporary criticism / edited by David L.
  Middleton.
          p.   cm. — (Critical studies in Black life and culture ; v. 30) (Gar-
land reference library of the humanities ; v. 1602)
      Includes bibliographical references and index.
      ISBN 0-8153-0869-8 (alk. paper)
      1. Morrison, Toni—Criticism and interpretation.   2. Women and litera-
ture—United States—History—20th century.   3. Afro-American women in
literature.   4. Afro-Americans in literature.   I. Middleton, David L.
II. Series: Critical studies in Black life and culture ; v. 30.   III. Series: Garland reference library of the humanities ; vol. 1602.
PS3563.08749Z915   1997
813'.54—dc20   96-43555
                                                                      CIP

Printed on acid-free, 250-year-life paper
Manufactured in the United States of America

GENERAL EDITOR'S PREFACE

Critical Studies in Black Life and Culture is a series devoted to original, book-length studies of African American developments. Written by well-qualified scholars, the series is interdisciplinary and global, interpreting tendencies and themes wherever African Americans have left their mark. The ideal reader for the series is one who appreciates the combined use of scholarly inquiry with a focus on a people whose roots stretch around the world.

Critical Studies is also a window to that world. The series holds out the promise of fulfilling the ideal of all scholarship by uncovering and disseminating the sources of a people's life-line. In relationship to this series, the untranslated Ghanaan narratives offering the earliest perspectives on African life and thought illustrate a scholarly need in this area. If and when they are published, we might have a clearer view of the past and of the consciousness of blacks in antiquity. The clarity would almost certainly contribute to a more detailed basis for understanding what the roots of "culture" and "civilization" are for African Americans in particular and for all of us in general.

Sometimes, however, the scholarly works published in Critical Studies remind us that the windows have not always been open or, if they were, the shades were pulled down, making it difficult if not impossible to see in or out. The series reaffirms forerunners who, by talent and determination, refused to be unseen or unheard: Phillis Wheatley, Anna Julia Cooper, Frederick Douglass, William E.B. DuBois, Zora Neale Hurston, Langston Hughes, and Ralph Ellison. They laid the aesthetic and intellectual foundation for Ralph Bunche, Albert Luthuli, Desmond Tutu, Martin Luther King, Jr., Wole Soyinka, and Toni Morrison to be awarded Nobel prizes. In addition to individual achievements, the outstanding examples of organized and permanent group life are to be found in the historic black church, black colleges and universities, and the NAACP; none of these, I might add, has received a comprehensive historical treatment, leaving sizeable gaps in any effort to conceptualize a total picture of multicultural America.

All of these achievements suggest a promising future in African American developments, pointing to a great deal of activity—some from those who have successfully peeked around pulled-down shades to look out, while others have found ways to peep in. Critical Studies in Black Life and Culture is committed to publishing the best scholarship on African American life.

C. James Trotman
West Chester University
1994

For Mary

Contents

Reading from Without and Within: Critical Argument and the Study of Toni Morrison

Now that Toni Morrison has been singled out by the world literary community and honored with the Nobel Prize, one expects her already very visible fiction to take its rightful place in the canon, hence to appear in standard American literature courses and on secondary school reading lists. Her individual texts have always been contested sites for general readers as well as academic critics, and the consequence of large numbers of persons thinking of her works as part of mainline American fiction has been an amazing diversity in interpretation. Whereas audiences were in the past drawn by various personal curiosities to Morrison herself as author and woman and source of meaning, now they look to the text as cultural artifact, as expression of ideology, or—when the medium is presumed to be the message—to the weave of language as symbol system. Upon occasion, even the reader her/himself becomes the foregrounded topic, as we shall see below.

Race (or, rather, *color*, as Albert Murray insists in *The Omni-Americans,* his persuasive argument about making honest, accurate distinctions) remains a substantial field of inquiry for critics, partly because of Morrison's own continual reinforcement of the fact that it shapes in central ways all she does. Nevertheless, interpreters coming to the novels with divergent interests and theorizing those works anew are making innumerable creative suggestions for how to read Morrison freshly and with integrity. Previously unremarked philosophical and ethical constructs in the novels are now set forward with increasing frequency. Connections between her work and other cultures and cultural phenomena than African American are explored as ways to stress universality in the fiction.

Morrison's creating within or in many ways "off of" mainstream literary tradition fascinates her critics as a means of identifying how her fiction is unique. Gender issues of all kinds mark the landscape of Morrison criticism as readers claim her texts for analyses of psychoanalytic meaning and for representations of the body and for theological speculations.

Perhaps one of the richest byproducts of this author/reader/text "process triangle" has been the recent flurry of publication related to the metafictional significance of her work. The same fascination with self-reflexivity that draws readers into Shakespeare's plays looking for the senses in which those pieces are "about" theater (where "playing" becomes both a metaphor as well as a method) now inspires readings of Morrison's fiction which assert that the fiction concerns primarily the "process" of making fiction.

This particular collection of essays aims to revise how we read Morrison's fiction but does not propose ultimately to shift attention away from the primary material itself to any of the numerous secondary contextualizations of it. As a whole, the following 15 essays, chosen and arranged to provide a comprehensive overview of Morrison's entire body of work, ask the reader to resist inferring the author's intentions (however strongly those may be stated in interviews), and instead to engage wholeheartedly in the ongoing interpretive struggle represented by arguments that stand in dialectical tension with conventional interpretations and even, in several cases, with each other. From such tension comes new insight and consequently intellectual progress.

At their best, these collected essays should present new ways of encountering what have become, for nearly all of us, familiar texts. Perhaps by verifying the craftsmanship and the highly controlled artistry of Morrison as author they will also rebut conclusively Stanley Crouch's assault on her as a writer with "no serious artistic vision or real artistic integrity" (*New Yorker*, November 6, 1995, p. 96). Crouch originally delivered that judgment in "Aunt Medea," in *The New Republic,* October 19, 1987, and then in the collection, *Notes of a Hanging Judge*, Oxford University Press, 1990.

Leading off the section of the book on *The Bluest Eye* and by implication setting a tone for the collection is Lynne Tirrell's philosophical inquiry into the value of storytelling. Tirrell's analysis of narrative foreshadows the recurring preoccupation with fiction as art running through other selections. Part of Tirrell's assessment opens up the moral implications of *The Bluest Eye* for those fictional figures who generate the story. Yet Tirrell also suggests that the moral act of storytelling, so creative, psychologically constructive, and survival-enhancing for Claudia MacTeer, the first-person narrator, simultaneously engages the reader as well as the author on the level of their being moral agents. While Claudia balances her personal perspective against another that is more objective (one moral perspective emerges), the reader too must hypothesize and interpret, and Morrison as author launches herself into what will be a continuing struggle in her writing over issues related to narrative authority.

In *Jazz*, which appeared 22 years after *The Bluest Eye*, narrative authority becomes all important, as we shall see below.

"Tracking 'The Look' in the Novels of Toni Morrison" is Ed Guerrero's dense study of gender and culture in Morrison's first five novels. "The Look," or "the gaze," is a function of patriarchal culture and has the effect of fetishizing and/or commodifying women. Morrison extends the typical construct shaped by the gaze by adding "whiteness" and "poorness" to the primary consideration of "womanness." Guerrero demonstrates in a sustained way how the black characters internalize dominant values related to race, class, and gender and construct themselves accordingly, almost always with disastrous results. The whole MacTeer family assumes a sense of inferiority and ugliness, or, as happens in the case of Pecola, experiences the ultimate negation and totally disappears. Guerrero's reading of Morrison is as moral in its implications as Tirrell's, for he shows us Toni Morrison as a charged critic and reformer writing in ways that agitate readers and heighten their awareness even if the fiction stops short of programatically demanding the dominant culture get over itself and change.

Closely related in terms of critical objectives is Timothy B. Powell's "The Struggle to Depict the Black Figure on the White Page." Like Guerrero, Powell mounts a cultural critique. Literary tradition in Western culture, particularly the symbol system of light and dark, with all the negative archetypes associated with dark, presents the African American writer with an enormously difficult challenge to create positive, whole, affirmative characters. Arguing semiotically as well as historically, Powell applauds Morrison for having succeeded triumphantly in this task with the body of her work completed during the 1970s. What she does with allusion, with unique characterization, with experimental structures exploiting oral narrative strategy is, in effect, to create a "(w)holy black text" and thus a new concept of reality identifiably different from that produced by Western phenomenology. Powell's punning use of "(w)hole" credits Morrison with countering the negation implicit in traditional archetypal assumptions (symbology) and in sociological practice (the gaze) through imaginative, original fiction-making that is both complete and spiritual. The epitome of her concept of black (w)holeness and identity is Morrison's *Sula* and *Song of Solomon*. So thoroughly associative is Powell's essay in its method that it's apt to have a decided ripple effect for readers, leading them outward from the primary text at hand to thoughtful consideration of a range of other materials.

Sula can be read as an explicit challenge to traditional male-centered ideology. Diane Gillespie and Missy Dehn Kubitschek, drawing on the work of women psychologists at the Stone Center at Wellesley College and on the explorations of literary critics who turn more and more frequently to women's fiction for evidence, offer a reading of *Sula* that demands one use female experience as the central paradigm. In *Sula,* the focus is on the inner dimensions of women's experience; women's voices tell the story, and women's psychological conceptions locate and order the crises represented. In particular, Gillespie and Kubitschek explore in their essay the relational senses in which the female experience of community structures the book. Helene and Nel, the Wright women, are set in contrast with three generations of nontraditional characters, Eva, Hanna, and Sula, the Peace women. Then the critics examine Nell and Sula intensely as "selves in relation" to each other who are in the process of developing into "selves in community." Conceptually key to this essay is the notion of empathy and the much-remarked-upon theme of friendship between women. However, other critical essays that deal with friendship—and such are numerous in the *Sula* literature—lack the theoretical base evident throughout "Who Cares? Women-Centered Psychology in *Sula.*"

David Cowart takes as his point of departure the commonly-heard suggestion that Morrison may be read most accurately in racial terms and offers instead an analysis based on literary history. In "Faulkner and Joyce in Morrison's *Song of Solomon*," Cowart argues that racial readings narrow one's focus unnecessarily. With reference to what he calls "a larger tradition" of Western writing generally, Cowart repositions *Song of Solomon* in the history of letters as "literature," not "black literature." Morrison adapts the central imagery of flight creatively from James Joyce, according to Cowart's findings. Furthermore, she constructs in her own unique fashion the profound web of associations related to naming by reconceiving William Faulkner's practices. In the end, *Song of Solomon* looms as a singular instance of fiction writing, belonging entirely to Morrison's consciousness, yet asking to be read within the framework of *Bildungsroman* tradition.

Gay Wilentz' work stands in immediate opposition to Cowart's. Her "Civilizations Underneath: African Heritage as Cultural Discourse in Toni Morrison's *Song of Solomon*" affirms the necessity of seeing Morrison as creating clearly from within the tradition of black storytelling and writing. Another example of historical criticism, "Civilizations Underneath" looks at the author's use of oral tradition as her technique for espousing "tribal" values, such as her Afrocentric concept of community. What Morrison wants, according to Wilentz' study of intentionality, is to make her readers participatory, and, she claims, by being thus involved the reader will necessarily discover the shaping influence of that "civilization underneath" the visibly present European one, the fundamental African heritage underpinning modern black consciousness.

Ashraf H.A. Rushdy, like several other commentators on Morrison's work in this collection, considers that the novels are highly interrogative. What they interrogate are the characters' self-knowledge and memory. Rushdy's psychoanalytic approach to narrative construction is based on an analysis of "primal scenes" in the fiction, "primal scenes" being a concept he derives by analyzing Wordsworth's notion of primal sympathy and Freud's notion of "constructed" fantasies. Morrison uses primal scenes, not primal fantasies, according to Rushdy, and in so doing keeps her prose focused on the duality of events as those are constructed. Memory, in *Sula* and *Song of Solomon* and *Beloved*, is personal and also communal property, and certainly it is most generative when shared.

Lauren Lepow's "Paradise Lost and Found: Dualism and Edenic Myth in Toni Morrison's *Tar Baby*" is a feminist critique of the book. By setting the criticism in a philosophical context, Lepow demonstrates that traditional dualistic thinking is seen by women theologians as negative in its necessary espousal of authoritarianism and sexism. For Morrison, then, confronting and overcoming dualism becomes a liberating way to grow beyond the traditional and confining dogma of sin and redemption. In *Tar Baby*, Morrison creates new myths by invoking Miltonic themes and structures but doing so critically. She subverts the authority of the old misogynist of English literature by shaping a story in which knowledge is not sin and original sin becomes the failure to discover one's own true nature. Reclaiming that nature, insisting on the authority of the self, *Tar Baby* articulates the essence of the feminist theology of wholeness. Jadine must be alone in the end. Neither sex nor romance is any part of what the book says she's about, finally, which is "self-creation and self-perpetuation against the odds of the dualistic world."

Sandra Pouchet Paquet, by employing a folkloric approach in "The Ancestor as Foundation in *Their Eyes Were Watching God* and *Tar Baby*," stresses the importance of reconnecting with one's ancient culture to achieve and then maintain psychic and spiritual health. For Janie Crawford, protagonist of Zora Neale Hurston's novel, the spiritual malaise that afflicts modern African Americans because of their upward mobility is counteracted by her discovery of ancestral roots. Yet Paquet's comparative analysis of Jadine Childs, Janie's literary descendant and namesake, reveals the extent to which *Tar Baby* scrutinizes the whole concept of the ancestor as foundation. Jadine has lost touch with her culture and suffers from alienation as a consequence. Like the powerfully presented Son, she needs to rediscover her fundamental being by learning and living the myths of the Isle de Chevalier. Whether she is capable of or interested in doing so remains doubtful, however, and the unresolved tension between Son and Jadine reflects Paquet's conclusion about rifts between the self and community in contemporary African American life.

"*Beloved* and the New Apocalypse" by Susan Bowers uses literary history and mythology as a means of assessing the value of apocalyptic writing as a context within which to see the book. Although the novel is "apocalyptic" in the traditional sense of being an "unveiling," African Americans share a culturally shifted sense of the meaning of the word. For white readers, the term points forward, and, by generating in them positive anticipation, excites the belief that the coming end will realize humankind's great hope. For black readers, whose history makes them feel excluded from this kind of millennial anticipation, the sense of glorious expectation resides in recovering what has been lost to them as a result of the diaspora that overwhelmed them. Any notion of apocalyptic struggle, then, involves a battle in the African American psyche, where racial memory has been taken hostage. Thus the battle for characters in *Beloved* is over "rememory," and hence recovery of their human dignity. Violence is the mode of the novel, as of course it is of the apocalyptic genre, yet acceptance of and release from psychological trauma are its transforming results.

For David Lawrence, another critic engaged in studying the motif of memory that pervades *Beloved*, both psychic and cultural considerations predominate just as they do in Bowers' analysis. "Fleshly Ghosts and Ghostly Flesh: The Word and the Body in *Beloved*," presents Lawrence's argument about the multiple significations of memory. In fact, Lawrence demonstrates, both memory and forgetting can be enslaving, so they must be delicately balanced. Lawrence works closely and carefully with the text to untangle the several meanings of Beloved both as fleshly, physical character, and as word/thought/deed borne forward destructively from the oppressive past. Control over one's own body is, in Lawrence's view, directly related to the authority one has over discourse in the book, and both Sethe and Paul D must undergo life-affirming rituals that involve language before they can be free within themselves and maintain the authority necessary to relate meaningfully to each other and their community.

Ann-Janine Morey, "Margaret Atwood and Toni Morrison: Reflections on Postmodernism and the Study of Religion and Literature," also uses *Beloved* as a platform to interrogate language. The traditional language of religion is for Morey a primary target, but in addition she interrogates all concepts of absolute authority and the egocentricity of man. Morey wants her readers to recognize Morrison's importance, along with other female authors such as Atwood, Mary Gordon, and Louise Erdrich, for a renewed study of the relation between religion and literature. Because writing by women typically questions traditional religious ideas and challenges conventional canonical universes, it has been systematically marginalized. Now, though, a book such as *Beloved* can be linked with Atwood's *Surfacing* and together those fictions are capable of promoting creative revisions of fundamental notions of boundary and authority. *Beloved* employs a narrative couched expressly in feminine concepts of bodily life, of sexual love, or time and memory, and each of these concepts is imaged in the work (also in *Surfacing*) in terms of water. Thus what Rushdy contextualizes in psychoanalytic terms and Bowers in apocalyptic ones, Morey treats along gender lines. For her, feminist postmodernism intentionally threatens the whole concept of a "phallocratic literary canon," in particular by challenging traditional language and ontological structures. So one of the main issues of *Beloved* is the way in which Morrison shows readers that the so-called "master tongue" is very much subverted because of its potential for domination and degradation.

A shift in method is evident in Barbara Williams Lewis' "The Function of Jazz in Toni Morrison's *Jazz*." Lewis raises issues of intertextuality by relating the novel to analogous art forms. She argues that the novel is composed like a version of "jazz literature" in that it takes primary qualities of jazz music (its flexibility of rhythm and time, its inventiveness of structure, its voices "jamming" on a central theme) and applies those ideas to the writing of prose fiction. Like other critics represented in this collection, Lewis engages theoretical concepts related to narrative, but her particular take on the stubbornly mysterious narrator of *Jazz* leads this culturally inclined reader to conclude that the uncertainty of that narrative voice is one more way in which the book remains "unresolved" in an appropriate, even calculated, jazzlike fashion. And, Lewis maintains, the reality of jazz is not only present as a thematic element in the novel but also serves as a metaphor for "conditions of life among migratory Negroes," an argument about the demographic shift of blacks from the South to the urban North which she unpacks in her presentation.

The facts of and the fallout from that population shift preoccupy Deborah Barnes, whose cultural studies approach applies the theory of commensalism to Morrison's fiction and produces the essay, "Movin' on up:The Madness of Migration in Toni Morrison's *Jazz*." Barnes analyzes the historical facts of migration as well as the representations of it in popular culture—particularly television shows—to present the dislocation experienced by blacks in their movement north to what was presumed to be socio-economic freedom. Joe and Violet Trace, who serve as microcosmic examples of the success achieved by large numbers of blacks, earned social mobility and moved upward through increasingly desirable neighborhoods in the City. Yet their success, invested as it is in literal and metaphoric mobility with all its consequent isolation, proves hollow because bought at the cost of cultural connectedness. The Traces, materially comfortable but melancholy and desolate at heart, are alienated without their community. Their hope lies in the ability to "rememory" their culturally rooted pasts.

Katherine J. Mayberry, in "The Problem of Narrative in Toni Morrison's *Jazz*," asks readers to step back from traditional interpretation problems involving character or context or language and to think rather about the relation between narrative and ideology. For Mayberry, the narrative function in all of Morrison's work is ambivalent not because it is derived from African American forms which are oral and open-ended but because of the capability of dominant culture to co-opt narrative and use it to inscribe hegemonic values. Toni Morrison's are nontraditional forms, though. She customarily works to give power back to historically silenced figures, and a novel such as *Jazz* may even "indict" the very concept of narrative authority, when, for example, its principal unnamed narrator self-consciously draws attention to the impossibility of her own knowledge, in the process granting imaginative power to the reader, whose authority ultimately controls the work. Finally, Mayberry's work becomes not only an analysis of narrativity in *Jazz* but a study of the function of criticism as well.

The essayists here presented wrangle with one another, and their assertions often clash. Such cacophany serves progressive ends, however, because, to use Jane Smiley's phrase, beneath that dissonance we may also hear "the sound of a new world being born" (speech at Simpson College, cited in *Chronicle of Higher Education*, June 7, 1996, B3). A new imaginative world, that is. Diverse in method and purpose, these studies agree completely on the importance of Toni Morrison's work.

Together they affirm the range of Morrison's ambition, the reach of her craftsmanship, and the real power—affective and intellectual—of her achievement.

PART 1

The Bluest Eye

Storytelling and Moral Agency

Lynne Tirrell

In fine, he gave himself up so wholly to the reading of Romances, that a-Nights he would pore on 'til 'twas Day, and a-Days he would read 'til 'twas Night; and thus by sleeping little, and reading much, the Moisture of his Brain was exhausted to that Degree, that at last he lost the Use of Reason. A world of disorderly Notions, pick'd out of his Books, crowded into his Imagination; and now his Head was full of nothing but Inchantments, Quarrels, Battles, Challenges, Wounds, Complaints, Amours, Torments, and abundance of Stuff and Impossibilities; insomuch, that all the Fables and fantastical Tales which he read, seem'd to him now as true as the most authentick Histories.

Cervantes, Don Quixote

The dangers of excessive reading are nowhere more brilliantly portrayed than in Cervantes's tale of the tragicomic *Don Quixote*.[1] A storyteller himself, Cervantes here displays the usual belief that if we want to learn about life from books, we should turn to history, not fiction. This bias runs so deep that even some novelists tend to justify fiction on the grounds of its inherent veracity; that is, they tend to make fiction a form of history. Henry James, for instance, has said that "the only reason for the existence of a novel is that it does attempt to represent life."[2] Some writers, less concerned with justifying fiction than James is, would nevertheless echo Virginia Woolf's claim that "fiction is like a spider's web, attached ever so lightly, perhaps, but still attached to life at all four corners."[3]

Quixote's world is attached to life, at least to its moral dimension. If we cannot draw a sharp distinction between fiction and history, and there is reason to think that we can't, then we'll have to look elsewhere for the significance of Quixote's situation. Quixote is good but misguided; his problems are epistemic but moral. Usually we ask how Quixote went so wrong, how he came to be confused about the nature of the world. I propose to ask how he went so *right*. After all, even though he seems silly, we give him credit for moral goodness. Even those who do not praise Quixote at least see him as a moral agent. Since participation in the practice of storytelling seems to be a key to Quixote's situation, and since we each may face the danger of becoming a crazed contemporary of Quixote, we must inquire into the moral value of storytelling itself.

I. STORYTELLING

It is useful to begin with an understanding of what a story is, and how it is distinct from other forms of discourse. I join Robert Scholes in taking a story to be "a narrative with a certain very specific syntactic shape (beginning-middle-end or situation-transformation-situation) and with a subject matter which allows for or encourages the projection of human values upon this material."[4] A story has a structure, and this structure is dynamic.

The question "why should we tell stories?" lends itself to several interpretations. Practical answers typically explain the value of stories and literature for increasing our knowledge of the world and our skill at perceiving the world.[5] Moral answers typically tend to focus on the content of the stories as providing moral examples. I know of no answer to this question that explains what narrative, particularly fiction, contributes to our becoming moral agents.[6] Accordingly, the question I address is whether storytelling is necessary to moral agency.

Since storytelling involves both a teller and a listener, our basic question breaks down into two: Why should anyone tell a story? Why should anyone listen to a story? The reasons for telling may be quite different than the reasons for listening.

Storytelling as a practice includes both constructing one's own story and performing that story or a story made up by someone else. When considering the teller of a story, I am not concerned with the performance of the story but rather with its construction, so I'll speak as if stories are always original. This isn't meant to deny the Brothers Grimm but simply to focus on the more difficult case. In telling an original story, one articulates what one thinks about a set of events, a particular character, a set of characters, an issue, a problem, or whatever. One has one's say. In addition, one presents a perspective, a character, and a set of judgments that delimit each.

In listening to a story, on the other hand, one confronts a perspective, a character, and a set of judgments. (For the listener, it may not matter whether the story is the teller's own or a "stock" story; what surely does matter is whether the listener has heard it before.) Sympathy and imagination help the listener to try that perspective on for size, while reason and comparison allow the listener to differentiate himself or herself from both the portrayer and the portrayed in the story.

I propose to explore the notion that telling stories to ourselves is necessary for being moral agents. As moral agents we must be able, in principle, to give an account of our own actions and the actions of others; however, such an account need not be a *story*. I will not argue that as a moral agent one must always in fact tell a story to account for one's own actions or those of others but rather that one must be capable of doing so. We will see that the minimal necessary features of moral agency involve the capacities necessary for articulation, and we will see that articulation is an important part of what we learn and practice through telling stories.

II. AGENCY AND ARTICULATION

Moral agency admits of two sorts of interpretations: on one it is categorical and on the other it admits of degrees.[7] As categorical, it is a status that one either has or lacks. Insofar as it admits of degrees, it is something that one can develop and refine. These are not competing interpretations, however, for just as one may completely fail to be a moral agent, once one *is* an agent, then one exhibits greater or lesser degrees of sophistication as an agent. In our discussion of agency, it will sometimes be useful to distinguish between a concern with what we call "categorical agency" and a concern with degrees of sophistication as an agent.

Moral agency is characterized by at least three features. First, one must have the capacity to *represent*, and that is, to take X as a Θ . Second, one must have a sense of *self*, which involves an ability to distinguish oneself from others. And third, one must be capable of making judgments marked by what we may call "authority." Without these three features one isn't even on the moral map; without them, one cannot be considered capable of taking the responsibility for one's actions. To lack these three capacities is to lack categorical agency.

To say that a moral agent must have the capacity to represent, to take something as fitting into categories or having certain features, is just to say that a moral agent is at least a minimally intentional being.[8] Moral agents have minds. This does not entail that one is to be able to *prove* that X is a Θ, nor does it require a keenly developed ability for abstract reasoning. Persons fail to be agents if they are incapable of representing their behavior. We can see how this applies to the Quixote case. The accuracy of Don Quixote's representations is not an issue in deciding whether he is a categorical agent but is at issue in deciding just how sophisticated an agent he is and what exactly he is responsible for.

A moral agent must have a sense of self and must be able to distinguish itself from others. This requirement is most often made explicit in discussions of personhood or theories of the self. Daniel Dennett, for example, argues that agents tend to resist their own dissolution, have (generally) a capacity to control things and themselves, a capacity for significant self-improvement (through learning), and have a capacity for self-evaluation and self-definition.[9] Careful examination of Dennett's list of capacities lends support to Annette Baier's claim that "persons are the creations of persons."[10] Baier argues that simple consciousness is not sufficient for personhood, which requires a more reflective and reflexive consciousness which she calls "Cartesian." This consciousness of oneself and one's world crucially involves not just a "consciousness of stimuli relevant to what in fact is self-maintenance in that world" but also a sense of oneself as a being in time, with a past, present, and future, with forebears and perhaps heirs (88). A person is essentially historical and social.

In addition to simply being able to make judgments, an agent must be capable of making judgments marked by what I shall call "authority." The notion of authority has both causal and normative aspects. First, one must be able to act according to one's decisions.[11] To be a moral agent, one must be capable of acting intentionally, of choosing an act and then doing it as chosen. The root of "authority" is "author," which the *Oxford English Dictionary* defines in its verbal form as "to originate, cause, or occasion." To be a moral agent, one must be capable of being the author of one's deeds; an agent is competent and has self-control.[12] This is the causal aspect. One cannot author one's deeds unless one makes judgments about oneself, one's place in society and in the world, and the similarities and differences between one's own situation and the situation of others. So this third feature presupposes the other two. The normative aspect of authority requires the ability to engage in the practice of *justifying* one's decisions (and actions) to others in one's community in terms of shared conceptions of both how things are and how things should be. (Of course, if one's actions are particularly evil or eccentric, one may not be able to justify these *particular* actions in terms of shared conceptions.) It is with respect to this normative aspect of authority that telling stories develops and refines our agency.

Telling stories does not necessarily help us gain the capacity to act according to our judgments but it does develop a sense of self, a sense of self in relation to others, and the capacity to justify one's decisions. Being a moral agent, after all, involves understanding or at least attempting to understand people. To understand people, whether others or oneself, one must put their actions into the appropriate context and produce hypotheses about their reasons for acting. That is, one must give an account. A story is a special kind of account, for it recognizes and essentially uses the fact that the agent is a particular person living at a time within a particular society. Although particular features of this person's context may be abstracted away, the very format of the story recognizes a person's social and temporal nature. Articulation, putting the story together, makes the story tellable and treats the actor as an agent.[13] Although actually telling any particular story aloud is not necessary for moral agency, the practice of storytelling is necessary, for it teaches us how to articulate people's lives. It is through the articulation of events, motives, and characters that we become moral agents.

One reason we tell stories is to see what sort of a story we can tell; in these cases, telling a story is a sort of self-examination by self-exposure. Often we find out what we think by listening to what we say. Telling stories helps us to find out who we are, as both Alasdair MacIntyre and

Martha Nussbaum have urged.[14] But stories don't just tell us who we are or who we have been. Stories tell us what we are capable of, and so they tell us who we might be. Stories provide a way of exploring, logically and emotionally, actions occurring in contexts and actions performed by agents with particular beliefs, motives, and desires, with which we sympathize or not.

The thesis under consideration is *not* the claim that the storyteller or novelist must tell only stories in which there are clear distinctions between the good and the bad, in which only morally good characters triumph and so on. This is the position of William D. Howells, for instance, who maintains that the novelist is "bound to distinguish so clearly that no reader of his may be misled, between what is right and what is wrong, what is noble and what is base, what is health and what is perdition, in the actions and characters he portrays."[15] In claiming that the novelist has a duty to present what is good *as* good and what is evil *as* evil, Howells is prompted by an imitation theory of the value of literature. Such a view echoes the Platonic theme that since art imitates life, and since life in turn imitates art, art should imitate only the best of life. Without rehearsing the host of familiar criticisms of this view, let us note that there is some truth in it. Surely we may admire literary characters and the way they cope with their circumstances, and we certainly may seek in ourselves traits we admire in our literary heroes and heroines. Literature which provides clear moral examples and which attempts, by way of examples, to address and solve moral crises, is certainly to be classed as "moral literature."[16] The moral value of literature (and storytelling) goes far beyond the confines of this set, however.

On Howells' account, what matters most is what the novelist or storyteller depicts; content reigns supreme. Howells keeps with tradition in emphasizing the effect of narrative on the reader. In doing so, Howells takes the *product* of the articulation to be the key to the relation between morality and literature.

There is a more basic way in which the very practice of telling stories is morally required. No matter what the novelist depicts and whatever judgments the narrator makes, engaging in the practice of storytelling contributes to the development of the moral agency of both the teller and the reader or listener. A morally corrupt narrator may make as positive a contribution to a reader's subsequent standing as a moral agent as may a morally good narrator. Storytelling, because of its narrative structure, is an aid to moral epistemology and so moral development. It is not the product but rather the *process* of articulation that is of the first significance.[17] The process of articulation provides a general enough focus to encompass both the readers and writers, for each articulates the tale by gauging the articulation of the other.

Articulation is not simply a matter of putting one sentence after another until one has set out a series of events in some sort of logical order. Consider, for example, Virginia Woolf's criticism of Percy Lubbock's *Earlham* as "a thoroughly bad book—not a book at all, in fact." Woolf explains that in *Earlham*

> Everybody is combed and clipped into their nice, portly, respectable waistcoats and flounces—that, to me, is the heart of the mischief—this conspiracy to misrepresent the human soul in the interest of respectability and, I suppose, of the defunct Henry James, until what with the mildew and the mold and the tone and the mellowness and the setting sun—the rooks cawing and so on and so on, nothing approaching bone or blood is left. . . . Never a venture or an oath or one word more important than another.[18]

The bone and blood of the story is in the structure of significances the storyteller imparts. The decisions the teller makes about what to say and what *not* to say, about what is central and what is peripheral, about *who* is central and who is not, and so on, are all part of the process of articulation. A story or a novel or a book that lacks clear justifiable decisions on these and related issues is only minimally articulated.

This first fact about articulation, that it presents a structure of significance, is closely tied to a second feature: every story is a story told from a perspective. Scholars of literature distinguish between first- and third-person perspectives and between omniscient and non-omniscient narrators.[19] Gerard Genette points out that the distinction between first- and third-person narrative is not primarily a grammatical one; an absence of sentences with "I" for the subject does not mean the narrative is not first person. In fact, only a *subject* can narrate, so in some sense *all* narratives are first person. Just the same, the traditional distinction does mark a difference between a narrator who is inside the story, who is a character in his or her own story, and one who is not.[20]

The distinction between first- and third-person perspectives has epistemological consequences for both the teller and the listener. First-person narrators, who are characters within their own stories, are usually limited to a fallible human perspective on the events of the story. A third-person narrator often takes the epistemic privilege of omniscience. Narrative point of view is not a mere formal element; it guides the reader to particular sorts of interpretive activities. When the narrative perspective is in the first person, for example, we tend to accept the narrator's claims about her or his own intentional states and to question impressions and judgments about others which we would accept more readily if the narrative were third-person omniscient. In reading a story we adopt, temporarily and to some extent, the perspective of the narrator.[21]

A first-person narrative is clearly a story told from a specific point of view. The narrator is a character who the reader comes to know more or less intimately. This case might lead one to think that the intimacy between the reader and the narrator is the source of the relevance of reading to moral agency. Iris Murdoch, for instance, champions the moral value of "unselfing," of paying close, deep attention to something outside oneself so that oneself and perspective are lost in the object of attention.[22] When one returns to her own cares and concerns, they are seen against a broader background and so may be seen with more accuracy. Applied to storytelling, this would be the view that reading or telling stories is good for fighting self-absorption. What is missing is the notion that stories, particularly stories in which we project ourselves into a future, can be an element in self-creation. Further, this "unselfing" may also be achieved in third-person narratives.

First-person narrative is often an efficient device for cultivating intimacy and concern, but it is just that—a device. First- and third-person narratives can each cultivate intimacy; the difference lies in the subjects of the intimacy. Through careful description, the third-person omniscient narrator, such as found in George Eliot's *Middlemarch*, may allow the reader intimacy with several characters while still remaining obscure. So although reading a first-person narrative may seem more of value for developing moral agency than reading a story told in the third person, there is really little difference. Hume, for example, writes that

> Our fancy easily changes its situation; and either surveying ourselves as we appear to others, or considering others as they feel to themselves, makes us enter, by that means, into sentiments, which no way belong to us, and in which nothing but sympathy is able to interest us.[23]

Through its articulation of characters and events, storytelling provides means for entering into sentiments not our own. This is among its most significant contributions to our development as moral agents.[24] Through telling and listening to stories, we learn to make subtle and not so subtle shifts in point of view, and these shifts are crucial to developing the sense of self and others so necessary to moral agency.

Storytelling helps us to develop what Hume calls "greatness of mind," which he takes to be required of moral agents. Greatness of mind requires two fundamental capacities of human nature: sympathy and comparison. And Hume's notion of sympathy is very like our notion of empathy, for it is the capacity to "receive by communication" from others "their inclinations and sentiments, however different from or even contrary to our own."[25] Comparison is a matter of judging objects not intrinsically but in relation to others; this is a very basic form of reasoning (Hume, 593). These capacities for sympathy and comparison may be considered aspects of the capacity for articulation. A similar distinction may be found in Shelley, who claims that "reason respects the differences; imagination the similitudes of things."[26]

Although Shelley was concerned with what makes us good or bad and not with our simply being moral agents and was concerned with all forms of poetry, not simply narrative, we should still pay attention to his claim that poetry is the greatest teacher of morality. He claims that poetry is far superior to the arid tracts of philosophers, for it "compels us to feel that which we perceive, and to imagine that which we know."[27] Poetry unites our faculties. Again, an important value of literature is the faculties and capacities it fosters. Shelley writes

The great secret of morals is love; or a going out of our own nature. . . . A man, to be greatly good, must imagine intensely and
comprehensively; he must put himself in place of another and many
others; the pains and pleasures of his species must become his own.
The great instrument of the moral good is the imagination.[28]

The notion that the essence of morality is "a going out of our own nature"
or a lack of self-centeredness is common to nearly all views of morality.
Shelley adds the claim that this is achieved through the imagination; for
Hume, it is achieved through sympathy. To be a moral agent, one must be
able to imagine the situation of others and live through it, if only in thought,
if only in feeling.[29]

Hume's claim that "moral good and evil are certainly distinguished
by our *sentiments*, not by *reason*" seems to be as far from a Kantian perspective on morality as one can get.[30] The Kantian places tremendous
emphasis on reason for determining morality, claiming that it is in the
exercise of reason that one develops one's moral faculties. The role of
storytelling in moral development is, however, no less important on
Kantian grounds. The difference between the Kantian and the Humean
with respect to this issue is one of emphasis. The Humean would emphasize the way a story engages our sympathy, while the Kantian would
emphasize the way a story explores concretely the rationality of particular actions in particular situations. Even the Kantian, however, would
agree with Hume's claim that reason is no guide to morality as long as
reason is very narrowly circumscribed. W.D. Falk, a contemporary
Kantian, points out that if we construe "reason" as calculation or deduc-
tion, reason will not be a guide to moral choice. He explains that "one's
proper choice is not found under the microscope or by calculation, but it
can be found; and not by the exercise of one special faculty, but, rather,
by the whole man testing *himself* out against an *objective* view of the
issues for choice."[31] Stories provide a way of testing oneself against experiences and points of view that are not one's own; as Wallace Bacon
and Robert Breen point out, "life and literature meet in their common
interest—the *forming and testing of personality.*"[32] What the Kantian
wants, however, is not merely a testing of oneself but a testing of oneself
against an *objective* view.

The Kantian emphasis on formal structures and objectivity seems to suggest that morality would be best served by reading and telling stories told from the third-person omniscient point of view. The first-person story may get one out of oneself but only to enter into something else. The reader or teller is still limited to a fallible perspective still hindered by subjectivity. The third-person omniscient narrative purports to be *objective*. The Kantian may concede Genette's point that every story has a subject behind it and so is first-personal in that sense, and yet claim that with a third-personal omniscient narrator we find a subject with an objective perspective. Although objectivity may be no more than a regulative ideal, it is clear that it is at least that.

Let us turn now to a literary example which raises the issue of a justification of first- and third-person accounts through the narrator's balancing her own personal experiences against an objective perspective. In *The Bluest Eye*, Toni Morrison shows how a moral sensibility may emerge from a text even though no explicit invocations of moral rules or ideals nor explicit final judgments of moral culpability are made by the narrator. Even more, the novel portrays a moral sensibility emerging *in the telling of the story*.

III. A LITERARY CASE STUDY IN THE DEVELOPMENT OF POINT OF VIEW: *THE BLUEST EYE*

Toni Morrison's *The Bluest Eye* is a story of a little black girl who prayed each night for the blue-eyed beauty of Shirley Temple. The novel is an artistic, often poetic, exploration of the complex relations between individual and community. Using vivid imagery, complex symbolism, and a multi-faceted point of view, Morrison creates a tragic and moving portrayal of the psychological destruction of Pecola Breedlove. The novel argues that Pecola is destroyed by the cultural values she adopts. Pecola has an impoverished sense of self and insufficient self-esteem because she accepts the values of the white community as (inadequately) filtered through the black community. The novel is also the story of young Claudia MacTeer, the narrator, who rejects just those values Pecola accepts, who grows up healthy and strong, and who tries, through the telling of Pecola's story, to understand herself, her community, and most of all, why she survived and Pecola did not.

The narrative point of view of *The Bluest Eye* is complex. Some sections of the text are grammatically and conceptually in the first person. Claudia herself is a character within the story she tells. Other sections of the text are third-person omniscient, suggesting a different narrator, or perhaps the authorial voice. This suggests that the author, but not the narrator, is struggling with the limits of the first-person narrator. When we get to the end of the novel, however, we find that the first-person voice and the third-person voice are the same narrator. This pushes Morrison, the author, further outside the story and makes the struggle over narrative authority a part of the story and not external to it. The struggle over narrative authority is the narrator's own. Since the author is removed from the question of narrative authority on this reading of the text, I join Morrison in treating the fictional Claudia as the teller of the tale for the remainder of the discussion.

The novel opens with the version of a child's beginning reader. The story of Dick and Jane and the green-and-white house is a classic normative statement of white middle-class American culture, which provides the context within which the lives of the Breedloves and the MacTeers are set. At the outset, we see how form lends content to the novel: At first the story is double spaced and follows the accepted rules of capitalization and punctuation. On the second telling, the lines are a half space closer, the words are closer together, and the capitals and punctuation are dropped. By the third telling, the words are not spaced and the lines are even closer together. With each repetition, this classic American child-reader's piece gets tighter and tighter and reads faster and faster until it forms a breathless and suffocating mass. It confuses and it constrains. Through the storybook reader, parts of which serve as headings to the "justified" sections of the book, white culture provides a background for Claudia MacTeer's story. Individual whites, however, are only bit players. At issue is the relation in which individual blacks stand to the particular norms of beauty and value imposed by white culture. Here we see the importance of what Baier calls "second person-hood," of seeing oneself and others in a social and historical context.

Following the children's reader, the narrator presents her own naturalistic interpretation of the events to follow. Her claim that no marigolds bloomed in 1941 because the earth itself was unyielding introduces the natural, earthy images that govern the novel and suggests that the environment was the supreme power governing the fate of the individual. This naturalism justifies the division of the novel according to seasons.[33] After the announcement of each season, Claudia's first-person narrative recalls what she takes to be the relevant events of her childhood and encounters with Pecola. Here the prose is set in unjustified print; she does offer judgments, but more important are the images she retains and recreates. As a child of nine she says she did not know the meaning of all that the adults said and did, so she would note "the edge, the curl, the thrust of their emotions" and "watching their faces, their hands, their feet" she would "listen for truth in timber"(16). The text here is filtered through the consciousness of the older Claudia, but it offers little analysis and is strictly in the first person. It is "truth in timber" that Claudia's youthful impressions offer, and against which she must judge her ultimate account.[34]

Following each section of unjustified prose by the young Claudia is a section of justified prose, headed by a relevant portion of the child's reader and narrated by the older Claudia. Speaking in the third person and with authority, she tells the story of the Breedloves, a family marked by self-hatred. Here the narrative point of view seems omniscient, for she is able to delve into the minds and hearts of the characters and unravel their pasts. In fact, the narrative of these chapters is so impersonal and objective that the reader does not find out that the narrator is Claudia until the end of the book.

A significant fact about the novel, for our purposes, is that its narrator does not seek an impartial or objective perspective on the events she recounts. She has found such a perspective and presumably found it lacking. This telling of Pecola's story interweaves the subjective, presented physically and metaphorically unjustified, with the objective, presented physically and metaphorically justified, and aims for a *first-person justified* account. Wrenching the notion of justification free from that of objectivity, Claudia wants to tell her own story *and* she wants it to be justified, to be right.

The Bluest Eye is not only a novel of "the horror at the heart" of a little black girl's longing for blue eyes (158). It is also the story of another little black girl who dissects white baby dolls to discover the charm they hold for others and who for a long time feels a "pristine sadism" for "the

Shirley Temples of the world" (22, 19). In telling Pecola's story the way she does, Claudia tells some of her own story too. Recognizing her own unsullied hatred for the little blonde who got to dance with Mr. Bo Jangles, Claudia later says "I had not yet arrived at the turning point in the development of my psyche which would allow me to love her" (19). Claudia scrutinized and sought justification for externally imposed standards; Pecola instead scrutinized herself (39). Later, Claudia comes to realize that she and her sister differ from Pecola crucially:

> Guileless and without vanity, we were still in love with ourselves then. We felt comfortable in our skins, and enjoyed the news that our senses released to us, admired our dirt, cultivated our scars, and could not comprehend this unworthiness. (62)

The young Claudia represents an automatic rejection of external standards which were impossible for her to meet. Many saw these standards as objective fact; Claudia and her sister did not. Even as a child, Claudia seemed aware that not everything that is external to the individual is objective.

Unlike Claudia, Pecola never loved herself. Always seeing herself through the eyes of others, she never saw anything to love. As the story unfolds Claudia comes to hold that it was Pecola's conviction that she was ugly, her deep internalization of white standards of beauty and value, that ultimately drove her mad. She believed the fiction of her own ugliness so fervently that she made it her reality and prayed for a miracle to release her from it. Tragically, the release came after her own father raped her, a rape which began as a misguided attempt to show her some tenderness and ended as an outlet for his rage and frustration. After that, Pecola Breedlove spent her days plucking her way

> among all the waste and the beauty of the world—which is what she herself was. All of our waste which we dumped on her and which she absorbed. And all of our beauty which was hers first which she gave to us. (159)

In the last two pages of the novel, when for the first time the first-person narrative is used in the justified text, Claudia still sees Pecola's destruction as "the fault of the earth, the land, of our town," explaining that "this soil is bad for certain kinds of flowers" (160). The black community would not nurture a twelve-year-old girl who had been raped by her father, and they would not wish for her baby to live.

> Certain seeds it will not nurture, certain fruit it will not bear, and when the land kills of its own volition, we acquiesce and say the victim has no right to live. We are wrong, of course, but it doesn't matter. It's too late. (160)

The story shows that it does matter, that such acquiescence is destructive. What Claudia's telling of the story shows, but does not say, is that the internalization of destructive standards can be avoided, Claudia speaks of her own progression of feelings toward white dolls and white girls and of a turning point as yet unreached by her nine-year-old self. Later she learned not to hate the little white girls who got to dance with Mr. Bo Jangles and whom everybody seemed to love. Learning this lesson later meant not having to hate herself.

IV. CONCLUSION: AGENCY AND POINT OF VIEW

This essay began with the question of "Why should we tell stories?" *The Bluest Eye* illustrates answers to that question for both the teller and listener or reader. I said earlier that *The Bluest Eye* shows how a moral sensibility may emerge from a text even though no explicit invocations of moral rules or ideals, nor explicit final judgments of moral culpability are made by the narrator and that even more, the novel portrays a moral sensibility emerging *in the telling of the story*. Now we are in a position to see how.

From the outset of the story, Claudia shows that she has categorical moral agency, for she represents some events from her childhood, she displays a clear sense of self, and she shows herself capable of both causal and normative authority. We can say this of the young Claudia within the story told by the older Claudia, and we can say it of the older Claudia who adopts the first-person voice. It is not so easy to say it of the voice of the third-person omniscient sections which is also the older Claudia. There the narrator tries to avoid self-exposure and does not display the sense of self and others and the capacity for authority characteristic of moral agents.[35] Failing to display these capacities is quite different from not having them. What is important to note here is that when the narrative is third-person omniscient, we have less obvious grounds for attributing moral agency to the narrator than we do when the narrative is first person.

Since Claudia begins with categorical agency, *The Bluest Eye* illustrates how telling a story may enhance the sophistication of the moral agent. The narrator begins with two different ways of articulating the events of 1941. The young Claudia was concerned with finding someone or something to blame for Pecola's destruction. Like William Dean Howells, she wanted to know who was good and who was bad. In writing the story later, Claudia can tell how it seemed to her at the time, or she can tell what she has since learned about the Breedloves and how they came to be who they were. Temporally, these perspectives are divided. Claudia does not, however, choose one way or the other. She structures her narrative to balance one perspective against the other. Rather than subsuming one account under the other, she seeks to establish a synthesis of them.

In finally telling the story, many years later, she tries to come to an understanding of the complexity of the issues and the difficulties of simple assignments of blame. She says that the novel is not so much an attempt to say *why* the events happened, since that is so difficult, but simply to say *how* (9). Still, it is much more than this. In attempting to say how and in struggling with the inadequacies of *her own stories*, one very impressionistic and one very objective and seemingly logical, Claudia tells yet a third story and emerges from that telling as a different (but related) agent. This third telling has enabled her to develop a distinctive point of view. She has something now that she didn't have before: she has a different and richer sense of the relation between the individual and the community, and she has a first-person justified story.

What is a first-person justified story like? Since it is first person, it is a story in which the narrator is a character who is involved in the events of the story. Claudia tries to tell a story in which her being a character, her involvement, does not undermine her very authority to tell the story. It is easy to read *The Bluest Eye* as an injunction to the black community to take care of its Pecola Breedloves. The young Claudia, whose prose is unjustified, rails against Pecola's situation and tries magic and prayer to effect change. The young, and not quite fully socialized, Claudia fully feels the injustice of Pecola's plight, but she has not learned to justify her views. The older Claudia, whose prose is justified, tells a more explicitly sociological and psychological story, claiming that Pecola went mad because the black community could not sustain her. Her view is at once more comprehensive than that of her younger self as well as more sympathetic to the conditions against which the community must fight. It is important to remember that justification is a social notion. We devise methods for discerning the truth which we hope will be reliable, but which we recognize as fallible because they are our own creations. A first-person justified story would make self-conscious use of these methods of justification without giving up responsibility for the tale and without giving up the "truth in timber" of the unjustified vision. A first-person justified story is not a story just anyone can tell.

What does the reader of *The Bluest Eye* gain from reading the novel? Toni Morrison has said that each of her books represents a study of the intricacies of character. She explains that "it's the complexity of how people behave under duress that is of interest to me—the qualities they show at the end of an event when their backs are up against the wall."[36] The stories involve situations which test characters, and the results give both the reader and the writer "something to feel and think about," not "something to swallow" (McKay, 421). In this we hear echoes of Hume: through sympathy and comparison a moral sensibility emerges. We see Claudia struggling to tell a story about Pecola which isn't oversimplified by too much involvement and too little distance, as in the first person, or too much distance and too little involvement, as in the third person.

If readers of *The Bluest Eye* are protégés of William Dean Howells, they will be disappointed by its paucity of clear moral examples. Howells's notion of reading is a rather passive and limited one. Compare it to Sartre's conception, for example, which is of a very active process. Sartre says that "in reading, one foresees; one waits. One foresees the end of the sentence, the following sentence, the next page. One waits for them to confirm or disappoint one's foresights. The reading is composed of a host of hypotheses, of dreams followed by awakenings, of hopes and deceptions."[37] To read is to anticipate. It is to compare one's own provisional understanding of the characters and what they would or would not do with that of the author. To read is to *interpret*. The reader does not simply accept wholesale whatever the author says but rather evaluates the author's credibility with each passing sentence.

Too much attention to the moral value of the actions and characters depicted in a narrative leads to a very limited understanding of the importance of storytelling and literature. Consider for a moment I.A. Richards's claim that "the artist is concerned with the record and perpetuation of the experiences which seem to him most worth having."[38] Is Richards then committed to saying that Toni Morrison thinks that ostracism, incest, and madness are experiences "most worth having"? Not only are these experiences presented in her novel but without them there would be no story. Or must Richards hold that Dalton Trumbo is committed, in *Johnny Got His Gun*, to the premium value of losing one's legs, arms, eyes, and ability to speak? That Hardy believes that ruinous marriages and impossible ambitions are most worth having? These questions rely on too narrow a view of Richards's claim and too narrow a view of the nature of stories and literature. Like Howells's view, this reading of Richards focuses too closely on the content of the story told. The experiences most worth having and the experiences recorded and perpetuated are not those of the characters within the stories but rather those of the artist. The artist is the articulator, and as Richards goes on to say, the artist is "the point at which the growth of the mind shows itself" (Richards, 61). In Morrison's novel, we see this growth of the mind in Claudia. We may experience some growth of our own if we read carefully and well.

Telling a story, a discourse with a beginning, middle, and end, with chronology and causality, with human or humanoid characters, is an exercise in articulation. To articulate is not simply to *say* or to *utter*. What is articulated consists of segments and joints, and the process of articulation involves fitting segments at the joints. Telling a story requires that we try to understand as much of the why and how of human events as we can and to articulate that understanding in a way that engages oneself and others. A fictional story is a sort of thought-experiment, for it is an exercise in devising characters and circumstances that quiet our initial objections to their unreality. A story is not just a *logical* exercise, however, and so the notion of thought-experiment falls short. Ideally, a story *engages* both the teller and the told intellectually *and* emotionally. This engagement requires articulating not just events and characters, but one's own point of view, either directly in telling the story or indirectly in listening.

Just as telling stories is an exercise in articulation, reading literature and listening to stories is also a way to learn how to articulate characters and incidents, for the reader follows the writer's articulation. In literature, descriptions of people and events are provided by the writer. In daily life we must provide our own descriptions of those we know, and we learn to do this, at least in part, from stories and literature. Don Quixote's problem was taking too uncritical an approach to the categories presented by the writers he read and too steady a diet of romance novels. Even when the social and moral categories presented are not so outlandish as those found in romances, it can be difficult to apply pre-established categories to new situations. Then one must tell one's own story one's own way. Claudia MacTeer struggles over whether Cholly Breedlove was a villain or a victim, and neither her perspective as a child nor her more objective perspective as an adult can quite encompass both. He is not simply a villain and not simply a victim, but how could he be both at the same time? She struggles to describe Cholly, Pecola, and all the Breedloves accurately, objectively, and yet to claim as her own her judgment of them.

Charles Altieri discusses a "thickened model of judgment" which involves "approaching one's deeds with a concern for the ways that one's reasons will establish one as a particular agent within a community, bound by certain commitments and characterized by certain qualities of concern."[39] Persons become selves by way of understanding their place within the community, as it is now, as they hope it can be, as others will and will not allow them to be. Without at least a minimally articulated notion of one's place in the community, one cannot be a moral agent. But it isn't just a matter of seeing one's place in the community *through the eyes of the community*. This is exactly what Pecola did and she ultimately lost both her sense of self and her sense of community. Altieri's notion of "thickened" judgment is a matter of projecting one's place in a community that one helps to reshape through the judgments one makes and the stories one tells. In telling the story that is *The Bluest Eye*, Claudia displays this sort of judgment. Poor Pecola does not.

In *The Bluest Eye* Morrison tells a story that captures an important aspect of the struggle of moral agency. Often we conceive the problem of moral agency to be a problem of leaping from the subjective to the objective, of gaining a clearer, better, impartial view of ourselves, our friends, our actions. We have seen that to be agents we seek authority for our judgments; we want judgments we can stand behind, and not just settle for saying, "well, that's how it seems to me." One message of *The Bluest Eye* is that this struggle for objectivity is followed by another even more difficult challenge. That challenge demands that we not lose our subjectivity in our quest for justification. In rising to this challenge, Claudia MacTeer shows us the importance of listening carefully to the stories of others and learning to tell one's own story.

It is through the articulation of events, motives and characters that we become moral agents. This is the sense in which storytelling is necessary for moral agency. In telling stories one develops a sense of self, a sense of self in relation to others, and a capacity to justify one's decisions. These features are necessary for being a moral agent in the categorical sense. Telling stories may also increase our sophistication as agents. We may begin with rudimentary stories that show a basic grasp of the moral, and sometimes we may eventually develop the thickened judgment that enables one to take control of oneself, one's place in one's community and to have a directed impact on that community.

NOTES

1. I am grateful to Douglas J. Butler, Thomas E. Hill, Jr., Richard L. Lippke, William G. Lycan, Benjamin C. Zipursky, and the members of the Triangle Ethics Discussion Circle for comments on an earlier draft of this paper.

2. Henry James, "The Art of Fiction," in *Literary Criticism* (New York: The Library of America, 1984), p. 46.

3. Virginia Woolf, *A Room of One's Own* in *The Feminist Papers*, ed. Alice Rossi (New York: Bantam Books, 1973), pp. 627-52.

4. Robert Scholes, "Language, Narrative, and Anti-Narrative" in *On Narrative,* ed. W. J. T. Mitchell (University of Chicago Press, 1981), p. 206.

5. See especially Julian Mitchell, "Truth and Fiction" in *Philosophy and the Arts,* Royal Institute Of Philosophy Lectures, Vol. VI (London: Macmillan, 1973), pp. 1–22.

6. In "'Finely Aware and Richly Responsible: Moral Attention and the Moral Task of Literature" (in *Philosophy and The Question of Literature*, ed. A.

Cascardi [Johns Hopkins University Press, 1987]), Martha Nussbaum is concerned to show that James's novel presents both a moral theory and a moral exercise but she does not argue that all storytelling promotes moral agency. MacIntyre's use of 'narrative unity' in *After Virtue* (University of Notre Dame Press, 1981) might suggest an answer to this question but is itself an answer.

7. I am grateful to Bill Lycan for help on this point.

8. See Donald Davidson, "Agency" in *Essays on Actions and Events* (Oxford University Press, 1980).

9. Daniel Dennett, *Elbow Room* (MIT Press, 1984), p. 100.

10. Annette Baier, "Cartesian Persons," in *Postures of the Mind* (University of Minnesota Press, 1985), p. 86.

11. Notice that authority, in the sense invoked here, is not a matter of being able to get others to obey one's commands.

12. See Aristotle's *Politics*, 1143a8.

13. Here the affinities between fictional and non-fictional narrative are apparent. Of course non-fictional storytelling involves articulation.

14. MacIntyre, *After Virtue*, esp. Ch.15. Martha Nussbaum, "Fictions of the Soul," *Philosophy and Literature* 7 (1983): 145–61.

15. William Dean Howells, *Criticism and Fiction* (New York: Harper and Brothers, 1891), pp. 98–9. For a similar but more sophisticated position, see John Gardner, *On Moral Fiction* (New York: Basic Books, 1978).

16. Such literature is moral because it attempts to indoctrinate its readers, not because it necessarily succeeds. Whether it succeeds depends in large part on the reader.

17. This focus on the process rather than the product also helps to avoid falling into Sartre's view that a writer cannot read his or her own text. Sartre holds this position because he takes the process of reading to be one of anticipating the unknown and since (once it has been written) the text is known to the writer, the writer cannot really read his or her own work. On the view being developed here, writers may read their own texts, but the products of subsequent readings may not always be the same as the products of earlier readings. What gets anticipated, once one learns the words and sentences and other structural elements of the text, is much more abstract.

18. Virginia Woolf, letter to R. C. Trevelyan, Dec. 29, 1922, in *The Letters of Virginia Woolf,* Vol. II: 1912–1922, eds. Nigel Nicholson and Joanne Trautmann (New York: Harcourt, Brace, Jovanovich, 1976), p. 601.

19. See for example, Gerard Genette, *Narrative Discourse: An Essay in Method,* trans. Jane E. Lewin (Cornell University Press, 1980), and Susan Sniader Lanser, *The Narrative Act: Point of View in Prose Fiction* (Princeton University Press, 1981).

20. Narrative perspective is rarely uniform through a given story. Stories are told in retrospect, and even most first-person narrators interject information

that they could not have known at the time of the action and do so using a third-person omniscient perspective. Nevertheless, most stories have a dominant narrative point of view.

21. The moral value of storytelling does not depend on the sincerity or reliability of the narrator, for it may be useful in literature as well as in life to have encountered the insincere and unreliable. Nor does it depend on the inability of the reader to distinguish himself or herself from the narrator while reading; such complete identification, if possible, would be beside the point.

22. See Iris Murdoch, *The Sovereignty of the Good* (London: ARK Paperbacks, 1985), p. 84.

23. David Hume, *A Treatise of Human Nature,* ed. A. Selby-Bigge (Oxford University Press, 1978), p. 589.

24. R.M. Hare, for example. maintains that a moral thinker *must* be able to represent and identify with the experiences and preferences of others. See *Moral Thinking: Its Levels, Method and Point* (Oxford: Clarendon Press, 1981), especially Chapter 5.

25. David Hume, *A Treatise of Human Nature,* p. 317.

26. Percy Bysshe Shelley, "A Defense of Poetry," in *Criticism: The Major Statements,* ed. Charles Kaplan (New York: St. Martin's Press, 1975), p. 355.

27. Shelley, "A Defense of Poetry," p. 377. See also Martha Nussbaum "Literature and the Moral Imagination" in *Philosophy and the Question of Literature.* Nussbaum argues that Henry James's *The Golden Bowl* both shows and elicits moral attention, which is our "moral faculty" (p.187). She takes James's view to be that "by identifying with them (his characters) and allowing ourselves to be surprised (an attitude of mind that story-telling fosters and develops), we become more responsive to our own life's adventure, more willing to see and be touched by life" (p. 87). This view is similar to mine, but it does not say what is *moral* about the attention and about the willingness "to see and be touched by life." This is also the view presented in Iris Murdoch's *The Sovereignty of the Good.*

28. Shelley, "A Defense of Poetry, " p. 362.

29. Wallace A. Bacon and Robert S. Breen in their *Literature as Experience* ([New York: McGraw-Hill, 1959], p. 101) argue that through literature "we undergo experiences we should not otherwise undergo, we assume dispositions of persons we should not otherwise come to know, we look from points of view different from our own and frequently more penetrating than our own and almost always more complete than our own." Because there is clearly a difference between events which really happen to me and those which I imagine, I do not share Bacon and Breen's enthusiasm for calling what we gain through literature "experience." At issue is the status of *imagined* experience.

30. David Hume, *A Treatise on Human Nature,* p. 589.

31. W.D. Falk, "Moral Perplexity" in *Ought, Reasons, and Morality* (Cornell University Press, 1986), p. 259.

32. Bacon and Breen, *Literature as Experience,* p. 61.

33. Toni Morrison's *The Bluest Eye* falls into six sections; its two introductory pieces are followed by Autumn, Winter, Spring, and Summer.

34. Notice the affinity between this concern for "truth in timber" and Woolf's view that it is "the blood and bone" that matter.

35. The third-person omniscient narrator displays sensitivity to these characteristics of characters within the story, and this may provide evidence about her own agency, but if so, it is indirect.

36. Nellie McKay, "An Interview with Toni Morrison," *Contemporary Literature* 24 (1983), p. 420.

37. Jean-Paul Sartre, *What Is Literature?,* trans. Bernard Frechtman (London: Methuen & Co. Ltd, 1950), p. 28.

38. I.A. Richards, *Principles of Literary Criticism* (New York: Harcourt Brace & Co., 1925), p. 61.

39. Charles Altieri, "From Expressivist Aesthetics to Expressivist Ethics," in *Philosophy and the Question of Literature,* p. 137.

Tracking "The Look" in the Novels of Toni Morrison

Ed Guerrero

In various papers, essays, and books over the past several years, a number of feminist and cultural critics have had much to say about what has come to be known as "the look" and its varied modes of inscription in films, literature, and the media, as well as in commodity/consumer culture in general. It is broadly argued in this body of theory and criticism that all forms of cultural production in a patriarchal, consumer-oriented society focus on the representation of woman as an eroticized, fetishized, and generally commodified object that is displayed for the enjoyment of a controlling male "look" or gaze. This process is best exemplified by Hollywood's creation of a circuit of visual pleasure that usually de-eroticizes the look at the male while displacing eroticism "onto the female—onto that which is already ideologically defined and accepted as an unproblematic sexual object" (Neale, 57). Evidence of this "look" and its commercial uses abounds on television as, for instance, when Brooke Shields is suggestively displayed to sell blue jeans or as one is subjected to the by now-cliched image of the eroticized female body offered up to colonize desire in the service of car sales: "Dodge boys have more fun." And, most certainly, magazines like *Vogue* and *Cosmopolitan,* or their black imitators, while vouching for the economic power of the fashion and cosmetics industries, also more than hint at the narcissistic and exhibitionistic pleasures of looking relations for women.

Because the list of examples of female objectification in the media would regress into infinity, for the purposes of this essay I would like to focus on how various modes of "the look" have been articulated in a most specific literary corpus, the novels of Toni Morrison. Moreover, because

27

Morrison is an African American woman, the inscription of looking relations in her novels *The Bluest Eye, Sula, Song of Solomon, Tar Baby* , and
Beloved assumes boundaries that encompass the sexual objectification of
women. And because of her positionality at the intersection of gender
and race, her explorations extend beyond this first issue to explore the
complexity of "the look" as the controlling gaze of a dominant, racially
oppressive society which constructs whiteness as the norm while view-
ing African Americans as "Other."[1] Understood from the perspective of a
black woman, the dominant society's gaze, constructed as white and male,
is driven by a layering of motivations that expresses not only sexual objectification but also racism and classism in its operations. But we must
push our analysis even further when it comes to Morrison's novels and
explore how "the look" of the dominant social order is internalized by her
black characters; that is, how they construct themselves and others through,
and in a few instances against, the gaze of the Master. Also pertinent to
this discussion is an insight of black feminist critic Barbara Christian,
who notes that "people of color have always theorized—but in terms quite
different from the Western form of abstract logic"—and that this "theorizing . . . is often in narrative forms, in the stories we create, in riddles
and proverbs, in the play with language, since dynamic rather than fixed
ideas seem more to our liking" ("The Race for Theory," 52). So it is through
her fictive or "narrative theorizing" that Morrison is critically aware of
how the dominant society's ideological and commercial apparatus maintains and holds "the look" in place to the detriment of her black characters. Put broadly, then, this essay will track down and interrogate some of
the diverse, and sometimes imbricated, meanings of "the look" articulated in Morrison's novels.

The tracks of "the look" have their origins and perhaps their most
focused representation in Morrison's first novel, *The Bluest Eye* (1970),
which holds as its central concern a critique of Western beauty and its
special destructiveness when imposed upon people of color in general
and women of color in particular. Morrison has these women in mind
when she asserts in the novel that the idea of physical beauty is one of
"probably the most destructive ideas in the history of human thought"
(97). One can discern much about the construction and workings of "the
look" by exploring the plight of the novel's principal victim and the most

poignant victim in all of Morrison's works, a twelve-year-old black girl named Pecola Breedlove. As the novel opens, the reader comes to understand that Pecola, by being born into a violent, impoverished, underclass environment, does not get much of a start in life. Pecola's sad situation is compounded, moreover, by a crushing sense of inferiority and ugliness inherited from her family and their own struggles with "the look" and by her attempts to ease her misery by retreating ever more deeply into a confused—and finally shattered psychotic—self-image.

Early in the novel Morrison locates Pecola and the Breedloves' problems with "the look" in the family setting and poses these problems as, ultimately, ideological. For while the suffocating poverty in which the Breedloves live is not unique, their self-perception as "aggressively ugly" people is. In a telling passage the author goes on to theorize in narrative form:

> You looked at them and wondered why they were so ugly: you looked closely and could not find the source. Then you realized that it came from conviction, their conviction. It was as though some mysterious all-knowing master had given each one a cloak of ugliness to wear, and they had each accepted it without question. The master had said, "You are ugly people." They had looked about themselves and saw nothing to contradict the statement; saw, in fact, support for it leaning at them from every billboard, every movie, every glance. "Yes," they had said, "you are right." And they took the ugliness in their hands, threw it as a mantle over them, and went about the world with it. (34)

Significantly, the "mysterious master" referred to is the dominant, hegemonic ideology which, with "the look" as its instrument, devalues the Breedloves, assigns them to their social place and, correspondingly, to their place in the hierarchy of physical beauty.[2] Equally as important, though, Morrison shows us the pervasiveness of the ideological apparatus, as "the look" is figured into billboard advertising, popular cinema, and other media and assimilated from "every glance," be it white or black.

Morrison develops the pathology of these revelations by working into the narrative a number of instances in which Pecola's and her family's self-esteem are literally destroyed by their encounters with varied expressions of the dominant society's gaze. Pecola's mother Pauline in an attempt to make some sense out of the drudgery, isolation, and poverty of her small-town, domesticated life, escapes, along with millions of others in the '30s and '40s, into the fantasies of Hollywood's "classic cinema." And here Morrison's fictive explorations are consonant with current theory about the construction of visual pleasure and looking relations in dominant cinema. Describing the alluring operation of cinematic fantasy, Pauline Breedlove tells the reader in her own voice: *"They'd cut off the lights, and everything be black. Then the screen would light up, and I'd move right on in them pictures"* (97). Here Pauline experiences one of the principal modes of "the look" in dominant cinema, that of the spectator at the screen. It is this "look" that Hollywood always tries to efface from the consciousness of the spectator so that one may identify with one's "ideal ego image" in the story world and deeply submerge into the film's verisimilitude.[3]

Uniquely, though, the operation of this look resides at the nexus of contradiction and irony for Pauline in ways that it doesn't for the white female spectator. For while many white feminist critics argue that women suffer negation of self by having to identify with a sexual object displayed for the pleasure of the male gaze at the screen, Pauline as a woman, and as one of color, must suffer this negation in a compounded sense, for her like hardly exists anywhere on the screen. She is therefore forced to look at and apply to herself a completely unrealizable, alien standard of feminine beauty and to experience the dissatisfaction resulting from the contradiction. The problem for Pauline with the dominant gaze built into classic cinema is that, in her specific situation, it conjures up the triple devaluation of being female, black, and poor.

Understanding the importance of dominant cinema in shaping looking relations and society's racially layered regimes of beauty, Morrison finally observes of Pauline: "She was never able, after her education in the movies, to look at a face and not assign it some category in the scale of absolute beauty, and the scale was one she absorbed in full from the silver screen" (97). What is more, this internalization of the cinematic "look" and its corresponding workings in Hollywood's "star system," extends to all of the novel's female characters. The black girls Claudia and Frieda are compared by their parents' boarder, Mr. Henry, to Greta Garbo and Ginger Rogers. The "high yellow dream child," Maureen Peal, points up the contradiction between black women's assimilated desires and their unattainability with a joke about a black woman wanting her hair done like Hedy Lamarr's while not having hair like hers. And, in a neurotic attempt to raise her value on the scale of beauty and love, Pecola turns Shirley Temple into a fetish, guzzling quarts of milk out of a cup marketed in the child star's image, in hopes of a magical transformation.

But if the women of *The Bluest Eye* suffer from "the look," so too does Pauline Breedlove's alcoholic husband Cholly. Originating in an incident in adolescence that permanently scars Cholly by showing him his "place" in a racist society and as an object of that society's sadistic, dominating gaze, "the look" contributes directly to the formation of Cholly's violent character and his undying mistrust of all women. In one of the few scenes in the novel in which Cholly begins to experience the possibilities that lie in discovering selfhood, a sensual appreciation of nature, and his nascent manhood, Morrison shows us that the pathology of "the look" also applies to men of color and that the gaze of hegemonic society is driven as much by reflex racism and the power dynamic of domination/subordination as it is by the exploitation of erotic pleasure.[4] Cholly's first romantic, sexual encounter, with Darlene, is set in a glen in the sensual, approving context of nature, as the reader finds Cholly's "mouth full of the taste of muscadine, listening to the pine needles rustling loudly in their anticipation of rain" (115). His amorous liaison is interrupted, however, by two racist white men who force him to copulate in the glare of their flashlights and their voyeuristic, sadistic gazes. As a result, Cholly displaces his rage onto the only target within his social grasp, his sexual partner Darlene, and by generalization onto all black women. This dominating, sadistic look, then, becomes one more instance in a casual chain of devaluations that culminates in disaster for the entire Breedlove family.

One can also discern a recurrent pattern here. For in the case of Pecola, Morrison constructs the possibility of her discovering a sense of self, of communing with nature. Then comes a shattering encounter with the gaze of the dominant society. On the way to the store to buy penny candy, Pecola attempts to unravel an enduring aesthetic paradox: whether dandelions are weeds or beautiful flowers. By symbolic implication Pecola struggles to discover whether she is a "weed" or has some value or undiscovered beauty beyond her depreciated position in the scheme of society's looking relations. While walking over a familiar route, Pecola enjoys the affirming innocence of a child's view of the world and the minute details in it that adults often overlook—cracks in the sidewalk, weeds, etc. In this moment of Pecola's reverie and unobstructed identification with things as they are, Morrison holds out the remote possibility of Pecola's gradually reversing the neurotic self-hatred that is already so deeply seated in her personality by this point in the novel.

For Pecola, however, this instant of childhood innocence and self-affirmation is all too brief, as Morrison has other things she wants to show the reader about Pecola's world. When Pecola enters the store to buy the ideal childhood, female image commodified in the form of Mary Jane candies from the storekeeper Jacobowski, Morrison evokes "the look" in one of its most detailed moments in all of her novels:

> Somewhere between retina and object, between vision and view, his eyes draw back, hesitate, and hover. At some fixed point in time and space he senses that he need not waste the effort of a glance. He does not see her, because for him there is nothing to see. How can a fifty-two-year-old white immigrant storekeeper with the taste of potatoes and beer in his mouth, his mind honed on the doe-eyed Virgin Mary, his sensibilities blunted by a permanent awareness of loss, *see* a little black girl? Nothing in his life even suggested that the feat was possible, not to say desirable or necessary. (41–2)

Here Morrison constructs the circuit of looking relations as that between Master and non-white Other, in which the Master looks upon the Other and sees an absence of humanity. In turn, the Other looks upon the Master and sees omnipotence and the negation of self. Thus the two create a circulating "look" in which they confirm their inhuman estimate of each "other" and, significantly, of themselves (Berger, 96).[5] Moreover, Pecola understands that the nucleus of the problem lies in her blackness, which "is static and dread. And it is the blackness, that accounts for, that creates, the vacuum edged with distaste in white eyes" (42). Pecola's encounter with "the look" ends with reflex self-negation, symbolized in her deciding that dandelions are ugly weeds after all. This incident is a psychological turning point for Pecola beyond which her self-esteem is increasingly eroded until the novel reaches its melancholy conclusion with her going completely insane.

In Morrison's second novel, *Sula* (1973), Morrison shifts her focus on "the look" to exploring in the actions of her characters the ethical differences between the verbs *to see* and *to watch.* The author shifts from *The Bluest Eye,* and how "the look" and ideology of its construction hold disastrous consequences for black folks' self-esteem, to *Sula,* where black folk as a community interrogate modes of "the look" within their own system of values. Although Sula and Nel, the two women at the center of the novel, are complementary opposites,[6] they are bonded forever together by the memory of an event that took place in their childhood and that must remain a shared secret. Here again, Morrison asserts her pattern of self-discovery, communion with nature, and a disruption which contains at its center the binary terror and pleasure of the gaze.

In an idyllic childhood scene, the blossoming adolescents Nel and Sula play on a hill overlooking a river. Morrison develops the scene with quaternary symbolism and reveals the culmination of the children's friendship set in deep communion with nature:

> They ran in the sunlight, creating their own breeze, which pressed their dresses into their damp skin. Reaching a kind of square of four leaf-locked trees which promised cooling, they flung themselves into the four-cornered shade to taste their lip sweat and contemplate the wildness that had come upon them so suddenly. (49)

Under the trees as they ritualistically dig a hole and cover it up again, Nel and Sula's friendship is inscribed in its most perfected moment. Yet this bond is solidified in an unexpected, horrifying manner when Sula accidentally throws a small boy, Chicken Little, to his death in the river below. The cause of his drowning is never openly known to the community, but it is this event, repressed but forever understood between Nel and Sula, that acts as a latent, hidden dynamic in the text. Finally, forty-three years later, in the novel's resolution, Eva, Sula's grandmother, asks Nel why she drowned Chicken, an accusation that Nel promptly denies, saying that it was Sula who did it.

For Eva, though, the shared responsibility and guilt for the event turns on her subtle ethical understanding of looking relations as she tells Nel, "You. Sula. What's the difference? You was there. You watched, didn't you? Me, I never would've watched" (145). Later, walking alone, Nel goes over Eva's accusation and uncovers an unanswered question that holds at its core her long-repressed sense of guilt and responsibility. As she dredges up the submerged fragments of childhood that have always tied her to Sula, she finally recognizes her real feelings about the drowning and the inner, driving mechanism of her voyeurism:

> What did Eva mean by *you watched?* How could she help seeing it? . . . But Eva didn't say see, she said *watched.* "I did not watch it. I just saw it." But it was there anyway, as it had always been, the old feeling and the old question. The good feeling she had had when Chicken's hands slipped. She hadn't wondered about that in years. "Why didn't I feel bad when it happened? How come it felt so good to see him fall?"
>
> All these years she had been secretly proud of her calm, controlled behavior when Sula was uncontrollable, her compassion for Sula's frightened and shamed eyes. Now it seemed that what she had thought was maturity, serenity and compassion was only the tranquillity that follows a joyful stimulation. (146)

Nel's realization that sadism motivated her "look" at the event completes our understanding of Nel and Sula as polarities of a single complex personality of which voyeurism is a significant feature. Correspondingly, this shared trait is revealed early on in the novel when Eva becomes aware of Sula's sadistic voyeurism when as a child Sula watches with great interest her mother Hannah burn in a yard fire.

Yet Morrison has much more to show us about the complexities of the looking relations in the trajectory of her work. When it comes to mirror gazes, there are two instances of "the look" in her novels, one in *Sula* and the other in *Song of Solomon,* that register gender difference in terms of male affirmation and female negation of self. In each case a gendered subject finds or loses him/herself in a reflective surface.

In *Sula* the mad Shadrack, in jail, looks at his reflection in a toilet bowl and rediscovers his blackness and himself. Upon confirming himself with the gaze as both black and real, Shadrack's schizophrenia eases, and he is content to fall into a primal sleep, a "sleep deeper than the hospital drugs; deeper than the pits of plums, steadier than the condor's wing; more tranquil than the curve of eggs" (11–12).

Here the male mirror gaze affirms and establishes Shadrack's sense of identity, and he is "reborn." This self-discovery is made all the more potent because Morrison constructs Shadrack as a mythical, proto-nationalist figure in the black community, functioning very much as what Mikhail Bakhtin calls a "chronotope."[7] The markers of Shadrack's proto-nationalism are evinced in the very order of the reformulation of his selfhood, the physical signs and powers that figure him in the novel, and his positionality in relation to the land itself. Shadrack discovers his racial essence in his reflection before gathering a sense of individual self. He is an atavistic primal being in the sense that his story opens the novel and that he wears his hair in the essentialist natural style of dreadlocks. And to further metaphorically demonstrate his connection to a formative, primal time/space, Morrison gives Shadrack the myth-making power to create his own holiday and weave it into the routine and folklore of the community. Finally, Shadrack's abode is rooted on ancestral land inherited from his grandfather. Shadrack, Nel, and Eva survive beyond the community's disintegration, into the '60s, privileged as witnesses in the novel's closure.

Conversely, Morrison in *Song of Solomon* (1977) recognizes that under patriarchy the female gaze into the mirror confirms a sense of lack or self-negation. For through the workings of narcissism and exhibitionism the mirror gaze entraps woman as the displayed object of male desire.[8] By relating how Hagar falls obsessively in love with her cousin Milkman, the author shows us the pathology of the mirror gaze while returning to explore the theme of the destructive, devaluing power of white standards of beauty when inflicted upon black women. In an attempt to pull Hagar out of a near-catatonic state of depression induced by Milkman's rejection of her fanatical attentions, Pilate gives her granddaughter a small plastic compact with gold trim. However, this proves to be a dangerous toy with which to entertain Hagar. For when she looks into the mirror of the compact, a deadly, ensnaring, self-reflexive gaze into an alien standard of beauty is invoked. Deluded, she thinks that Milkman isn't attracted to her because she lacks the straight hair and blue eyes that white society has constructed for all as the commodified norm. Thus Hagar rejects the "natural" self that she finds reflected there, the self shaped by the traditions and lifestyles of her grandmother Pilate and mother Reba, both of whom represent Nature in the novel and energetically work against the allure of outward appearances and the colonizing powers of "the look."[9] Hagar fantasizes a persona that she imagines will make her more desirable to her projected lover, Milkman.

And it is precisely because woman in the consumer system bears the burden of sexual and gender-focused exploitation that Hagar rushes off to obtain a mad list of commodities and beauty treatments in order to transform herself into the objectified spectacle worthy of male attention and romance.[10] Among the many things she buys are "a Playtex garter belt, I. Miller No Color hose, Fruit of the Loom panties, and two nylon slips—one white, one pink—one pair of Joyce Fancy Free and one Con Brio" (314). In tragic contrast to Shadrack's rebirth and affirmation of self in the mirror, Hagar loses herself and literally dies of a fever brought on by self-hatred and the disappointment of not being able to make the magical transformation promised by the goods so frantically consumed.

It is, however, in Morrison's next-to-last novel *Tar Baby* (1981) that we see woman, figured in the character Jadine, totally depicted as the narcissistic, exhibitionistic, commodified, and professional object of the male gaze. In a look similar to that into a mirror, both she and her black admirer Son stare at her commodified picture as a fashion model, "playing to the male look" in a French magazine. Morrison emphasizes the voyeuristic quality of the male gaze and reveals Jadine's reification[11] when Son finds it easier to gaze upon the high fashion picture of her in the magazine than look at the real Jadine standing next to him. Moreover, Jadine's narcissism and exhibitionism are made clear as she translates to Son, from French, her biography in the article that, when taken with the "four-page spread" of photos, signifies her total objectification. This latter point is further stressed by the incomplete, fragmented way that she reads her history: "Mademoiselle Childs . . . Graduate of the Sorbonne . . . an accomplished student of art history. . . . a degree in. . . . An American now living in Paris and Rome, where she had a small but brilliantly executed role in a film by . . ." (99–100). Of course, the irony of this biography is that, in the context of the magazine, none of her accomplishments as an educated black woman has meaning in itself; they are only packaging to valorize the object, Jadine, displayed in the pictures, making it more desirable to the spectator/buyers.

As a high-fashion model raised in a white, wealthy household that is completely isolated from the black community which in some manner always asserts itself in the verisimilitude of Morrison's novels, Jadine is figured as more the object of "the look," in accordance with white feminist and cultural criticism's definitions, than any of Morrison's other characters. This issue is underscored with yet another "look" in *Tar Baby,* one that further points up Jadine's shallowness and reification. While out shopping, Jadine chances upon a stunning African woman whom she perceives as a "woman's woman . . . mother/sister/she" (39) with jet black skin wearing a canary yellow dress. However Jadine's admiring gaze at this "unphotographable beauty" is returned with the counter-hegemonic "look" of resistance and rejection. The African woman meets Jadine's gaze with utter contempt as she spits on the street.

Jadine's individualist, careerist ideology and outlook, as well as her professional exhibitionism, signal her construction as the reified end result of a trajectory of situations, characters, and attitudes that critique and explore "the look" in its varied modalities throughout Morrison's first four novels. It is, however, with the production of *Beloved* (1987) that Morrison disrupts the rough temporal continuum of her novels, whose historical settings range from 1919 to the present, to focus a whole novel on an earlier historical moment, that of slavery and its immediate aftermath. And perhaps it is because the mass media in all of its cinematic and electronic, sophisticated representational forms has not yet emerged at the moment of *Beloved'* s historical setting that Morrison's narrative exploration of looking relations does not surface so sharply as it does in her other novels. Yet, perhaps because Morrison is so concerned with rediscovering the socially repressed horror of slavery for a contemporary audience, there is one telling moment in *Beloved* when in a brief description she historicizes "the look" of the oppressor and its genocidal implications for black folk. Noting the elemental power of this "look" by inscribing it with a capital *L,* Morrison tells of slave catchers crossing the Ohio River to recapture the runaway Sethe and her children. On their way to Sethe's house, 124 Bluestone Road, they are instantly spotted by the black community, which discerns their diabolic intentions by "the righteous Look every Negro learned to recognize along with his ma'am's tit. Like a flag hoisted, this righteousness telegraphed and announced the faggot, the whip, the fist, the lie, long before it went public" (157). Finally, then, Morrison reveals to the reader the cruel, arrogant "look" that lies beneath the layered surface of all the varied rationalized "looks" of domination that of naked, violent power lashing out under the thin pretense of "righteousness."

In conclusion, and to return to the subtle "looks" of a contemporary society now more into seduction than brutality, it is interesting to remark upon one final point about Jadine as the perfected object of voyeuristic male desire, an object that stands in contrast to the representation of nearly every other black woman in the trajectory of Morrison's work. In this regard it is significant to note that *Tar Baby* takes as its setting an exotic, isolated island that is a colonial outpost of the French Empire, for both the island and Jadine's body represent the same exotic, colonized fantasy space in the dominant ideology. Moreover, the terms of this isolation and domination extend to all women, for it is Judith Williamson who so eloquently points out this same relationship: "Woman is an island because she is mysterious, distant, and a place to take a holiday; but she is also an island within ideology—surrounded and isolated, as the colony is by the colonizer, held intact as the 'Other' within a sea of sameness" (107).

NOTES

1. Sylvia Winter discusses "the Place of the Norm" which is "constituted by and through the definition of certain desired attributes. The most desired attribute was the 'intellectual faculty.' The sign that pointed to one's possession of this attribute was whiteness of skin. The sign that pointed to its nonpossession was blackness of skin, which revealed non-human being" (152). Richard Dyer argues effectively that the representational power of "whiteness" resides in its ability to be "everything and nothing," to be constructed as the norm against racial difference.

2. Bill Nichols puts it succinctly in his introduction to *Ideology and the Image:* " Ideology operates as a constraint, limiting us to certain places or positions within these processes of communication and exchange. Ideology is how the existing ensemble of social relations represents itself to individuals; it is the image a society gives of itself in order to perpetuate itself. These representations serve to constrain us (necessarily); they establish fixed places for us to occupy that work to guarantee coherent social actions over time. Ideology uses the fabrication of images and the processes of representation to persuade us that how things are is how they ought to be and that the place provided for us is the place we ought to have" (1).

3. Laura Mulvey discusses three "looks" in illusionist, narrative cinema: the look of the camera at the filmic event, the look of the spectator at the screen, and the look of the actors in the narrative. "The conventions of narrative film deny the first two and subordinate them to the third, the conscious aim being always to eliminate intrusive camera presence and prevent a distancing awareness in the audience" (208). Also see Robert Ray, 32–45. Ray agrees that all marks of a film's production are effaced or subordinated "both to establish the cinema's illusion of reality and to encourage audience identification with the characters on the screen" (34).

4. James Baldwin's short story "Going to Meet the Man" with its graphic horror and deep psychological insight into the mind of the violent racist, by showing the spectacle of a black man's torture and murder at the hands of a white mob, makes a powerful narrative argument for looking relations' applying to people of color in ways not explored by the original discourse on "the look." The lynch mob scene in Richard Wright's "Big Boy Leaves Home" also narrativizes this same issue. More generally, it is interesting to note that, as Paul Willermen argues, ". . . In patriarchy the direct object of scopophilic desire can also be male" (43).

5. Judith Williamson notes that "the most likely Other for a white working-class man, is either a woman . . . or a foreigner—in particular somebody black. It is not likely to be someone from the class which controls his livelihood" (103).

6. Here Walter Benjamin articulates a concept that helps us to further understand the Nel/Sula polarities when he says that storytellers are divided into those who "come from afar" and those who stay at home. He continues: "If one wants to picture these two groups through their archaic representatives, one is embodied in the resident tiller of the soil, and the other in the trading seaman. Indeed each sphere of life has, as it were, produced its own tribe of storytellers." Nel has left Medallion only once in her life and represents the traditions of the community. On the other hand, Sula has traveled afar and represents that worldly perspective that is critical of "the second[-]hand lonely" of the women of the town who have seen nothing outside of it (84–5).

7. Here I draw upon Bakhtin's influential essay "Forms of Time and of

the Chronotope in the Novel," in which he defines the chronotope as a process, character, or figuration by which historical time/space is assimilated into the novel, where "time, as it were, thickens, takes on flesh, becomes artistically visible; likewise, space becomes charged and responsible to the movements of time, plot[,] and history" (85). Bakhtin gives special attention to rogues, clowns, and fools and says of them that they "create around themselves their own special little world, their own chronotope" (159). It is precisely in this manner that Shadrack functions in *Sula*, as he represents an earlier, mythical time/space in the formation of black consciousness and culture.

8.   Kaja Silverman observes that "the image of a woman in front of the mirror, playing to both the male look and her own, has become a familiar metaphor of sexual oppression" (139).

9.   In her essay "Community and Nature: The Novels of Toni Morrison," Barbara Christian insightfully points up the polar opposition between Pilate and her brother Macon Dead. Whereas Macon represents "the ideology of a rising northern middle class," so "Pilate, his sister, represents the tradition that identifies with Nature; it has no desire for material things. Pilate is presented in the novel as the healer of the spirit, the guide to essences beyond outward appearance or material things. Born without a navel, she learns how important, though misleading, appearances are to people" (55).

10.   W. F. Haug argues that women are encouraged by advertising to consume in order to transform themselves and become worthy of romance. Haug adds, "Where love succeeds, brought about by this fashionable packaging, and leads to encounters which under existing conditions appear in the form of a commodity-cash nexus, the cost of clothes can be interpreted as 'capital investment'" (73).

11.   Drawing on Lukacs, Fredric Jameson defines the process of reification as "a complex one in which the traditional or 'natural' unities, social forms, human relations, cultural events, even religious systems, are systematically broken up in order to be reconstructed more efficiently, in the form of new post-natural processes or mechanisms" (62–3). Specifically, under the pressure of the commodity system the perception of Jadine is "broken up," abstracted into a series of photos that Son can look at and relate to more easily than the real person. This point is made in another way when Morrison describes the African woman who opposes Jadine as an "unphotographable beauty" (39).

WORKS CITED

Bakhtin, Mikhail. "Forms of Time and of the Chronotope in the Novel." *The Dialogic Imagination: Four Essays by M.M. Bakhtin*. Ed. Michael Holquist. Austin: University of Texas Press, 1981. 84–259.

Benjamin, Walter. "The Storyteller," *Illuminations*. 1955. New York: Schocken, 1969. 83–109.

Berger, John. *Ways of Seeing.* London: Penguin, 1972..

Christian, Barbara. "Community and Nature: The Novels of Toni Morrison." *Black Feminist Criticism.* New York: Pergamon, 1985. 47–65.

———. "The Race for Theory." *Cultural Critique* 6 (Spring 1987): 51–63.

Dyer, Richard. "White." *Screen* 23 (Autumn 1988): 45–64.

Haug, W.F. *Critique of Commodity Aesthetics.* 1971. Minneapolis: University of Minnesota Press, 1986.

Jameson, Fredric. *The Political Unconscious.* Ithaca: Cornell University Press, 1981.

Modleski, Tania, ed. *Studies in Entertainment.* Bloomington: Indiana University Press, 1986.

Morrison, Toni. *Beloved.* 1987. New York: Plume, 1988.

———. *The Bluest Eye.* 1970. New York: Pocket, 1972.

———. *Song of Solomon.* 1977. New York: Signet, 1978.

———. *Sula.* 1973. New York: Bantam, 1975.

———. *Tar Baby.* New York: Signet, 1981.

Mulvey, Laura. "Visual Pleasure and Narrative Cinema." 1975. *Narrative, Apparatus, Ideology.* Ed. Philip Rosen. New York: Columbia University Press, 1986. 198–209.

Neale, Stephen. *Genre.* London: British Film Institute, 1980.

Nichols, Bill. *Ideology and the Image.* Bloomington: Indiana University Press, 1981.

Ray, Robert B. *A Certain Tendency of the Hollywood Cinema 1930–1980.* Princeton: Princeton University Press, 1986.

Silverman, Kaja. "Fragments of a Fashionable Discourse." In Tania Modleski. 139–54.

Willermen, Paul. "Voyeurism, The Look, and Dworkin." *Afterimage* 6 (Summer 1976): 41–50.

Williamson, Judith. "Woman Is an Island: Femininity and Colonization." Modleski. 99–118.

Winter, Sylvia. "Sambos and Minstrels." *Social Text* 1 (1979): 149–56.

PART 2
Sula

Toni Morrison: The Struggle to Depict the Black Figure on the White Page

Timothy B. Powell

> The problem, for us, can perhaps be usefully stated in the irony implicit in the attempt to posit a "black self" in the very Western languages in which blackness itself is a figure of absence, a negation. Ethnocentrism and "logocentrism" are profoundly interrelated in Western discourse as old as the *Phaedrus* of Plato, in which one finds one of the earliest figures of blackness as an absence, a figure of negation.
>
> —Henry Louis Gates, Jr. (7)

This problem of how to represent the black self on the white page, how to overcome the inherent ethnocentrism of the Western literary tradition, is one with which both the critic and the novelist of Afro-American literature must struggle to come to terms. As Gates points out, it is a tradition which dates all the way back to Plato's metaphor of the soul—of a white horse which is described as a "follower of true glory" and another, "of a dark color," which in turn attempts to lead the soul "to do terrible and unlawful deeds." For those who are able to control the dark horse and allow the white one to lead the way, Plato promises a vision of the soul which goes on to "live in light always," whereas those charioteers who cannot control the black horse are condemned "to go down again to darkness," to a life below the earth.

It is this symbology of light and dark, in which blackness becomes the archetype of absence, negation, even evil, which must be overthrown if the "black self" is ever to become understood as presence, affirmation, and good. For centuries blacks in America have effectively undercut the white *logos* by "signifying," or playing upon the meanings of the traditional (white) understanding of the Word. Forced to live in a state of incarceration, wherein they could not express themselves explicitly, the earliest black Americans were impelled to adopt a dualistic and duplicitous form of the white man's language that would allow black meanings to be secretly imbued in the language of the Master. In *The Souls of Black Folks,* W. E. B. Du Bois tells of how slaves were able to turn the words of their oppressors' own songs against them with "veiled and half-articulate messages." In spirituals like "Swing Low Sweet Chariot," it would be clear to the slaves that the "home" to which the chariot carries the listener is not the tranquil green pastures of the twenty-third psalm or even Plato's realm of eternal light, but instead the original home of the slaves—Africa and the promise of freedom which that continent has held for generations of black Americans. For the soul that drives the spirituals is distinctly different from that of Plato's chariot. This "chariot" is not led on by a pure white steed towards a pure white reward but is instead a vehicle for black meaning.

What remains is to bring these meanings to the fore. In the time of slavery the black *logos* (the reasoning, the logic, the Word of black American culture) necessarily had to remain hidden in the semantic shadows of the Master's language. Sadly, for a long time after the Emancipation Proclamation, the black self was still confined to the shadows, the black logos to nuance. Houston Baker, in his book *Blues, Ideology, and Afro-American Literature*, has aptly captured this phenomenon in the critical phrase *black (w)hole.* For it is precisely in a hole on the edge of Harlem where the protagonist of Ralph Ellison's *Invisible Man* eventually finds his wholeness: "The point is that I found a home—or a hole in the ground, if you will" (Ellison, 6). Whether it is literally a hole in the ground in which the protagonist finds his wholeness, as in Richard Wright's "The Man Who Lived Underground," or the kind of shadowy hole in which Bigger Thomas finds himself at the end of his quest for wholeness in *Native Son*, Houston Baker's phrase captures the experience of a generation of Afro-American novelists who have struggled to overcome the dilemma of how to inscribe the black self on the white page. For these are novels and stories of souls who chose to allow the black horse to lead, only to find, as the white *logos* dictates, that their way leads "down again to dark-ness," to a life under the earth.

The battle becomes, for the critic and novelist of Afro-American lit-erature, to de-center the white *logos*, to create a universe of critical and fictional meanings where blackness will no longer connote absence, ne-gation, and, evil but will come to stand instead for affirmation, presence, and good—a struggle for the right/write/rite of Afro-American literature to exist. It is for this reason that critics like Henry Louis Gates and Hous-ton Baker have directed us back to the vernacular, for if the black *logos* can be said to exist at all, it must lie in oral texts like spirituals, blues, and folktales. The task which lies ahead, to my mind, is to lift the black self out of the hole, to bring black meanings out of the semantic shadows of the Master's language and to affirm these meanings in a medium which can truly be called a black text, a text whose margins are ruled by the black *logos*.

No one, to my mind, has accomplished this more fully than Toni Morrison. Her triumph has not come without a struggle, and it is this ongoing quest over the course of her first three novels which I will at-tempt to delineate here. From the pain and dissimulation chronicled in *The Bluest Eye* (1970), to the grief and sadness of *Sula* (1974), Toni Morrison embarks on a journey which ends with the soaring affirmation of black selfhood in the last lines of *Song of Solomon* (1977). It is a quest not only to de-center the white *logos*, but finally to rebuild the center, to dis-cover the powers which lie hidden in the black *logos*. In the course of discussing these three novels, I will attempt to show how Morrison rises out of what Houston Baker calls the black (w)hole to create what I will call, in a signifying riff on Baker's term, a (w)holy black text.

Ironically Morrison's quest for the black *logos* begins with the con-summate example of the *white* text—the Dick-and-Jane reader:

Here is the house. It is green and white. It has a red door. It is very pretty. Here is the family. Mother, Father, Dick, and Jane live in the green-and-white house. They are very happy. . . . See Mother. Mother is very nice. Mother, will you play with Jane? Mother laughs. Laugh, Mother, laugh. See Father. He is big and strong.

Father, will you play with Jane? Father is smiling. Smile, Father, smile. (7)

It is, however, a highly significant beginning, since it points to the fact that all Afro-American writers have, willingly or not, been forced to begin with the Master's language. The Dick-and-Jane reader comes to symbolize the institutionalized ethnocentrism of the white *logos*, of how white values and standards are woven into the very texture of the fabric of American life. And for the protagonist of Toni Morrison's first novel, Pecola Breedlove, it is precisely these standards which will lead to her tragic decline.

The all-too-familiar lines of the Dick-and-Jane primer also serve as an important contrast, pointing out an essential difference between the cold, clear logic of the white text and the often irrational pain of the black text which is to follow. In Langston Hughes's poem "Theme for English B," the poet asks the white instructor, "So will my page be colored that I write?" Hughes' answer is ambiguous—"Being me, it will not be white. / But it will be / a part of you, instructor, / you are white" (640)—intimating that the black poet's page will indeed be different and yet also suggesting that it is never possible to avoid fully the influence of the white instructor. It is the same question which Morrison puts before us at the outset of *The Bluest Eye*. For here again we are confronted with the white instructor—the essential text from which we all learned to read. By prefacing the novel, and subsequent chapters within the novel, with the text of the elementary Dick-and-Jane reader and self-consciously juxtaposing this original or primary white text with her own black text, Morrison is presenting the reader with a challenge, calling immediately into question not only the difference between the white and black text but also how we as critics are going to read what follows.

While the anonymous author of these children's books never explicitly states that these cardboard characters are white, it is nevertheless clear, since the mythos which they embody ("Here is the family. Mother, Father, Dick, and Jane live in the green-and-white house. They are very happy") is so clearly the ideal of Western culture, which is to say white culture. The happiness which is to be taken for granted within the family structure of this (white) family stands in stark contrast to the pain and dissimulation which defines the family life of Pecola Breedlove, one of the central characters in Morrison's "black text." Pecola's family has been ripped apart by alcoholism and anger. There never was a Breedlove house, let alone a "green-and-white" one wallpapered with happiness. The Breedloves are renters, and when Cholly Breedlove, Pecola's father, lands himself in jail, the Breedloves are put outdoors, a condition which Morrison sees as a definitive margin marking the edge of the precipice on which these black families find themselves precariously situated:

> There is a difference between being put *out* and being put out-*doors*. If you are put out, you go somewhere else; if you are out-doors, there is no place to go. The distinction was subtle but final. Outdoors was the end of something, an irrevocable, physical fact, defining and complementing our metaphysical condition. Being a minority in both caste and class, we moved about anyway on the hem of life, struggling to consolidate our weaknesses and hang on. . . . (18)

It is interesting to note, in terms of Toni Morrison's project to discover the black *logos*, that the "hem of life" on which Pecola and Claudia find themselves is measured here relative to a white center or an ethnocentric standard. This is not a novel which inscribes its circle of significance around a black center but instead offers a view of "being a minority" forced to define itself in terms of the ethnocentrism of white culture. Therefore, when Morrison writes here of "our metaphysical condition," she does not refer to a uniquely black metaphysical standard but is in fact speaking of "our . . . condition" relative to the "metaphysical" paradigm (or what Derrida calls the white mythology[1]) of Plato and the rest of Western culture. That the black and Western paradigms are inherently different is, I think, implicitly suggested when Morrison notes that it is a "*physical*" (as opposed to metaphysical) "fact" which defines "our . . . condition." The ethereal, Platonic mythos of truth and goodness is a promise remote and inaccessible to this black family faced with the corporeal concerns of having to spend the night sleeping on the cold, hard ground.

And yet one is always aware in *The Bluest Eye* of the haunting presence of that singular (white) eye of the title, the view from the center which keeps these black characters feeling as though they have been consigned to live on "the hem of life." For example, when Pecola menstruates for the first time and Claudia and Frieda take her outside to hide the mysterious accident from their mother, there are the "fascinated eyes in a dough-white face" of their neighbor Rosemary, who immediately rushes to tell Mrs. MacTeer that "Frieda and Claudia are out here playing nasty!" (27). And when Pecola strolls down to the neighborhood candy store, she confronts, in the eyes of the white shopkeeper, that glare of "glazed separateness" which she has felt "lurking in the eyes of all white people" (42), making her feel ugly and unwanted. For Cholly Breedlove, Pecola's father, these cruel blue eyes intervene in the form of two hunters, shining their flashlights on his nakedness as he is caught in the midst of his first sexual encounter. The anger and humiliation which boils up in Cholly is never reconciled, and his hatred becomes displaced through transference: "For some reason Cholly had not hated the white men; he hated, despised, the girl" (37). Like Cholly, Pecola's mother also comes to see herself through blue eyes—preferring the identity which her white employers give to her, as the "ideal servant" who always keeps their house in order—rather than acknowledge the emotional ruins of her own life: her brutal marriage to Cholly and her cruel relationship with her own daughter, into whom she beats a "fear of life" (102). By looking at themselves through the eyes of a white culture, the Breedlove family lose all notion of their own black identity: "It was as though some mysterious all-knowing master had given each one a cloak of ugliness to wear, and they had each accepted it without question" (34).

Despite the fragility of her characters' self-images, Morrison has not failed, here in her first novel, in her quest to posit a black self. *The Bluest Eye* is meant to be a novel of failure; it is a portrait which depicts how a young black woman's idea of what constitutes a true self is de-centered by the implicitly ethnocentric tenets of the society into which she is born. Pecola Breedlove fails to discover a true self precisely because she allows her values to be dictated by the white mythology. As Claudia says, "All the world had agreed that a blue-eyed, yellow-haired, pink-skinned doll was what every girl child treasured. 'Here,' they said, 'this is beautiful, and if you are on this day "worthy" you may have it'" (20). But whereas "Claudia rebels against the dictates of the white mythology, destroying and dismembering the dolls she is given for Christmas, Pecola allows herself to be wooed (finally into insanity) by the dream of the bluest eye, a panacea for all of her earthly woes. She becomes convinced that, if only she had blue eyes like the painted, all-too-cheerful eyes of Shirley Temple that stare back at her each morning from her milk mug, then she too would be accepted into the world of "green-and-white" houses and families that are "very happy" which has been promised to her in the "white text" wherein she first learned to read about the world. Shirley Temple, Dick and Jane, the blonde Christmas doll—these are the embodiments of the white logos, the templates which society holds up for Pecola to judge herself against. These figures of the white mythology to which she compares herself are the catalysts which precipitate Pecola's psychic disintegration, leaving her alienated from any sense of an authentic black self.

In terms of Morrison's quest to inscribe the black figure on the white page, to raise her characters out of the black (w)hole, *The Bluest Eye* can be seen as a direct confrontation with the white *logos*, a necessary first step towards clearing the way for the (w)holy black text to appear. For it is Morrison's shattering contrasts between the "big and strong," "smiling" Father of the white text and broken-spirited Cholly, the father in the black text, which make clear the inadequacies of the white mythology for representing the black self. Morrison literally is deconstructing the essential white text, removing capitalization, punctuation, and finally the spacing until the white text is nothing more than a fragmentation of its former self at the beginning of the chapters:

SEEFATHERHEISBIGANDSTRONGFATH
ERWILLYOUPLAYWITHJANEFATHER
ISSMILINGSMILEFATHERSMILESMILE (105)

The deconstruction of the white text complete and the black text clearly differentiated, Morrison is then able to move on to the greater challenge of attempting to affirm blackness as present and valuable, to write the black *logos*.

In *Sula*, Morrison attempts to move her focus outside the sphere of influence of the white *logos* by centering her novel around a black com-

munity. Gone are the "fascinated eyes in a dough-white face" which be-
little and demean the black self. By conscientiously removing these white
eyes, Morrison brings into focus a world which revolves around a black
cultural center, a community governed by black mythology. And yet she
is not quite able, in her second novel, to wrench herself and her characters free from what Jacques Derrida calls "the imperialism of the logos."
For even though the plot of the novel unfolds in a small Midwestern town
inhabited solely by black folk, the tyranny of the white *logos* and the
power which it exerts through its ability to name remain strongly, if implicitly, present. The town is called "the Bottom," and the origin of its
name comes, Morrison writes, from "A joke. A nigger Joke." A "good
white farmer" promises freedom and "a piece of bottom land" to his slave,
provided the slave performs a particularly difficult task. Once the slave
has complied, instead of delivering a plot of fertile valley property, the
farmer gives the black man his freedom and a tract of land "high up in the
hills." When the slave queries his master on the name *Bottom*, the white
man tricks him, justifying his actions by explaining that, yes, the land is
high up in the hills, "but when God looks down, it's the bottom. That's
why we call it so. It's the bottom of heaven—best land there is" (5).

More than just a malevolent prank at the expense of a presumably
uneducated slave, Morrison's anecdote is an insightful testimony as to
how blacks have been manipulated by the white *logos*. The black slave is
disenfranchised of the fertile valley land that should rightfully be his, not
because of his ignorance but because of the duplicity inherent in the white
man's logic and language, that controlling power which the white man
wields in the form of the *logos*. The slave is in no position to argue, since
it is a verbal contract to which he has committed and the *logos* (i.e., law,
logic, word) is controlled by the white master. The final irony is that,
when the valley community becomes economically prosperous enough
to be able to move from an agrarian to a service-oriented society, the
whites buy back the elevated property and the blacks once again wind up
on the bottom. The moral of the story is, of course, that the dominance of
white society has not been halted by the eradication of slavery or the
advent of civil rights, since neither of these actions dispels the primacy of
logocentrism in Western civilization.

In "The Quest for Self," Dorothy H. Lee has correctly noted that each of Morrison's novels embraces the theme of the main character's search for identity. As Lee points out, *Sula* is, like *The Bluest Eye,* the story of a failed quest, a tale of Sula's inability to create for herself a true sense of self-worth. She loses Nel, her childhood friend in whom she sees another "version of herself," through her own callous and self-centered desire for satisfaction when she takes Nel's husband to bed. Later she loses her lover Ajax, the man who sets her free from her endless wandering from man to man, ironically, because Ajax senses that his own freedom is in danger from her obsessive love. She dies, finally, unable to fulfill her quest, unable to find and hold onto a truly black self.

Again and again in *Sula*, Morrison returns to the image of the river with a "closed place" in the middle. The initial significance of this figure relates to an episode early in Sula's life in which she and Nel are playing along the banks of the river, swinging a young boy around and around by the arms when accidently his hands slip away and he is hurled into the muddy water. Unable to swim, Sula and Nel watch helplessly as the boy's black head disappears beneath the water and the river embraces him, leaving a dark "closed place in the water" (52). As the novel wears on and Sula's life is lived out in its recurring patterns of loss and despair, this "closed place" becomes an image of the void within Sula, of the absence at her very center, for as Morrison writes "she had no center, no speck around which to grow" (103). Thus in the final analysis, it becomes clear that, although *Sula* is a novel centered around black people and black culture, the power of the white *logos* is still very much in evidence. Blackness is still being used here to mean absence or negation: *Black center* is read here as "no center."

In her first two novels, Toni Morrison seems to reside within the critical sphere inscribed by Houston Baker's term *black (w)hole,* for both novels describe a search for wholeness in the shadowy periphery of a society dominated by the white logos. And yet to attempt to apply the term *black (w)hole* critically to Sula or Pecola is to miss much of Morrison's irony. Unlike the Invisible Man who, with a pride born of struggle, calls his hole on the edge of Harlem "home," or Bigger Thomas who, in digging himself into the hole in which he finds himself at the end of the novel, at least feels that he has succeeded in temporarily asserting his manhood, neither *The Bluest Eye* nor *Sula* is meant to claim that the situation of their respective protagonists is to be construed as wholeness. Pecola's and Sula's quests for identity are of ironic proportion, with no heroes, no victories, no redemption.

And yet the movement from "on the hem of life" to "no center" is, in the context of Toni Morrison's own project to write the black *logos*, a step forward. Unlike the authors of the great novels of Ellison and Wright, Morrison does not ask the reader to accept these characters as being portraits of black (w)holeness.[2] Sula Peace's quest for identity ends, like Pecola Breedlove's, in frustration. Both of these characters, like the town in which Sula grew up, have been ironically (and rather heavy-handedly) misnamed, for they know neither peace nor love, only struggle and alienation. They are not whole, but fragile and fragmented. And yet if the critical reader is able to accept the logic of Morrison's project—that is to say, to take an active part in un-learning the white *logos*—then it becomes possible to see this move from a white center to "no center" as progress, for in doing so Toni Morrison has rejected the compromise implicit in the term *black (w)hole* —the idea that wholeness is possible, provided the black self is willing to remain confined to the shadowy realm of basements in Harlem or abandoned tenements in Chicago.

In *Song of Solomon*, Toni Morrison continues her ongoing quest to free herself and her characters from the imperialism of the white *logos*. Like *Sula*, the novel begins in a black community ("the part of the world that mattered") in which blackness is still judged by the standards of the white *logos*, which is to say as absence, negation, and evil. The protagonist's subservience to the white *logos* is symbolized by his name. Milkman has been marked with the brand of the white *logos* at birth— given the name Macon Dead III. It is a familial scar inherited from his grandfather who, upon emancipation from slavery, was mischristened by a drunken Yankee soldier who grossly reinterpreted his grandfather's statement that he was born in Macon, Georgia, and that his father was dead. The black community attempts to signify away the brand by renaming the boy *Milkman*, although this name too is stultifying in that it originates out of an incident in which his mother is caught nursing her only son well past the age when city blacks consider a child sufficiently grown to feed himself. Both names arrest Milkman's maturation. Incarcerated within this linguistic prison, he dreams despondently of some ancestor, some lithe young man with onyx skin and legs as straight as cane stalks, who had a name that was real. A name given to him at birth with love and seriousness. A name that was not a joke, nor a disguise, nor a brand name. But who this lithe young man was, and where his cane-stalk legs carried him from or to, could never be known. No. Nor his name. (17–18)

As in Toni Morrison's first two novels, the central storyline of *Song of Solomon* is a quest for black identity. In Milkman's case it is a metaphorical struggle for life, for in order to become un-Dead he must somehow regain "the name that was real." Like Morrison's own project, Milkman's quest is to dis-cover the originary black *logos* and the mythical powers it holds.

Whereas Pecola Breedlove and Sula Peace seem sentenced from birth to a life of despair, Milkman seems fated from the first to achieve a greater destiny. He is the first black to be born in Mercy Hospital, and his entrance into the world is harkened by the ill-fated flight of Robert Smith, Southside's seemingly innocuous insurance salesman, who fashions himself a pair of blue silk wings and leaps to his death in an aborted attempt to fly, as the townspeople watch from below and Milkman's aunt, Pilate, sings:

> *O Sugarman done fly away*
> *Sugarman done gone*
> *Sugarman cut across the sky*
> *Sugarman gone home . . . .* (5)

With Mr. Smith's failed though spirited attempt to conquer logic and gravity, Milkman is welcomed somewhat auspiciously into the world, fated it would seem from birth to carry on this vision, this dream of flying back "home." Before he can fulfill his destiny, however, he must first recover his original name. To do so requires his first unlearning the white *logos* in order to recover the power imbued in a truly black identity.

His quest is an interpretive one, the fragment of the blues song which

Pilate sings at the birth/death being the essential text which will lead him to his goal. But before he can learn to read this truly black text (and it is significant that the text is sung and therefore unwritten), he must first free himself from the linguistic bondage into which he was born. It is Pilate who becomes the boy's tutor in unlearning the white *logos*, who, even if she cannot free him, at least teaches him to love to be free. For Pilate is a figure who defies (white) logic and thereby challenges Milkman to drop the precepts of the white *logos*. Pilate's conjuring powers can be seen in the police station where, before Milkman's very eyes, she is able to transform herself into a withered hag, old and shrunken beyond her years. Furthermore, she possesses the power to communicate with the ghost of her dead father, although she continually misinterprets the spectral text which her father reveals in his visits from the other side of the grave, believing his only words, "Sing, sing," to be a command rather than an attempt to communicate to his daughter the now-forgotten name of his bride.

The origin of Pilate's mystical powers would appear to lie in her possession of the original text of her name, inscribed on the piece of brown paper to which her father copied it, "as illiterate people do, [with] every curlicue, arch and bend in the letters" (18), that she keeps hanging from her ear in a small metal box. Again it is significant that her name has been written by a father who is illiterate, for it suggests that the original text to which Milkman's interpretive quest aspires is in fact pre-lexical and thus beyond the margins of the *logos'* s field of power.

It is a quest which leads Milkman back to the small farming community of his father and Pilate's youth—a quest fed, at least initially, by both emotional need (ignited by Pilate's spiritual fostering) and material greed (inflamed by his father's tales of lost gold). However, once Milkman returns to Montour County and experiences the elation of being surrounded by folk who know, remember, and speak lovingly of his "people," he loses sight of his avarice and becomes completely absorbed in his quest to find his true name, his familial identity. Having escaped the narrow confines of his hometown, Milkman discovers that the first level of his misnaming is stripped away, and he becomes not "Milkman" but Macon Dead's son. It is here that he encounters the second tutor in his ongoing education to learn how to unread the white *logos*. Circe, like Pilate, is a conjurer figure, a keeper of spirits, a vessel of secrets from the past, a figure so utterly beyond the pale of the white *logos* that Milkman finds himself having to "take a chance" when he invokes "logic" to try to understand even her very existence:

> Milkman struggled for a clear thought, so hard to come by in a dream: Perhaps this woman is Circe. But Circe is dead. This woman is alive. That was as far as he got, because although the woman was talking to him, she *had* to be dead. Not because of the wrinkles, and the face so old it could not be alive, but because out of the toothless mouth came the strong, mellifluent voice of a twenty-year-old girl. (242–3)

It is from Circe that Milkman learns the first names of his grandmother and grandfather, although Circe's knowledge, like Pilate's, is fragmented and unsure. Circe, however, is able to provide Milkman with the direction he needs in order to continue his quest, telling him that his grandfather's "people" came from "down around Culpepper somewhere. Charlemagne or something like that" (246).

When Milkman arrives in the rural hill country of Virginia, in his ancestral home of Shalimar, the brand of the white *logos* is immediately evident to the town folk:

> He hadn't found them fit enough or good enough to want to know their names, and believed himself too good to tell them his. They looked at his skin and saw it was as black as theirs, but they knew he had the heart of the white men who came to pick them up in trucks when they needed anonymous, faceless laborers. (269)

These toothless, poverty-stricken men who look sideways at him with scorn and attempt to slit his throat are, however, to be the teachers who erase the last vestiges of the white *logos* from Milkman and instill in him the knowledge necessary to be able to interpret the truly black text. Walking through the woods, following the bobbing lantern ahead as they trail the hounds, Milkman finally comes to realize the intuitive, almost primordial understanding which these men possess. For they are the keepers of a language unknown to him, a lexicon which has been lost beneath the veneer of civilization. As he struggles to keep up with the other hunters, trying to keep the light of the lantern in sight, he catches his first glimmer of understanding:

> The men and the dogs were talking to each other. In distinctive voices they were saying distinctive, complicated things. . . . And the dogs spoke to the men. . . . It was all language. . . . No, it was not language; it was what there was before language. Before things were written down. Language in the time when men and animals did talk to one another. (281)

There is a degree of authenticity to their use of language, to this inherently oral text, which Milkman had never previously imagined. And when the men in the mountains of Virginia finally shoot the bobcat from his perch atop the tree, Milkman is given his final initiation into the rites/rights/writes of his race which will enable him to interpret faithfully the semantic nuances of the truly black text. The men cajole him to reach into the carcass saying, "Don't get the lungs, now. Get the *heart*" (286, emphasis added).

It is only by grasping the heart of the black idiom that Milkman is able to complete his interpretive quest. Only after this ritual has been performed does he realize that the song which he has heard the children of Shalimar singing over and over again, in what he takes to be an incessant, senseless children's game, is not, as he had initially thought, merely a "meaningless rhyme" but rather a fuller version of the essential text which Pilate misinterpreted as her father's telling her to "Sing, sing." Here, in the oral text passed on from generation to generation through children, Milkman learns that the interpretive trail which has led him from "Sugarman" to "Charlemagne" to "Shalimar" and finally to "Solomon" holds the secret true ancestry and revives a long subsumed desire in Milkman for flight. He returns to Southside to collect Pilate and the sack containing his grandfather's bones, whereupon they return together to the place in the mountains of Virginia where his great-grandfather leapt from the bonds of slavery into the arms of freedom.

With Milkman's leap Toni Morrison raises Afro-American fiction out of the black (w)hole, giving us instead a (w)holy black text. It is "whole" in the sense that Milkman has escaped the linguistic prison into which the drunken Yankee soldier wantonly threw his grandfather and all subsequent generations of his family. He has recovered that "name that was real" and with it an identity based on blackness as an affirmation, a source of wondrous power and heartfelt pride. By *holy* I mean to suggest that Morrison has been able to draw upon the soul of the spirituals, to bring out of the semantic shadows the true meaning of "home" in the blues passage "Sugarman done fly away . . . / Sugarman gone home," and with it the true feelings of strength and joy which have always resided in the black *logos* and yet which have for too long remained confined to black (w)holes. I would also like to expand the conventional religious connotations of *holy* to include Toni Morrison's ability to raise folktales like the South Sea Islands' myth of the flying Africans on which the story of Milkman is based and the blues passages which provide Milkman with the oral history of his ancestor to a level worthy of being called sacred texts of the Afro-American tradition.

With the writing of *Song of Solomon,* Toni Morrison thus successfully achieves her quest to overthrow the white *logos,* to escape the "glare of glazed separateness" that Pecola finds "lurking in the eyes of all white people" (*Bluest Eye,* 42), making her feel small and ashamed of her blackness, and to free herself and her characters of the duplicity and power that the white landowner wielded over the ancestors of the Bottom. Morrison is effectively able to draw upon the power of the black *logos* to inscribe a black figure, a black reality upon the white page. It is a reality defined not by the mythos of (white) Western culture, the phenomenological "things-in-themselves" of Hegel or Heidegger or the naturalistic "realism" of Zola or Balzac but instead a reality governed by the black *logos*—a magical realism. "Black people believe in magic," Toni Morrison has said, "it is part of our heritage" (Watkins, 50). It is this heritage which Toni Morrison has drawn strength from in order to depict blackness as affirmation, presence, and good in the creation of a (w)holy black text.

NOTES

1. See Jacques Derrida. "White Mythology: Metaphor in the Text of Philosophy." *Margins of Philosophy.* Trans. Alan Bass (Chicago: University of Chi-

cago Press, 1982). For Derrida's thoughts on the influence of logocentrism, see Jacques Derrida, *Of Grammatology*, trans. Gayatri Chakravorty Spivak (Baltimore: Johns Hopkins University Press, 1976).

2. I do not mean to contend here that the element of black wholeness which Ellison and Wright describe is not without ironic overtones. Rather I wish to point out that Toni Morrison, still early on here in her quest for the (w)holy black text, at no time allows the reader to be content with considering these characters as whole.

WORKS CITED

Baker, Houston A. Jr. *Blues, Ideology, and Afro-American Literature.*Chicago: University of Chicago Press, l984.

Ellison, Ralph. *Invisible Man.* New York: Vintage, 1972.

Gates, Henry Louis, Jr. "Criticism in the Jungle." *Black Literature and Literary Theory.* Edited by Henry Louis Gates, Jr., New York: Methuen, 1984. 1–24.

Hughes, Langston. "Theme For English B." *The Norton Anthology of Modern Poetry.* Edited by Richard Ellmann and Robert O'Clair. New York: Norton, 1973. 640–41.

Lee, Dorothy H. "The Quest for Self: Triumph and Failure in the Works of Toni Morrison." *Black Women Writers: A Critical Evaluation.* Edited by Mari Evans. Garden City: Anchor. 1984. 346–59.

Morrison, Toni. *The Bluest Eye.* 1970. New York: Pocket, 1972.

———. *Song of Solomon.* New York: Knopf, 1977.

———. *Sula.* 1973. New York: Bantam, 1975.

Plato. *Phaedrus. The Works of Plato.* Trans. Benjamin Jowett. Edited by Irwin Edman. New York: Random, 1928.

Watkins. Mel. "Talk with Toni Morrison." *New York Times Book Review* 11 (September 1977): 50.

Who Cares? Women-Centered Psychology in *Sula*

Diane Gillespie and Missy Dehn Kubitschek

In the 1970s and '80s, an explosion of creativity in Afro-American fiction has made famous Ernest Gaines, David Bradley, Toni Morrison, Alice Walker, and Gloria Naylor, to name only a few. As the last three names suggest, this "second renaissance" of fiction has a strong female component. In these same decades, a new psychology of women has emerged, in part through the research of Nancy Chodorow, Carol Gilligan, and the Stone Center psychologists at Wellesley College. In that it focuses on women's rather than men's experiences and derives its interpretative categories from women's own descriptions of their experiences, this body of research may be described as women centered. These researchers have listened to and analyzed women's voices; as part of this exploration, they have turned to literature by and about women where emerging psychological conceptualizations of female development are, as Carol Gilligan notes, well represented ("Moral Orientation," 29). Women-centered psychologists have found caretaking and its associated values of empathy, affiliation, nurturance, and a collective vision of social life to be central to female experience. This new psychology of women challenges the traditional male idea of the self-in-relationship. In order to explore this self-in-relationship, women-centered psychology has privileged the continuing mother-daughter relationship, an important expansion of the male model of the self. This new paradigm, in turn, requires expansion.

As yet, most of the literary models used in women-centered psychology have been of middle- or upper-class Euro-American origin (for example, see Jean Wyatt's analysis of *Mrs. Dalloway*). Minority literature offers women-centered psychology another expansion of the female self beyond the Euro-American mother-daughter or friend-friend dyad; Afro-American literature often explores a self-in-community. The mother-daughter relationship is certainly crucial in the development of the female self, but powerful social and economic forces affect that central relationship and female development as a whole. In their depiction of female characters, minority women authors delineate experiences and psychological processes described in the new women-centered psychology; they also challenge its limited assumptions about self-in-relation.

Toni Morrison's *Sula,* a contemporary novel about female friendship, offers a view of female psychological development that defies traditional male-centered interpretations of female development and calls out for an expansion of the women-centered paradigm. Both the novel's subject (minority experience) and its treatment implicitly critique the psychology's usual focus on the experiences of middle-class white women who are often bound by conventional social relationships. Nancy Chodorow's theory of the reproduction of mothering, Carol Gilligan's work on women's moral and psychological development, and the continuing work of the Stone Center offer a paradigm through which to perceive the novel, while *Sula's* exploration of women's experiences fleshes out the still-emerging psychological schema of these researchers.

Sula demonstrates the inadequacy of traditional male-centered psychology's idea of the self by showing that men raised to be autonomous, contained selves become alienated and unhappy; though the women's lives do not run smoothly, they are raised to be selves-in-community and, except for Sula, have more fulfilling lives. In showing these two modes of self-definition, the novel anticipated the findings of women-centered psychology. Nancy Chodorow's *The Reproduction of Mothering* provided the basis that women-centered psychologists have since used to discuss the origins of gender-identity differences between men and women. Significantly, although Chodorow explores individual psychological development, her theory explicitly rests on the social fact of women's having been the primary caretakers of children. Like Toni Morrison, she sees the construction of an individual, gendered self as the result of inescapable social context.

In her groundbreaking 1981 essay on female friendship in five novels including *Sula,* Elizabeth Abel disputes the sufficiency of Chodorow's theory of the reproduction of mothering. Chodorow argues that because women, historically, have reared children, boys have had to differentiate themselves from their mothers in order to establish firm gender identities. In contrast, girls have identified with their mothers, and the resulting attachment has established the basis for empathic understanding of others' needs and experiences. Critical to the girl's preoedipal experience is her mother's double identification. In "Family Structure and Feminine Personality," Chodorow states, "A woman identifies with her own mother and, through identification with her child, she (re)experiences herself as a cared-for child" (47). In addition, a girl forms her gender identity by observing female role activities that are "immediately apprehensible in the world of her daily life" (51). She does not have to repress or reject this preoedipal identification with her mother in developing. Instead, she continues to identify with her mother and other women in her social world after the preoedipal period: "Sex role training and social interaction build upon and reinforce the largely unconscious development" (54) so that girls become relationally oriented.

In her analysis Abel identifies and describes a common underlying psychological process or emotional pattern that, she argues, transcends "the diverse cultural situations" of the several novels. She criticizes Chodorow's theory for overestimating the degree of mother-daughter identification and undervaluing the role of women's friendships in "fulfilling the desire for identification" (418). In this framework, several of the friendships exemplify women's tendency toward identification as a source of personal growth. *Sula,* in contrast, exemplifies "the tensions generated by the conflict between identification and autonomy" (426); the novel highlights this issue of "ambivalence and separation" in female friendships (443).

Abel presents a thoughtful case for the importance of identification in female friendships, largely unexplored terrain at the time of her essay. Her approach, however, has a fundamental weakness which limits her interpretation: her analysis decontextualizes female friendship. The scope necessary for a psychological theory of engenderment has been the occasional subject of feminist critical exchanges. Literary critic Judith Gardiner pointed out immediately that Abel's analysis isolated Nel and Sula's relationship. Psychologist Harriet Lerner criticizes feminist psychoanalytic theory from a family systems perspective that attempts to restore social context.

Overlooking the context of female friendship particularly distorts *Sula,* the only Afro-American novel in Abel's analysis. In limiting her discussion to Nel and Sula, she assumes *a priori* that *Sula* centers on self-in-relation rather than self-in-community The Afro-American tradition has, however, always been steeped in context, assumed self-in-community (Levine; Genovese). Hazel Carby, for example, distinguishes the nineteenth-century Afro-American women's tradition in fiction from the Euro-American women's tradition on just these grounds: "But [Iola Leroy's] future was perceived as social, a transformed individual committed to a definition of self in relation to community" (75). *Iola Leroy* was, of course, long thought to be the first novel by an American black woman; *Sula's* immersion in social context partakes of a long tradition. Morrison refuses to privilege the individual female in relation to any particular other. For female residents of the Bottom, the self exists in relation to the entire community; there is no alternative.

Abel's exclusive focus on the friendship makes invisible or uninteresting two major components of the novel: first, the interaction of male and female perspectives and, second, the social and economic influence on female identity. Relocating the critical focus from the dyad of a friendship to this social context reveals *Sula's* exploration of the interaction between traditional male and female visions of sociality and hence of the self. It recognizes *Sula's* challenges to current women-centered psychology limited by class and race: What happens when rigidly held social conventions, such as those characteristic of the middle class, determine the course of female psychological development? What happens to female psychological development when poverty and racism intervene in the process of mothering?

Nel and Sula's friendship forms part of an interchange between male and female versions of the community. A return to Chodorow's theory offers a means of analyzing *Sula's* presentation of the traditional male vision of sociality. In her postulation of two very different gender-determined visions of the self, Chodorow concludes that "masculine personality . . . comes to be defined more in terms of denial of relation and connection . . . whereas feminine personality comes to include a fundamental definition of self in relationship" (169), a perception borne out in Gilligan's *In a Different Voice* and Jean Baker Miller's *Toward a New Psychology of Women*. Because boys must successfully separate from the mother, individuation becomes the overriding issue in the development of masculine identity, while connection and involvement with others are denied. Not surprisingly, then, male-centered developmental theories, such as those of Freud and Erikson, designate the achievement of separation as a prerequisite for intimate relationships.

Sula's narrator clearly finds this separation inimical to personal fulfillment, but she depicts male sociality, as she does female sociality, in the total social context of the novel. An interpretation like Abel's decontextualizes the girls' friendship not only from the other women in the novel but from the men also. A holistic interpretation of gender must admit and analyze *Sula's* interactive, transformative interchanges between male and female visions.

I. THE MALE VISION OF COMMUNITY

Women-centered psychologists cast doubt on the assertion "that separation leads to attachment and that individuation eventuates in mutuality" (Gilligan, *Different Voice,* 155*)*. The narrator's depiction of male characters in *Sula* shares their skepticism. In achieving identity through maintaining distance, the males experience a diminished capacity for intimacy and interdependence. Nel's father's occupation becomes a synecdoche for his position in the family—rarely at home, he's "a seaman." When their relationships become troubled, BoyBoy, Jude, and A. Jacks[1] leave Medallion. Such a need to distance themselves fits with Chodorow's assumption that, "for boys, identification processes and masculine role learning are not likely to be embedded in relationship with their fathers or men but rather to involve the denial of affective relationship to their mothers" (177). In *Sula,* with the single exception of A. Jacks, men who do not physically remove themselves from their mothers or mother surrogates cannot maintain their identities. The Deweys' individual identities dissipate completely to merge into one, and they not only stop growing physically but remain boys in mind, "mischievous, cunning, private and completely unhousebroken" (73). Tar Baby and Plum "lose" themselves in alcohol and heroin, respectively. In this women-centered portrayal, nearly all men are impoverished in their ability to relate to others. Separation "dislocates" men, dissipating the community; closeness suffocates them, dissipating the self.

In contrast to other male characters, Shadrack does participate in the community, albeit from a distance. Unlike his Biblical namesake, Shadrack emerges from his inferno, W.W.I, neither personally nor socially triumphant. He is alienated, "with no past, no language, no tribe, no source, no address book . . ." (10). The community recognizes his distance by considering him crazy. A self, "a grave black face" unconnected to anyone else, he alone of the male characters "struggle[s] to order and focus experience" (12) and in so doing stakes out "a place for fear" so that he can control it. His ordering principle, National Suicide Day, becomes a recognized ritual in the community.

Though Shadrack's degree of alienation differentiates him from the other characters, his thinking nevertheless shows two traits which Gilligan considers central supports for the male model of a completely independent and detachable self: an extreme respect for others' autonomy and an overarching abstraction as the basis for all moral action. Shadrack only once directly interacts with another member of the community (with Sula, after Chicken Little's death). The annual National Suicide Day parade welcomes any participant but requires none; its form is fixed whether it involves only Shadrack or half the town. Shadrack thus lives a vision that requires nothing of others, a position that links him to the men of Gilligan's study: "By limiting interference, [men tend to] make life in community safe, protecting autonomy through reciprocity, extending the same consideration to others and self" (*Different Voice*, 37–8). In expressing fear through his ritual, Shadrack fulfills his responsibility to himself; by allowing others to participate, he extends it. By remaining physically isolated, he cordons off aggression in himself and limits any possible interference with his own or others' autonomy. Shadrack thus sustains somewhat tenuous connections rather than severing them, as BoyBoy and Jude do; in absorbing this man and his bizarre insight, the Bottom coheres as a community.

This alienation, perhaps of necessity, makes Shadrack's moral vision abstract. When Sula stumbles into his shack after Chicken Little has drowned, Shadrack sees "the skull beneath" Sula's face—a truth which abstracts from the context of Chicken Little's death (with which Sula is preoccupied) to the human condition. Shadrack understands that the presence of death makes human connections fragile, ever-changing, dangerous, especially if one attempts to live in proximity to others. In this same scene the narrator sets the background for contrasting the morality of abstraction with the morality of social connection. Shadrack attempts to comfort Sula with a single word, "always"—without further context, a cryptic abstraction of maddeningly contradictory meanings. Sula, on the other hand, discovers Shadrack as an individual through an empathic response to his situation; unlike the rest of the town, she sees a neat, orderly, unthreatening person whom she dubs "Shad." Because she recognizes him as an individual, her visit leaves an impression on him. As women-centered psychologist Janet Surrey might explain, through Sula's presence, Shadrack recognizes his "need to be seen . . . for who [he] is and [his] need to see and understand the other with ongoing authenticity" (9). Shadrack treasures his only post-war experience of self-in-relationship.

Shadrack's impersonal truth transcends his social context until Sula's death, when the certainty of "always" crumbles and the narrator exposes the depth of his loneliness. Complete autonomy and its guardian abstract morality have been made bearable by the complementary experience of being "recognized and seen" by Sula. Deprived of the hope of continued relationship, Shadrack cannot maintain his role. In the canonical American novel, Shadrack's type of independence, with its concomitants of alienation and abstraction, has been privileged; its accompanying loneliness has in fact been valorized (Chase; Baym). In the usual pattern, Shadrack's moral vision and its development would dominate and Sula's would recede. The narrator of this women-centered novel, however, portrays Shadrack's world view in a reciprocal interchange with a female vision of moral connection.

II. THE FEMALE EXPERIENCE OF COMMUNITY

As Chodorow emphasized the source of different male and female conceptions of the self, Carol Gilligan has traced the processes of this gender development. Complemented by Stone Center research, Gilligan's paradigm offers an illuminating vocabulary for a beginning discussion of *Sula's* female characters. At the same time, *Sula* delineates moral problems and paradoxes for which women-centered psychology has as yet no language, limited as it has been by its focus on the white middle class.

Working from interviews with women about moral dilemmas in their lives, Gilligan traces a distinctive development in the moral thinking of her female subjects quite different from that identified in dominant developmental theories based on studies of boys and men. Whereas the male models value individuality and abstract principles, such as "justice," which apparently safeguard it, the female voice emergent from these interviews speaks of the primacy of emotional connection and its preservation. Women's concern for this continuity leads them to exercise care in their interactions with others to make decisions not on the basis of abstractions but with regard to a particular context. Outside of psychology, discussions of "particular context" have frequently used different terminology, "community" being the most common. The centrality of this concern to Afro-American fiction is apparent from Susan Willis's remark on "the single most common feature in fiction by black women writers: that of return to the community" (116). In her discussion of selfhood in Paule Marshall's 1959 *Brown Girl, Brownstones,* Mary Helen Washington accents the contextual model and its implications for individual identity: "Selfhood is not defined negatively as separateness from others, nor is it defined narrowly by the individual dyad—the child and its mother—but on the larger scale as the ability to recognize one's continuity with the larger community" (159).

Women developing this ethic of care progress through three stages, Gilligan suggests, which are characterized by unique definitions of moral responsibility to others; first, an unsocialized selfishness; second, submersion in others; third, an authenticity in relationship. Self-centered and isolated, a woman in the first stage conceives of morality as imposed from without; in this unsocialized state, her primary concern is survival. In the second stage, she selflessly immerses herself in other people; defining morality by social conventions and traditional feminine goodness, she concerns herself with service. Selfishness is equated with immorality, with not "being good." In the third stage, a woman includes responsibilities to herself as well as to others, an inclusion that forms the basis for authentic emotional connections.

After Chodorow, most women-centered psychologists recognize the preeminent influence of the mother-daughter relationship, its quality an important determinant of the young girl's successful passage through Gilligan's stages of moral development. This primary relationship is widely recognized in feminist (or womanist, to use Alice Walker's term) writing and criticism (Christian, Walker, and Rich). Several prominent black women novelists have attributed their artistic successes to their mothers' and grandmothers' empowering influences (Washington). These real-life stories, of course, embody the extraordinary rather than the usual life. Gloria Wade-Gayles speaks movingly of black women's ambivalences in reading fiction about the mother-daughter relationship, indicating that they are

> often disappointed by the recurring image of the cold, distant and domineering mother. We want to see mothers embracing their daughters—loving them openly and unashamedly. We want to see mothers and daughters sharing laughter and bearing [sic] their souls to each other in moments of intimacy. And yet, we want the truths of our mothers' lives even if those truths are sometimes "cruel enough to stop the blood." We must see them first as persons with dreams and needs no less important than ours, and then as mothers who sacrificed their dreams in order to put our hands on the pulse of freedom and self-hood. (12)

Wade-Gayles's comment reiterates Chodorow's social concern: the social context of the mother-daughter relationship structures female personality and relational capabilities. Toni Morrison has consistently delineated the results of mother-daughter relationships damaged by racism and poverty. In *The Bluest Eye,* Pauline Breedlove psychically abandons her daughter Pecola, who goes mad; in *Song of Solomon,* First Corinthians becomes whole despite her mother; the heroine of *Tar Baby* is a deracinated orphan, in *Beloved,* Sethe's household is haunted by an unresolved mother-daughter relationship. *Sula* explores the mother-daughter experience in the Bottom's equivalent of the middle class, the Wrights' milieu, and in its poorest sector, the household of the young Eva Peace. Further, the novel's portrayal of the mother-daughter relationships is firmly contextualized in the larger society.

Women-centered psychological interpretations of female experience emphasize the web-like nature of women's social relationships. The connections represented in the web, interdependence and affiliation, are critical to the emergence of a secure sense of female self. As Gilligan notes, "The ideal of care is . . . an activity of relationship, of seeing and responding to need, taking care of the world by sustaining the web of connection so that no one is left alone" (*Different Voice*, 62). Partially because male psychology and literature have denigrated women's caretaking roles as impositions on male autonomy (consider Sigmund Freud, Erik Erikson, and James Thurber), women-centered psychology has tended to reclaim caretaking by focusing on its empowering, generative aspects. The dangers of a self-image based upon a morality of care, however, have not been extensively explored from within a women-centered framework. True, feminist literary critiques of caretaking have often focused on the degenerative aspects of this role for the women themselves, their stunted personal or artistic growth. This criticism, however, has generally been founded on conceptions of the self more in line with the independent male model than the self-in-relationship.

The greatness of *Sula* lies partially in its commitment to the complexity of women's experience of caring. Exploring the degenerative and generative versions of female morality, *Sula* exposes the paradoxes of women's individual efforts to participate in the collective life. Predating Gilligan's work by eight years, Morrison's depiction of the Wright women's progression is almost a textbook illustration of Gilligan's critique of the second stage of women's moral development, degenerative goodness. *Sula* simultaneously shows the development of empathy possible within such financial security—a condition for eventual authentic selfhood—and the hibernation of the female self in the middle class.

WRIGHTEOUSNESS: THE MIDDLE CLASS AND DEGENERATIVE GOODNESS

Sula traces through the Wright women the complexities of the second stage of women's moral development. Taking on responsibility for others to the exclusion of the self, a woman with this perspective venerates the feminine conventions of self-sacrifice and martyrdom. As Gilligan states, "The woman at this point validates her claim to social membership through the adoption of societal values. Consensual judgment about goodness becomes the overriding concern as survival is now seen to depend on acceptance by others" (*Different Voice,* 79). The tension between responsibility to others and responsibility to self, however, creates a feeling of duplicity in relationships, an "underground world" (53) where opinion and judgment are reserved. In reserving the self, the woman fails to develop her own adult voice. Without a reconciliation between femininity and adulthood, the conflict between self and other "cannot be resolved. The 'good woman' masks assertion in evasion, denying responsibility by claiming only to meet the needs of others, while the 'bad woman' forgoes or renounces the commitments that bind her in self-deception and betrayal" (71). Women generally cannot articulate these degenerative aspects of caring because caring constitutes the whole social definition of their being good; they are psychically unable to forego social approval and to imagine alternatives that are "not good."

For most of *Sula,* the adult Nel Wright personifies the degenerate aspects of conventional female morality; her mother largely shapes this lengthy phase of Nel's development. Helene Wright epitomizes the immorality of conventional feminine "goodness." Her many social concerns are not genuine; rather, her unconscious aim is to control by "manipulating her daughter and her husband" (16). When Helene smiles at the white conductor who has just insulted her integrity, Nel sees the "custard" which social propriety masks. Helene represents the meltdown of the self that occurs when women unconsciously adhere to social convention. She is the spider "blind[ed] to the cobalt on [her] own back" (104), unaware of her own nature and capabilities. Helene fears her repressed self—for example, her "rage at the folded leaves she had endured" (23) after relieving herself during her train trip home. Her fear of the social truths of her past—her "much handled" mother, "who never said a word of greeting or affection" (23)—prevents her from developing a moral perspective. Acting from this fear, she stifles the threatening development of her daughter's self. Her insistence on clothes-pinning Nel's nose symbolizes her powerful need to channel her daughter's development in socially acceptable directions. Her ostensible attention to others' needs is motivated by her own need for social approval. This option of conforming through service is, however, available only to a woman with sufficient income. Eva, trapped with three hungry children and no money, must make a genuine sacrifice as opposed to Helene's bogus productions. Eva gives of herself, literally, to secure food for her children, while Helene feeds on her child. Middle-class status thus allows the development of patterns of caring, which, carried to an extreme, blind one to the authentic needs of the self. Poverty and racism, on the other hand, often prevent predictable social patterns from developing or recurring, as the Peace women's experiences demonstrate.

From her mother, Nel learns middle-class self-righteous immersion in others. From the time that she meets Jude Greene, Nel embodies the limitations and paradoxes of such immersion. As Gilligan makes clear, this goodness, ostensibly freely offered to others, is in fact a bargain: "Childlike in the vulnerability of their dependence and consequent fear of abandonment, they claim to wish only to please, but in return for their goodness they expect to be loved and cared for" (*Different Voice*, 67). Nel's husband shows an awareness of this social contract, and his image of wifely subordination indicates one of its usually unspecified costs: "Whatever his fortune, whatever the cut of his garment, there would always be the hem—the tuck and fold that hid his raveling edges; a someone sweet, industrious and loyal to shore him up. And in return he would shelter her, love her, grow old with her" (*Sula*, 71). The obliteration of the serving woman's personality becomes explicit in his complacent forecast: "The two of them together would make one Jude" (71). The marriage bargain breaks down, of course, when Nel discovers Sula and Jude having sex. After several years Nel confronts Sula with what she defines as Sula's betrayal, protesting, "I was good to you, Sula, why don't that matter?" (124). Sula's reply exposes the diseased motivation in Nel's reasoning: "It matters, Nel, but only to you. . . . Being good to somebody is just like being mean to somebody. Risky. You don't get nothing for it" (124–25). But the traditionally good woman expects something for all that she has given up.

Nel's concept of goodness damages her and those she serves. To ensure that her husband remains dependent on her goodness, that he needs her, Nel encourages his worst traits. Morrison's diction indicates her disgust with the male childishness and female manipulation engendered by this process:

> [Jude] told them a brief tale of some personal insult done him by a customer and his boss—a whiney tale that peaked somewhere between anger and a lapping desire for comfort. He ended it with the observation that a Negro man had a hard row to hoe in this world. He expected his story to dovetail into milkwarm commiseration, but before Nel could excrete it, Sula said that she didn't know about that—it looked like a pretty good life to her. (88–9)

Sula's humorous rejoinder that the whole world is obsessed with his privates makes Jude aware of a viewpoint other than his own and moves him toward self-recognition as Nel's coddling can never do.

When Nel discovers Sula and Jude on the floor of the bedroom, she approaches the acceptance of her own needs, which characterizes moral maturity and authenticity:

> Hunched down in the small bright room Nel waited. Waited for the oldest cry. A scream not for others, not in sympathy for a burnt child, or a dead father, but a deeply personal cry for one's own pain. A loud, strident: "Why me?" She waited. The mud shifted, the leaves stirred, the smell of overripe green things enveloped her and announced the beginnings of her own howl.
>
> But it did not come. (93)

Nel's inability to admit her needs and feelings takes a terrible toll. Deprived of her husband, Nel focuses on her children, and here too the narrator's judgment of traditional goodness is unsparing: "But it was a love that, like a pan of syrup kept too long on the stove, had cooked out, leaving only its odor and a hard, sweet sludge, impossible to scrape off" (142). Or, again, Nel's overwhelming intensity toward her children is "bear-love" (119). Destructive because of its dishonesty, this love enables Nel to evade her responsibilities toward understanding her own experience; consequently she preserves an immature and incomplete saintly self-image based on a denial of her real self.

Nel's submerged needs are embodied in a gray ball of fur floating just outside her field of vision, and "that was the terrible part, the effort it took not to look" (94). Repression devours Nel's energy, but Morrison's portrayal, while sympathetic, neither excuses nor evades Nel's motivation, which is cowardice: "It was so nice to think about their [her children's] scary dreams and not about a ball of fur. . . . It just floated there for the seeing, if she wanted to. . . . But she didn't want to see it, ever, for if she saw it, who could tell but what she might actually touch it, or want to, and then what would happen . . ." (94). The hair ball represents an extreme of the repression which Nel has practiced all her life to preserve a self-image of goodness which has a nasty flavor of complacency. Sula challenges this assumption with her deathbed statement, "About who was good. How you know it was you? . . . I mean maybe it wasn't you. Maybe it was me" (126). At this point, self-deluded by a "vision of an innocence attained by the denial of self" (*Different Voice,* 145), Nel cannot admit that Sula's point has any validity; preoccupied with her own goodness in overcoming selfish resentment of the betrayal, Nel glories in being the only woman in town willing to visit the dying Sula.

Eva's much-later reiteration of the same idea forces Nel to a self-recognition because Eva includes specific details which Nel cannot refute. Again enveloped in a glow of self-approval, Nel visits Eva in the nursing home as an act of charity. Instead of conforming to the social conventions of being grateful for Nel's sacrifice, Eva rudely demands, "Tell me how you killed that little boy" (144) and refuses to accept Nel's disclaimer with "You. Sula. What's the difference? You was there. You watched, didn't you? Me, I never would've watched" (145). Eva identifies the same image of passivity characteristic of the second-stage women of Gilligan's studies, women "drawn unthinkingly . . . by the appeal of avoiding responsibility by sinking [like Nel], into an 'ice age of inactivity'" (143).

Eva jolts Nel into remembering that she did in fact watch as opposed to merely seeing; that is, she did in some way enjoy the excitement of the event: "All these years she had been secretly proud of her calm, controlled behavior when Sula was uncontrollable . . . . Now it seemed that what she had thought was maturity, serenity and compassion was only the tranquillity that follows a joyful stimulation" (146). Immediately after this recognition, she becomes very angry with Eva, considering her a bad woman, mean and spiteful. Her self-image has been shaken, however, and revisiting Sula's grave provides the psychic impetus necessary to her self-recognition and acceptance:

> Leaves stirred; mud shifted; there was the smell of overripe green things. A soft ball of fur broke and scattered like dandelion spores in the breeze.
> "All that time, all that time, I thought I was missing Jude." And the loss pressed down on her chest and came up into her throat. "We was girls together," she said as though explaining something. "O Lord, Sula," she cried, "girl, girl, girlgirlgirl." (149)

In this scene, the last of the novel, Nel abandons the conventional fiction of her supreme attachment to her husband to mourn her greater losses, Sula's friendship and Sula herself. No longer oversimplifying her experience and denying her feelings and her own needs, Nel has the potential to attain moral maturity and enjoy authentic relations with others.

Nel breaks out of the conventional vision of goodness, which, in its preoccupation with propriety, fails to nurture truthfulness necessary to relationships that clarify the self. Nel's socialization, however, does teach her to empathize with others so that she can serve them. Her capacity for empathy extends to situations that fit conventional social dictates—an older woman in a nursing home, children, a sick friend. Her empathy reaches its limit when another's actions are unconventional—a friend sleeping with her husband. Nel's early friendship with Sula provided her with an alternative vision of the good, which, in Sula's absence, she could not sustain on her own—until the end. The models of women-centered psychology can comfortably accommodate the Wright women; the Peace women, however, in their experiences of poverty, challenge the presumed universality of the self-in-relation model, as *Sula* insists on an expansion to self-in-community.

THE PEACE WOMEN: NECESSARY EXPERIMENTATION

As with Nel, Sula's relationship with her mother psychically structures her conception of morality and self. In the Peace household three generations of mother-daughter relationships work out their responsibilities to themselves and others in nontraditional terms. Because these women are largely indifferent to social convention, they can articulate an honest self-in-relation that avows responsibility for action; such honesty promotes mutuality that eventuates in self-knowledge, knowledge necessary to achieve the authenticity of Gilligan's final stage. In taking responsibility for their actions, however, the Peace women struggle with developing emotional connections to other people and to each other. They tell social truths that cut through illusory, fragile, or superficial connections; these truths force redefinition of the self-in-relationship, as with the mothers who suddenly parent their children in Sula's presence. But in this process the Peace women fail to develop empathy, a capability necessary to harness truth with care.

Unlike the middle-class Helene Wright, Eva does not turn to custard in order to survive but maintains an integrated self-in-relation with other people. In the poverty which constructs her reality, the survival of Eva's children is constantly threatened, and her emotional connections with them are thus frequently heightened (hence the fiery nature of her relationships). Paradoxically, in order to deal practically with this threat, Eva must distance herself (hence the ice imagery which also characterizes her). In order to feed her children after BoyBoy's desertion, for example, Eva leaves town for eighteen months. This physical separation is sign and symbol of an analogous emotional distance, for Hannah asks at one point, "'Mamma, did you ever love us?'" (58). In indignant reply, Eva demands to know if she "'was supposed to play rang-around-the-rosie'" while her daughter was "'shittin' worms'" (60). To Eva, the knowledge that she made herself live in order that they might live should suffice without softer manifestations of love. Eva bequeaths to Hannah, and Hannah, in turn, bequeaths to Sula, a capacity for emotional distance that allows for the creation of a female self. Through Eva, Morrison delineates the paradoxes of a morality of care when self and relations are threatened by social and economic annihilation.

For much of her life Eva embodies and evangelically promotes conventional service to others. Thus, she sacrifices her leg for insurance money to feed her children and throws herself out a window in a vain attempt to smother the flames killing her daughter Hannah. Eva's efforts extend from her immediate family to the larger community. Indeed, Eva's house becomes a kind of extended family when she takes on the matriarchal role of demanding that the young married women rooming there prepare timely suppers for their husbands and otherwise pay attention to conventional niceties. The house becomes a kind of social center for men, who leave intellectually and emotionally refreshed. Further, Eva takes in homeless waifs. In all these ways she becomes a connective force in the community, her traditional goodness a generative force for those around her.

The models of women-centered psychology do not yet include this expanded caretaking which does not erode the caring self. The Stone Center researchers do, however, suggest an explanation for the fate of three of the waifs. Three boys of disparate ages, races, and temperaments under Eva's tutelage gradually merge into one entity. Seeing them in her house for the first time, when their differences are still evident, Eva names each one Dewey. Questioned about how others will be able to tell them apart, Eva answers, "'What you need to tell them apart for? They's all deweys'" (32). This chilling obliteration of individuality permanently stunts the boys: Not only do they become physically indistinguishable, they stop growing at 48 inches and never learn toilet training. Like Sula's later attempt to manipulate A. Jacks, Eva's mangling of the Deweys grotesquely parodies Nel's "good" treatment of Jude. This suffocation of individuality through a conventional maternal morality reinforces male fears of intimacy. Eva's care of the waifs, lacking an understanding of their individuality, lacks empathy, a crucial element in completing the process of female development.

Women psychologists at the Stone Center have just begun to elucidate the role of empathy in the morality of care. In working out a psychology of women, they assume that the self develops "in relation" with other people, that psychological growth occurs by "participating in and fostering the development of others" (Miller, "The Development," 13). In these researchers' view, "Relationship implies a sense of knowing oneself and others through a process of mutual relational interaction and continuity of 'emotional-cognitive dialogue' over time and space" (Surrey,

10). Mutuality and reciprocity in relations lead to an unfolding of intersubjective worlds in which the self is seen and clarified; in a sense, there is no self apart from relationship.

Critical in the development of the relational self is the capacity for empathy, "the central organizing concept in women's relational experience" (Surrey, 2). In "Empathic Communication," Alexandra Kaplan identifies two dimensions in accurate empathic responses, the cognitive and the affective. Affectively the empathic experience is one of interconnection, "an interpenetration of feeling" (14). Once one has perceived affective cues in the other, one "surrenders to affective arousal in oneself—as if the perceived affective cues were one's own" (Jordan, "Empathy," 3). The cognitive part of empathy recognizes that the self is separate from the other and from what has happened in the momentary identification. Both dimensions must coexist if "a genuine sense of understanding and being understood" (Jordan, "Empathy," 3) is to occur. The one experiencing empathy has her experience validated by the affective response from the other yet feels her differences accepted. As Jordan states, "Growth occurs because as I stretch to match or understand your experience, something new is acknowledged or grows in me" ("The Meaning," 7). But Eva's lack of empathy does not allow for growth or change.

Unlike Helene and Nel Wright, however, Eva maintains a self in her relations with others. Her autonomy and her independence of others' judgments rest on ability to perceive and admit truth about herself and her relations. Her morality, then, extends beyond conventional definitions of self-sacrifice. Remaining within the network of her family, friends, and community, she takes responsibility for her choices, a critical component of a morally mature vision: "To be responsible for oneself, it is first necessary to acknowledge what one is doing. The criterion for judgment thus shifts from goodness to truth when the morality of action is assessed not on the basis of its appearance in the eyes of others, but in terms of the realities of its intention and consequence" (Gilligan, *Different Voice,* 83). Eva alone, of all the female characters, demonstrates this commitment to a sometimes very painful truth. Unlike Shadrack, who distances himself on the basis of his knowledge, she both weaves the filaments of the communal web and lives among them.

This truthful dimension of Eva's morality appears most strikingly when she discusses her decision to kill her drug addict son Plum. Eva's shocking action has, in the absence of critical analysis of the psychology of caretaking, given rise to some odd interpretations. Philip Royster refers to "Eva's *fantasy* that her son, Plum, an alcoholic [sic] veteran of World War I, wanted to return to her womb" (161–2, emphasis added), while Barbara Christian calls Eva's homicide "presumptuous" and opines that Eva has recurrent dreams of incest with Plum (160). Critics have by and large simply ignored Eva's own rationale (for exceptions, see Faith Pullin and Elizabeth Ordonez). This rationale refuses to temporize about Plum's degeneration, a threat both to Eva's individual self and to the community of the household:

> There wasn't space for him in my womb. And he was crawlin' back. Being helpless and thinking baby thoughts and dreaming baby dreams and messing up his pants again and smiling all the time. I had room enough in my heart, but not in my womb, got no more. I birthed him once. I couldn't do it again. . . . and he'd be creepin' to the bed trying to spread my legs trying to get back up in my womb. (62)

Eva's language hardly expresses sexual desire nor does the metaphor of returning to the passivity of the developing fetus seem fantastic when applied to the parasitic junkie. (Plum has regressed completely; almost entirely passive, he becomes active only to steal from everyone in the house.) At his bedside, Eva identifies the contents in a soda bottle as blood and water—a birth image connected, of course, with Plum's attempted re-entry. Eva claims that her own needs must be primary, that she cannot again take on the all-sustaining maternal role which she has already performed for Plum. Eva's refusal to accept an adult baby is reminiscent of Edna Pontellier's less articulate summation in Kate Chopin's *The Awakening* that she would give up her life for her children but not her self. Eva's consideration of her own needs as well as Plum's indicates that at this point her connections are authentic, based on a solid self rather than the need to serve.

The critical disapproval of Eva's perception of Plum stems, we believe, not only from her action but from the critics' discomfort with the notion that extreme circumstances warrant extreme reactions to defend the individual self—Malcolm X's "any means necessary"—when that self is female. Although Eva's actions in sacrificing her leg for insurance money and throwing herself out a window in a vain attempt to save Hannah are as violent as her murder of Plum, they do not occasion the same attacks because they defend *others*, Eva's children rather than Eva herself. The critics imply that Eva's action arises from thinking characteristic of Gilligan's first stage, where all attention is focused on individual survival and amoral perception makes external punishment the only brake on behavior. Eva mourns Plum, however, before she burns him, grieving that her child's personality has died. Her consideration and her decision simply do not seem the act of a panicked and selfish individual lightly denying another's rights. Crucially, when Hannah asks why she has killed Plum, Eva does not lie. Unlike Nel, Eva forces herself to recognize the truth of her own needs, to act on them, and to communicate the truth when asked.

Of the three Peace women, Eva has the most capacity for authenticity in caretaking. The extremity of her early life as a caregiver forced her to recognize her own as well as others' needs. She neither leaves the community permanently nor compromises herself in her relation with others. In large measure she dictates the terms of social life in the community for young married couples, the Deweys, and the men who come to court her. Only Sula is sufficiently independent to rebuff her prescriptions. When Eva asks Sula about plans to marry and have children, Sula replies, "I don't want to make somebody else. I want to make myself." Eva inveighs with the verdict used against women who do not conform: "Selfish. Ain't no woman got no business floatin' around without no man." Ironically, as Sula points out to her, "You did" (80). And in fact Eva has, like her daughter Hannah and now her granddaughter, made herself without depending on others but at the expense of supportive emotional connections that allow for the expression of a full range of intersubjective experiences.

Whereas Nel must distance herself from her mother's dominance and shallow social vision to gain her identity, the Peace daughters must find some way to connect with each other, to close distances between them that vary with the generations and have variant effects. Although Hannah is not a fully developed character, the reader notices a continuity between Eva and her daughter—after her husband Rekus's death, Hannah eschews a definite commitment to any one man. She does, however, move back into Eva's house "to take care of it and her mother forever" (35), precisely the commitment which Sula refuses both when her mother burns and when she sends Eva to the nursing home. This difference may reflect Hannah's and Sula's divergent experiences with their mothers. Hannah may have been in doubt about Eva's feelings for her, but Sula learns early the true state of her mother's affections, having overheard Hannah say that she loves her but cannot like her. This rejection unfits her for conventional female morality, which assumes that care irrevocably connects individuals through empathic understanding. The distance between Peace mothers and daughters in *Sula,* then, allows the daughters considerable freedom in creating a self, but it restricts the daughters' capacities for emotional nurturing, empathy, and connection.

A true ethic of care, in women-centered psychology and moral development, requires reciprocity between the person cared for and the person who cares. Eva rarely experiences being cared for, i.e., being interdependent; generally, she performs the caring activities, i.e., is depended upon. As she withdraws more and more, her daughter and granddaughter learn few caretaking skills. The clumsiness of the untrained caretaking impulse is noticeable in one of the few links between Eva and Sula: As Eva sacrifices her leg to feed her children, so Sula slashes her finger to protect Nel, but Eva's desperate solution is appropriate to desperate circumstances while Sula's is wildly disproportionate to the threat—ordinary means are simply not part of Sula's vocabulary because she has not experienced traditional care. Unlike Nel, who has inherited from her mother what Gilligan terms "the conventional feminine voice" (*Different Voice,* 79), Sula has inherited an unconventional feminine voice for which there is no consistent understanding audience. As a result of growing up in Eva's chaotic household where she is "never scolded or [given] directions," Sula "could hardly be counted on to sustain any emotion for more than three minutes" (45). Sula will thus have difficulty in sustaining connections, a difficulty foreshadowed when Chicken Little, having "slipped from her hands" (52), drowns. This inability to experience connection is most obvious in Sula's experience of sex, which she pursues in order to feel most intensely her loneliness and isolation. Although free, Sula lacks nurturance and the training to care for others, experiences which could give her freedom connected meaning.

Morrison clearly identifies the two most formative events for Sula as hearing Hannah's avowal of dislike for her and losing Chicken Little's grip: "The first experience taught her there was no other that you could count on; the second that there was no self to count on either" (103). Sula thus lacks both the terms necessary to any ethic of service; without either a coherent self or a consistent other, the exchange of caring cannot exist. Sula's moral voice develops out of a shock of recognition of her separateness from others. Unlike Nel, who cannot differentiate sufficiently (first from her mother and later from her children), Sula experiences fortified boundaries, both with her mother and with the community as a whole. Thus the intersubjective worlds of other women do not unfold for Sula, except, of course, briefly during her relationship with A. Jacks and more continuously in her adolescent relation with Nel.

Women-centered psychology has discovered the importance of empathy and described the process of its growth; its next task is to confront the effects of poverty and racism on caretaking and its necessary precursor, empathy. Morrison's social vision does not, however, show poor women as crushed, with nothing to offer, even if they are not empathic. In fact, partially because poverty has forced social experimentation and made conventional falsities impossible, poor women may provide middle-class women (and researchers) with impetus toward self-recognition. Their unconventional voices do not, in Morrison's view, become masculine: Unlike BoyBoy and Jude, Eva returns for her children; unlike Shadrack, Sula returns to Nel. The unconventional female voice remains essentially female—and essential.

III. NEL AND SULA: MUTUALLY CREATIVE SELVES-IN-RELATION

The friendship between Sula and Nel in many ways nurtures both girls by supplying the lacks in their mother-daughter relationships. Nel, for example, finds support for her nascent separation from her mother: basking in Sula's approval, she stops using the clothespin which her mother hopes will reshape her "too-broad" nose. Sula, on the other hand, finds companionship to replace the distance in her family; Nel sees her fully. The attachment to Nel prevents Sula from operating totally out of unsocialized selfishness, Gilligan's first stage. Without Nel, she would be, to use Gilligan's terms, "constrained by a lack of power that stems from feeling disconnected and thus, in effect, all alone" (*Different Voice*, 75). Although Sula considers Nel and herself identical, Nel is at crucial moments aware of their boundaries. When Sula sacrifices the top of her finger to scare off hoodlums frightening the two girls, Nel notices as they walk away that Sula's face is "miles and miles away" (47).

In their childhood friendship, Nel's and Sula's antithetical strengths and weaknesses assure them mutual dependency and thus equality of participation. Sula's preservation of her self allows Nel to limn boundaries between herself and her mother; in turn, Nel's attention to details of connection and her calm consistency allow Sula's rigid boundaries to become more fluid, as when they work together digging holes in the earth or when Sula empathically discovers "Shad." In describing the relationship, the narrator points to the development of individuality necessary to any moral maturity: "In the safe harbor of each other's company they could afford to abandon the ways of other people and concentrate on their own perceptions of things" (47). After identifying with each other in the areas they define as fundamental (Abel), they, nevertheless, complement each other in a way that anticipates the possibility of a mature moral vision; both Sula's freedom of self-expression and Nel's consistent regard for others are necessities for authenticity. Their friendship empowers them until the end of their adolescence, when caretaking must be extended to the adult world of love and work.

This marvelous friendship does not exist in a social vacuum, however, and just as the girls' images of themselves are modified by the surrounding society, so is the course of the friendship. Although Sula and Nel value each other highly, they realize that their valuations are eccentric—they know that they are not white or male, the social elites. As the surrounding society bears in, they internalize social contempt. While buying ice cream, they are deemed "pig meat" (43), a phrase replete with the ambiguous compliments of a sexist society. Afterwards, they dig circular holes with sticks, enlarge the holes so that they join in a larger circle, and then fill the entire "grave" with trash (50). The scene shows clearly their subconscious recognition of their femininity in their construction of the yonic symbols and their conception of themselves as one (either defined by gender or joined sexually—for an interpretation of *Sula* as a lesbian novel, see Barbara Smith). Unfortunately, they cannot rejoice in this unity; their actions recreate the social trashing of their female identity. The surrounding society impinges on the friendship in another way. Nel's conventional response to Jude causes her first lasting divergence from Sula, who has not been trained in the usual ways of keeping a man. In a heterosexual society, Nel is expected to refocus her commitments from her female friend to her husband, an expectation so strong that Nel thinks for years that she has done so.

The primary force that ruptures the friendship is not the direct impact of the surrounding society, however, but Nel's and Sula's conflicting modes of moral perception. The confrontation occurs in a particularly damaging way because neither woman is aware even of potential divergence. Nel thinks that talking with Sula has always been like talking to herself (82), while Sula thinks of "Nel as the closest thing to both an other and a self" (103). In Sula's ten-year absence, Nel has developed into the very conventional feminine voice "proclaiming its worth on the basis of the ability to care for and protect others" (Gilligan, *Different Voice,* 79) for which her family has trained her. Sula, in contrast, has learned to take care of only herself and to take responsibility for her actions. Working from this conceptual framework of independence, Sula objectively evaluates degenerative goodness in a critique resembling Gilligan's description of women in the second stage of moral development. Although Sula has not learned conventional caretaking behaviors, she has "scrutinize[d] the logic of self-sacrifice in the service of a morality of care" (*Different Voice,* 82), a capacity critical to authenticity, in which "the morality of action is assessed not on the basis of its appearance in the eyes of others, but in terms of the realities of its intention and consequence" (83). Sula's lack of interest in social appearance unfits her for social conversation "because she could not lie" *(Sula,*105). Significantly, among the lies that she cannot tell are those denying the costs of women's self-sacrifice in their service to husbands and children (105).

Some truths also escape her, notably, the possibility of authentic connections in which neither individual is forced to mirror the other. Thus, Sula cannot conceive of the possibility of hurting Nel if Sula herself is pleased, and she has sex with Jude with no idea of the likely consequences to her friendship with Nel. Nel, on the other hand, sacrifices her real feelings for those socially expected and earns Sula's disgust for her dishonesty. As Gilligan notes of the two modes of self-definition, "These divergent constructions of identity, in self-expression or in self-sacrifice, create different problems for further development—the former a problem of human connection and the latter a problem of truth" *(Different Voice,* 157). Nel joins with the community to view Sula as a "pariah" (105), a "selfish" woman who has only her own interest at heart. Sula, for her part judges Nel as "one of *them.* One of the spiders whose only thought was the next rung of the web. . . . It had surprised her a little and saddened her a good deal when Nel behaved the way the others would have" (103–4) Exposing both modes of perception to the scathing critique of the other, Morrison refuses to sentimentalize or deny their inherent limitations: both necessary to authenticity, they remain in their isolated states, destructive to both themselves and their community.

Nel's rejection of Sula is a microcosm of the community's rejection, for the Bottom's judgment of a woman living an experimental life is severe. Sula's functions as Scapegoat (Royster) and as negative definition for the community (Christian; Ogunyemi; Pullin) have often been the subject of critical commentary. The quality of life in the community improves when Sula becomes the embodiment of a threatening evil and individuals unite to defend themselves. The community might, however, have adopted another means of incorporating Sula, that of listening to her insights. Instead, Sula's actions speak louder than her words; that is, the community reacts to its definition of her actions while her voice, speaking its radical re-definition of her own acts and those of others, remains inaudible. As Nel reflects in remembering Sula's effects, Sula "simply helped others define themselves" (82).

The community cannot listen to Sula because she does not care for it, either literally or figuratively. Sula's general failure to develop empathy—temporarily accepting another's perspective as one's own—leaves her moral vision incomplete and inaccessible to the community. Remaining incapable of empathizing with real individuals (the trapped Nel, the aged and ill Eva, Hannah on fire) Sula weeps instead "for the deaths of the littlest things" (106), like children's cast-off shoes and wedding rings in pawn shops, sentimental representations unconnected to known individuals.

Empathy by itself, of course, does not guarantee the integrity of a moral system or its use to the community. Without reciprocity, it becomes a tool of pity or venom. As Nel's degenerative goodness clearly indicates, empathy may be used to bind another in dependency. In one of her few empathic moments, during her relationship with A. Jacks, Sula feels "flooded with an awareness of the impact of the outside world on Ajax" (115). Instead of using this insight to understand his subjective truth, though, Sula says the fatal "Lean on me" (115). When A. Jacks bolts from this blatant attempt to violate his independence and make him into another Jude, Sula recognizes her own failure, as Nel never does: "I did not hold my head stiff enough when I met him and so I lost it just like the dolls" (111). Earlier Sula muses on women's difficulties with emotional boundaries while making love with A. Jacks: "*I will water your soil, keep it rich and moist. But how much? How much water to keep the loam moist? And how much loam will I need to keep my water still? And when do the two make mud?*" (113). Caring for others, whether individually or communally, requires a giving of one's self and "selfless" effort to experience with the other, yet these very acts can both entrap the self in the "restriction [they] impose on direct expression" (Gilligan, *Different Voice*, 79) and exploitatively convert the vulnerability of another into dependency. Moral authenticity requires both truth and empathy. Without truth, degenerative goodness co-opts empathy in the service of control. Without empathy, truth destroys the possibility for connection.

Morrison's exploration of the female voice struggling toward maturity and authenticity climaxes in Sula and Nel's discussion at Sula's deathbed. There they confront the limitations of their respective moral visions. Frightened by Sula's detachment, even in the face of death, Nel is unable to hear Sula's truth; irritated by Nel's self-sacrifice in the name of conventional goodness, Sula fails to appreciate Nel's pain. In their final actions, Sula and Nel openly and reciprocally care for the other in a recognition of interdependence: *After* Sula dies, her first thought is to tell Nel of the experience; years after Sula's death, Nel feels her presence and makes a crucial step toward authenticity. The emotional connections between Sula and Nel transcend the hostility of their immediate society and the vagaries of their conflicting moral perceptions. Death cannot sever the only genuine emotional connection that Sula experiences, nor can it obliterate the influence that moves Nel toward authentic emotional and moral maturity.

IV. COLLABORATIVE CONCLUSIONS: TOWARD SELVES-IN-COMMUNITY

In *Sula* the moral work of the women caretakers—work ignored or devalued by the male world—sustains both personal and community identity. Yet as the tunnel scene suggests, none of the conventional caretaking has prevented damage to individuals or ultimately obliteration of the Bottom community. Unlike Sula, Nel, and Shadrack, many in the Bottom hoped for someone else to save them from the grips of racism and poverty. (For discussion of this passivity, see Lounsberry and Hovet.) Thus, conventional caretaking encouraged passivity rather than mature activity: Hoping for abatement of their pent-up anger, the townsfolk crawl into the tunnel-womb, and like Plum in his desire to retreat to the safety of total dependency, they suffocate. However, Nel's final synthesis of the two necessary constituents of authentic selfhood, empathic caring and self-assertion, argues for actual individual growth and potential interdependence among members of a community. Morrison hopes to create a different community, one composed of the readers of her novels ("Rootedness," 341). Thus, the exchanges between women-centered psychologists, minority women writers, and readers of both might constitute the speech of a new community.

Significantly, this community is not solely female. *Sula* shows damage done to both male and female characters: the isolated Shadrack and Jude, the conglomerated Deweys, the melted Helene, the lonely Sula. Furthermore, A. Jacks and Nel, the only two successfully integrated personalities, represent both genders. The end of the novel, often read solely as Nel's recognition of her bond with Sula, in fact also shows a continuing dialogue between male and female points of view: Just before Nel's recognition, she passes Shadrack (the male who reminds her of Sula); just before she articulates her insight, she smells "overripe green things," surely a reference to Jude Greene. Female bonds do not exist in isolation but in a community that necessarily includes men.

Both the community within the book and the community of readers outside the book communicate in an erratic and flawed manner, of course. Witness the broken relationships of the novel, on the one hand, and the gap between women-centered models of middle-class white female development and Eva's experiences on the other. Morrison demonstrates how much she values these attempts at communication, however, by contrasting the imperfect community of the Bottom with its replacement, the archetypal symbol of white suburbia—the golf course. Nel recognizes the loss when she thinks, "Maybe it hadn't been a community, but it had been a place. Now there weren't any places left, just separate houses with separate televisions and separate telephones and less and less dropping by" (143). This separation has resulted from the monologue of the controlling voice in the Western social context, a male definition of sociality in search of abstract principles to guarantee individual autonomy and freedom. Morrison suggests that dialogue with the female perspectives of self-in-relation and self-in-community will both empower women and offer a chance for stronger communities. The dialogue between women writers and women psychologists, therefore, not only elaborates theoretical moral perspectives for women's experiences but also takes on particular urgency in a society operating largely on abstraction, separation, and detachment.

NOTES

1. In a crucial scene, Sula discovers from his driver's license that the man whose name she has always heard as "Ajax" is in fact named "A. Jacks." The novel offers some justification for literary critics' unanimous choice to use "Ajax"— "Ajax" occurs not only in Sula's consciousness but once in the narrator's usage *after* Sula's death (page 139 lists among the victims of the tunnel disaster "some of Ajax's younger brothers"). Morrison often depicts the interaction of myth with quotidian reality, and in *The Bluest Eye* the myth is specifically Greek. The mythological implications of "Ajax," however, seem a poor fit with this character, who does not resemble either of the *Iliad's* two Ajaxes. Barring the discovery of another Ajax to offer enriching characterization, then, the critics' preference for "Ajax" ignores Sula's discovery.

On the large scale, this usage obscures Morrison's exploration of ambiguities in language; on the smaller, it devalues Sula's self-examination and screens

Morrison's connection of Eva and Sula. Morrison begins here a concern that figures more prominently in her next novel, *Song of Solomon* (the double meanings of "You can't just fly off and leave a body" and "Sing"). The whole incident offers a fascinating opportunity for discussing the complex interactions of oral and print traditions: Sula accepts a printed document's correction of her oral understanding of her lover's name, but that oral understanding was based on the printed version of an originally oral epic poem.

Within the context of *Sula's* characterization, "A. Jacks" underlines the limitations of both Sula's and Eva's characters. Contemplating why she has lost her connection with Albert Jacks, Sula considers her misidentification of his name as emblematic of her inability to know and respect his true self. As this essay argues later, Eva's misnaming of the Deweys indicates a similar failing, her inability to perceive and value their separate selves.

WORKS CITED

Abel, Elizabeth. " (E)Merging Identities: The Dynamics of Female Friendship in Contemporary Fiction by Women." *Signs* 6.3 (1981): 413–35.

Baym, Nina. "Melodramas of Beset Manhood: How Theories of American Fiction Exclude Women Authors." *The New Feminist Criticism.* Edited by Elaine Showalter. New York: Pantheon, 1985. 63–80.

Carby, Hazel. *Reconstructing Womanhood.* New York: Oxford University Press, 1987.

Chase, Richard. *The American Novel and Its Tradition.* Garden City: Anchor,1957.

Chodorow, Nancy. "Family Structure and Feminine Personality." *Woman, Culture, and Society.* Edited by M.Z. Rosaldo and L. Lamphere. Stanford: Stanford University Press, 1974. 43–66.

———. *The Reproduction of Mothering: Psychoanalysis and the Sociology of Gender.* Berkeley: University of California Press, 1978.

Christian, Barbara. *Black Women Novelists: The Development of a Tradition.* Westport: Greenwood, 1980.

Gardiner, Judith Kegan. 'The (US)es of (I)dentity: A Response of Abel on '(E)Merging Identities.'"*Signs* 6.3 (1981): 436–42.

Genovese, Eugene. *Roll, Jordan, Roll.* 1974. New York: Vintage-Random, 1976.

Gilligan, Carol. *In a Different Voice: Psychological Theory and Women's Moral Development.* Cambridge: Harvard UP, 1982.

———. "Moral Orientation and Moral Development." *Women and Moral Theory.* Edited by Eva Feder Kittay and Diana T. Meyers. Totowa: Rowman, 1987. 19–33.

Homans, Margaret. "Her Very Own Howl: The Ambiguities of Representation in Recent Women's Fiction." *Signs* 9.2 (1983): 186–205.

Jordan, Judith. "Empathy and the Mother-Daughter Relationship." *Women and Empathy: Implications for Psychological Development and Psychotherapy.*

Edited by Jacquelyn H. Hall. Works in Progress 82–02. Wellesley: Stone Center for Developmental Services and Studies, 1983. 2–5.

———. "The Meaning of Mutuality." Works in Progress 23. Wellesley: Stone Center for Developmental Services and Studies, 1986.

Kaplan, Alexandra. "Empathic Communication in the Psychotherapy Relationship." *Women and Empathy: Implications for Psychological Development and Psychotherapy.* Edited by Jacquelyn H. Hall. Works in Progress 82–02 Wellesley: Stone Center for Developmental Services and Studies, 1983. 12–16.

Lerner, Harriet G. *Women in Therapy.* Northvale: Aronson, 1988.

Levine, Lawrence. *Black Culture and Black Consciousness.* Oxford: Oxford UP, 1977.

Lounsberry, Barbara, and Grace Ann Hovet. "Principles of Perception in Toni Morrison's *Sula.*" *Black American Literature Forum* 13 (1979):126–9.

Miller, Jean Baker. "The Development of Women's Sense of Self." Works in Progress 12. Wellesley: Stone Center for Developmental Services and Studies, 1984.

———. *Toward a New Psychology of Women.* Boston: Beacon, 1976.

———. "What Do We Mean by Relationships?" Works in Progress 22. Wellesley: Stone Center for Developmental Services and Studies, 1986.

Morrison, Toni. *Sula.* 1973. New York: Bantam, 1974.

———. "Rootedness: The Ancestor as Foundation." *Black Women Writers (1950–1980).* Edited by Mari Evans. Garden City: Anchor, 1984. 339–45.

Ogunyemi, Chikwenye Okonjo. "*Sula:* 'A Nigger Joke.'" *Black American Literature Forum* 13 (1979): 130–3.

Ordonez, Elizabeth J. "Narrative Texts for Ethnic Women: Rereading the Past Reshaping the Future." *MELUS* 9.3 (1982):19–28.

Pullin, Faith. "Landscapes of Reality: The Fiction of Contemporary Afro-American Women." *Black Fiction: New Studies in the Afro-American Novel Since 1945.* Edited by A. Robert Lee. New York: Barnes, 1980. 173–203.

Rich, Adrienne. *Of Woman Born.* New York: Norton, 1976.

Royster, Philip M. "A Priest and a Witch Against the Spiders and the Snakes: Scapegoating in Toni Morrison's *Sula.*" *Omoja* 2 (1978):149–68.

Smith, Barbara. "Toward a Black Feminist Criticism." *The New Feminist Criticism.* Edited by Elaine Showalter. New York: Pantheon, 1985. 168–85.

Surrey, Janet. "Self in Relation: A Theory of Women's Development." Works in Progress 13. Wellesley: Stone Center for Developmental Services and Studies, 1985.

Wade-Gayles, Gloria. "The Truths of Our Mothers' Lives: Mother-Daughter Relationships in Black Women's Fiction." *Sage* 1.2 (1984): 8–12.

Walker, Alice. "In Search of Our Mothers' Gardens." *In Search of Our Mothers' Gardens.* New York: Harcourt, 1983. 231–43.

Washington, Mary Helen. "'I Sign My Mother's Name': Alice Walker, Dorothy West, Paule Marshall." *Mothering the Mind: Twelve Studies of Writers and Their Silent Partners.* Edited by Ruth Perry and Martine Watson Brownley. New York: Holmes, 1984. 142–63.

Willis, Susan. *Specifying.* Madison: University of Wisconsin Press, 1987.

Wyatt, Jean. "Avoiding Self-Definition: In Defense of Women's Right to Merge (Julia Kristeva and *Mrs. Dalloway*)." *Women's Studies* 13 (1986):115–26.

PART 3
Song of Solomon

Faulkner and Joyce in Morrison's *Song of Solomon*

David Cowart

Critical response to "black" literature tends to overemphasize the adjective and to neglect the claims of the noun it modifies. In doing so, critics can seem unintentionally patronizing, as if black prowess with pen or typewriter somehow confounded expectation. The ethnic, like the regional writer, often requires rescue from labels that imply diminished importance, for just as the critic effectively qualifies all praise of a writer labeled "Southern," so does the qualifier "black" or "Afro-American" tend subtly to disparage. William Faulkner, for example, had once to free himself from the regionalist tag; Toni Morrison, whose work resembles Faulkner's in interesting ways, deserves emancipation from her own literary ghetto.

To be sure, Morrison's 1977 novel *Song of Solomon* concerns the black experience in America over four generations, and in what follows I mean to consider this novel's exploration of black themes. But I wish to introduce and provide a context for these subjects with a consideration of Morrison's accomplishment within a larger tradition. One can argue—without qualifying one's admiration for Morrison's talent and originality—that her themes of history, identity, and freedom deserve consideration as something more than the self-absorbed, even solipsistic expression of black desire. They deserve consideration as part of a dialogue or intertextual engagement with certain literary precursors, among the most important of whom are Faulkner and Joyce.

My task is not source-hunting, and only marginally does it concern influence. I seek a pair of presences in the work of a novelist whose Afro-American sensibility strikes me as overdetermined. Morrison imagines freedom, for example, in images of flight, images "grounded," she asserts, in the myth of the Flying African.[1] But these same images invite comparison with those of Joyce in *A Portrait of the Artist as a Young Man*. History she projects as the knowing of names almost lost in the past. If like Ellison she suggests that knowing who you are depends on knowing where you are,[2] she also suggests, like Faulkner, that identity has its roots in the past, and one recognizes stylistic debts to Faulkner in passages of speculation about a lost or obscured personal history.

I am aware that Morrison might disapprove of the discussion undertaken here. Indeed, in an interview she inveighs specifically against suggestions that she bears a resemblance to the authorial presences I have adduced: "I am not *like* James Joyce; I am not *like* Thomas Hardy; I am not *like* Faulkner. I am not *like* in that sense. I do not have objections to being compared to such extraordinarily gifted and facile writers, but it does leave me sort of hanging there when I know that my effort is to be *like* something that has probably only been fully expressed in music. . . ."[3] But the critic must not be dictated to by politically or ideologically motivated avowals of the supreme importance of a black cultural orientation. In another interview Morrison remarks that from age seventeen, when she left for school, "the things I studied were Western and, you know, I was terrifically fascinated with all of that, and at that time any information that came to me from my own people seemed to be backwoodsy and uninformed. You know, they hadn't read all these wonderful books. . . . the consciousness of being Black I think happened when I left Cornell."[4] In other words, her literary interests and the literary influences on her from the end of high school to the time she left Cornell University with a Master's degree at age twenty-four were not Afro-American. I argue, then, the need to examine Morrison's affinities with the writers she would have encountered as a student of literature in the early 1950s—before the advent of Afro-American studies. After all, her Master's thesis dealt in part with Faulkner, and surely (like Wright, Ellison, and Baraka before her) she would have encountered the powerful gravitational field of Joyce—a writer hard to avoid in graduate school. The question, then, is: How does

Morrison compare with these writers? Does she execute meaningful variations on the themes—freedom, identity, history—she inherits from them?

Morrison's encounter with her precursors takes place in the story of a young man named Macon "Milkman" Dead who undertakes a quest into his personal history and encounters his own precursors: Jake and Sing, Solomon and Ryna. Milkman's quest reveals parallels, first, with similar quests in the works of Faulkner.[5] Faulkner, writing about a culture obsessed with history, turns often to the individual's encounter with a genealogical as well as cultural past. In *Go Down, Moses,* for example, Isaac McCaslin discovers the corruption in his family's past and refuses to come into his inheritance. Morrison offers something like a complementary genealogical quest: the search for a black integrity, if the word be taken in its original sense of "completeness." Unlike Faulknerian history, which—at least at the personal level—can tend to be a terrible revelation, the past that Milkman Dead comes to know liberates him, once he has risen above a dream of easy riches in the form of recovered treasure. Like Faulkner's Lucas McCaslin, who also looks for buried treasure, Milkman must renounce this potentially corrupting cupidity to achieve the wholeness attendant on self-knowledge and maturity.

Milkman recovers a "treasure" in the form of a lost past, a lost myth, a lost name. Indeed, the name-theme, a subject of considerable interest to critics,[6] figures prominently from the very beginning, where the narrator's bitterly comic meditation on "Not Doctor Street" poignantly comments on the yearning for some linguistic validation of black achievement and professional cachet. This reflection also registers the subversive resources of language (or of "notlanguage," to borrow the Faulkner coinage a construction like "Not Doctor Street" resembles); this subversiveness is a well-known feature of language as spoken by the oppressed or socially marginalized (Faulkner's "notpeople," in effect). The name-theme receives its most extensive development in terms of the enforced pseudonymity of the main character and his family. This pseudonymity is a persistent concern for a family that must subsist without an authentic name. "Macon Dead," a name conferred by a contemptuous white man, has displaced some more genuine name. The bogus appellation even hints at its own ultimate effect: it "makes dead."

Thus in Faulknerian cadences the narrator introduces the senior Macon Dead early in the novel, reflecting on names and what they mean:

Surely, he thought, he and his sister had some ancestor, some lithe young man with onyx skin and legs as straight as cane stalks, who had a name that was real. A name given to him at birth with love and seriousness. A name that was not a joke, nor a disguise, nor a brand name. But who this lithe young man was, and where his canestalk legs carried him from or to, could never be known. No. Nor his name. His own parents, in some mood of perverseness or resignation, had agreed to abide by a naming done to them by somebody who couldn't have cared less. Agreed to take and pass on to all their issue this heavy name scrawled in perfect thoughtlessness by a drunken Yankee in the Union Army. A literal slip of the pen handed to his father on a piece of paper and which he handed on to his only son, and his son likewise handed on to his.[7]

The debt to Faulkner here is considerable, not only in the centrality of a character's brooding on the past but in the very syntax in which the author describes it. One notes the fragmentary sentences beginning now with an iterated participle ("Agreed to take and pass on to all their issue . . ."), now with some elliptical appositive ("A literal slip of the pen . . ."), and continuing with a relative pronoun that sets in motion a train of subordinated polysyndeton ("and which he handed on . . . and his son likewise handed on"). Such syntax, not to mention the vocabulary ("issue," "scrawled," "a drunken Yankee"), is highly characteristic of Faulkner and serves, as in his work, to enact grammatically a mental journey into a misty and potentially painful past.

Another meditation on the larger meaning of names and naming comes in a comic catalogue of the nicknames that constitute such a distinctive feature of black culture, nicknames representative of

yearnings, gestures, flaws, events, mistakes, weaknesses. Names that bore witness. Macon Dead, Sing Byrd, Crowell Byrd, Pilate, Reba, Hagar, Magdalene, First Corinthians, Milkman, Guitar, Railroad Tommy, Hospital Tommy, Empire State (he just stood around

and swayed), Small Boy, Sweet, Circe, Moon, Nero, Humpty-
Dumpty, Blue Boy, Scandinavia, Quack-Quack, Jericho,
Spoonbread, Ice Man, Dough Belly, Rocky River, Gray Eye, Cock-
a-Doodle-Do, Cool Breeze, Muddy Waters, Pinetop, Jelly Roll,
Fats, Leadbelly, Bo Diddley, Cat-Iron, Peg-leg, Son, Shortstuff,
Smoky Babe, Funny Papa, Bukka, Pink, Bull Moose, B.B., T-bone,
Black Ace, Lemon Washboard, Gatemouth, Cleanhead, Tampa Red,
Juke Boy, Shine, Staggerlee, Jim the Devil, Fuck-Up, and *Dat
nigger*. (330)

Though comic, this catalogue offers powerful testimony to the need
for names that confer distinction and "bear witness." Such sobriquets
embody a primitive means of circumventing the galling fact that nearly
every regular name is inauthentic. The practice invites comparison with
the naming of women in the Dead family. Their names are chosen ran-
domly from the Bible—a not altogether unefficacious attempt to be guided
by a source of authority older than and superior to that of white men. The
greater authenticity of these names contributes to the sense that the dis-
taff evinces the greater moral authority within the black community—a
suggestion that again echoes Faulkner.

The obsession with authentic names culminates in Milkman's consideration of a children's rhyme. Like Faulkner's Ike McCaslin interpreting the ledger entries one December midnight in the plantation commis-
sary, Milkman interprets a strange historical record when he analyzes the
rhyme and discovers something about the past and about his identity. The
rhyme preserves the names of his grandparents, Jake and Sing, as well as
those of his Miltonic "grand parents," Ryna and the eponymous Solomon.
Thus the larger significance of the theme of names and naming comple-
ments the theme of history. True names are indispensable to the sense of
identity, that great goal of all who, their humanity denied, must struggle
for a sense of their own value as human beings. To know oneself and
one's real worth, one needs at least to know one's name.

To the extent that Faulkner chronicles the "formation" of Ike McCaslin
in *Go Down, Moses,* he produces, like Morrison, a *Bildungsroman.* Indeed, she has described her novel as "a male story about the rites of passage."[8] But in this regard one finds the more convincing analogue to *Song*

of Solomon in a novel often invoked in discussions of Wright and Baraka: *A Portrait of the Artist as a Young Man.* Joyce's great novel also concerns the formation of its protagonist's character, and it, too, develops the theme of the family romance. Stephen Dedalus, like Morrison's hero, finds himself at odds with his immediate family and looks to a remote figure of legend and myth as his authentic parent.

Both Joyce and Morrison depict a protagonist in search of a principle of cohesion or order. Joyce ends each of his five chapters with the achievement of some kind of comforting stasis for his autobiographical hero. But each succeeding chapter reveals some inadequacy in the ordering previously arrived at. The final achievement, the embracing of an artistic vocation, is supreme for Stephen Dedalus, whether or not Joyce ironically undermines him at the end (as many critics argue, especially when they consider the beginning of *Ulysses*). Morrison's novel, however, is not a *Kunstlerroman*,[9] and so it cannot conclude with a vision of supreme aesthetic ordering. Morrison's ephebe, Macon "Milkman" Dead, can achieve in life only the precarious order available to one who disciplines selfish appetites and recognizes the supremacy of love. Milkman does, however, seem to end with something like Stephen's sense of vocation: He will search for another good woman like Pilate.

Joyce and Morrison also define their respective cultures. In a formula that Ellison's invisible man cites, Stephen Dedalus announces his intention to "forge in the smithy of my soul the uncreated conscience of my race."[10] In other words, he sets himself the task of defining and focusing the culture—morally inchoate—that produced him, and he makes this announcement at the end of the novel in which his creator, the artist who has depicted himself as a young man in Stephen, has effected precisely this act of cultural definition, this refining of a national ethos. Morrison anatomizes black mores less harshly than Joyce does those of his countrymen, but she, too, suggests a something unforged and uncreated about a newly nascent black America.

Much of the richness of *Song of Solomon* lies in the originality with which its author, like Joyce, organizes her project of cultural definition around a myth of flight. Joyce's novel, highly involved with its own aesthetic, depends on the myth of Daedalus, "fabulous artificer" and patron saint of the craft whereby one, according to the traditional image for artistic creation, takes to the air. But Morrison's myth of flight concerns not art but simply freedom. The novel opens and closes with flying, from the insane flight of Robert Smith, which precipitates the birth of Milkman, to Milkman's own ambiguous flight to Guitar on the last page. In between, the motif recurs numerous times. Milkman notices the winged ornament on his father's car at an early age. He takes an interest in flight from earliest infancy, but "when the little boy discovered, at four, the same thing Mr. Smith had learned earlier—that only birds and airplanes could fly—he lost all interest in himself" (9). When he meets Pilate for the first time she shows him the sky in a gesture of profound importance (42, 209). Under the influence of his avaricious father and the embittered Guitar, Milkman flirts with becoming a peacock like the one he and Guitar see as they plot an act of thievery—flirts, that is, with becoming a gaudily winged creature incapable of sustained flight. The motif of flight dictates Milkman's exhilarating plane flight (220) and the dream of flight in Sweet's bed (398). Most important, he discovers in Solomon, the eponymous progenitor, a miraculous bird-man. But the wonder of Solomon's feat—he left his wife Ryna and flew away to Africa, his place of origin—is qualified by the suffering he causes. Milkman, too, a latter-day bird-man, causes suffering when he flies away from certain responsibilities: "while he dreamt of flying, Hagar was dying" (332). At the end of the novel Milkman realizes that Pilate could fly without leaving the ground, and he even witnesses her name take literally to the air as one of the birds present at her burial swoops down and bears off the little box she has worn as an earring—the box that contains the scrap of paper bearing her name. Shortly after this sequence, Milkman himself takes flight as he flings himself through the air towards the waiting Guitar.

But Milkman's flight is as problematic for Morrison as Stephen Dedalus' is for Joyce. For Morrison especially, there are responsible and irresponsible modes of flight, depending on what one is attempting to transcend or escape. Stephen discovers that he must fly clear of the "nets" of family, nation, and church if he is to enjoy sufficient autonomy to create, to become "a priest of eternal imagination."[11] Milkman, too, must escape the nets that would make him morally and spiritually earthbound. His nets include his own selfishness, for which all too often the women around him must pay (Hagar, First Corinthians, Pilate): the narrow bourgeois materialism of his benighted father; and the self-defeating violence and machismo of black militancy.

But Morrison does not borrow from or rewrite Joyce. She merely undertakes a similar act of ethnic definition, and at times she urges her program in terms virtually antithetical to those of Joyce. Where Joyce endorses Stephen's resistance to familial imperatives and Irish nationalism, Morrison deplores the Dead family's failure to cohere and its petit-bourgeois attempts to distance itself from a larger idea of ethnic community. At the same time, however, the novel's action and characters depict the agon of competing models of black social progress. Milkman and Guitar—and before them Solomon—symbolize black options for escaping the labyrinth of social injustice. The question, as for Stephen Dedalus and his mythic progenitors, is whether they can fly without tumbling from the sky.

As I noted at the outset, Morrison is no epigone. If Joyce and Faulkner figure as presences in this novel, they do so without impairing or qualifying Morrison's ultimate originality and autonomy. They do, however, help to define this novel's mythic side at the same time that they buttress or make more resonant the moral seriousness with which she meditates the fate of a particular ethnic community. I conclude, therefore, with a consideration of certain points in *Song of Solomon* where archetype intersects with concrete historical moment.

Though Morrison concentrates not on conflict between blacks and whites but on the black experience, she does provide a broader social context for Milkman's coming of age. Born, like Milkman, in 1931, she herself grew up in a "racist" household: Her father and grandparents thought whites genetically prone to violence and morally inferior.[12] Her character Milkman, at once a surrogate for the author and a representative black man of his day, faces momentous choices. The reader for the most part encounters Milkman during his belated maturation in 1962 and 1963, the period of germination for the seeds of both the Civil Rights movement and black militancy. Black leaders invited their followers— and sympathetic whites—to make a choice between nonviolent civil disobedience and an often violent counter-racism.

During the period of this novel's major action, many blacks felt impelled to embrace a tendentious ideology of the type espoused and promulgated by men like Malcolm X and Elijah Muhammad, both mentioned briefly in Morrison's novel. Black militancy—and occasionally terrorism—began to manifest itself in organizations like the Black Panthers and in a new generation of leaders that included Huey Newton, Angela Davis, Stokely Carmichael, H. Rap Brown, Bobby Seale, and Eldridge Cleaver. Members of these organizations espoused violence to acquire political power—and sexism to recover or reconstitute black manhood. Ron Karenga, for example, openly preached the idea that black women's role was properly to "complete" or "complement" black men. This notion continues to polarize black men and women, and its presence contributes part of the dramatic tension in Morrison's novel.

Morrison sketches in these currents at their most extreme in her terrorist brotherhood, the Seven Days. Although she allows the reader to see the reasons behind this organization in the various forms of gratuitous violence visited by whites on blacks, she gradually allows the reader to see also that the violence of the Seven Days merely breeds madness and more violence. Thus in the course of the novel she reveals repeatedly the mental toll of membership in the Days. Henry Porter, for example, puts in his first appearance as a shotgun-brandishing drunk; he evidently manages to restore his equilibrium only by getting out of the terrorist organization and by falling in love with First Corinthians. As for Guitar, he eventually becomes virtually psychotic and, attempting to kill his own racial brother, kills the innocent Pilate instead.[13] Morrison's point is unmistakable: Violence by its own nature fails to discriminate; it rebounds on the heads of the perpetrators and their people. She allows the reader a certain amount of sympathy and even satisfaction at the idea of secret militancy, but gradually she reveals the real cost of such short-term gratification. Only well into the novel does the reader learn that Robert Smith, the crazed insurance salesman who attempts to fly from the roof of Mercy Hospital, was a member of the Days. The account of his death introduces and frames another narrative: the birth of a black man who will learn alternatives to the routes Smith takes to achieve 1) justice and 2) flight.

Yet Milkman, in the novel's last sentence, also leaps desperately from a high place, and the author leaves the reader to interpret this final, cryptic image: Milkman suspended above his adversary and symbolic brother. After fleeing Guitar's violence, Milkman now meets him head-on, with a dawning awareness that Guitar represents a challenge he must meet if he is to continue to grow, to know, to fly, and to survive. Guitar, then, is something more than a symbolic brother. Like Conrad, Poe, Wilde, and Nabokov, Morrison exploits the theme of the *Doppelganger* or psychological double. Guitar represents the Jungian shadow of Milkman's developing consciousness—that part of the self that one most dreads, least wishes to admit—yet the part with which one must come to terms in the interest of psychological wholeness. Symbolically, Milkman represents a black middle class that must encounter the denied or sublimated rage embodied in Guitar. If the rage is not faced, it will, like other forms of the repressed, reassert itself in various pathologies of consciousness, perhaps even take over and dictate behavior that will result in self-destruction. Thus the novel's ambiguous conclusion, with Milkman poised in the air on his way to grappling for his life with Guitar, implies that the character of black aspiration remains to be defined and resolved: violent self-assertion or a maturational striving for self-knowledge, love, and legitimate forms of social consequence or "power," to use the word that was so pervasive in the era in which the novel's main action transpires.

The author of this novel, then, presents actions representative of two ways of raising black consciousness and promoting justice: one public and violent, the other private and personal. The alternatives come into focus in the scene in which Pilate saves Milkman and Guitar from the law after they have tried to rob her in the name of their foolish, self-serving, and mutually exclusive ideas of justice. Pilate plays Aunt Jemima and thereby disgusts the militant Guitar at the same time that she moves and shames the selfish Milkman,[14] who is brought to understand something of love and familial solidarity. He continues to learn the lesson, and Pilate's love, capable of transcending even the death of her granddaughter, becomes symbolically the basis on which Morrison imagines, if not the millennium of the oppressed, at least the conditions that would alone make meaningful any improvement in their economic and political lot.

The ethic of love this novel promotes—which finds its embodiment in Pilate the life-saver, the nurturer, the family-preserver—returns us to the subject of literary affinities, for Pilate's monumental and archetypal qualities recall those of characters in Joyce and Faulkner. Like Molly Bloom, she affirms; like Dilsey, she endures. Through Pilate, too, Morrison hints at a messianic theme that constitutes another link to Joyce and Faulkner. Though ironically undercut by their creators, both Joyce's Stephen Dedalus and Faulkner's Isaac McCaslin are Christ-figures. Stephen sees himself as the literary savior of his country, and he sees as a rival the leader of an international peace movement who "has the face of a besotted Christ."[15] In the last part of *Portrait,* the reader encounters him in the midst of an apostolic twelve fellow students, one of whom Stephen thinks will betray him. Ike McCaslin, on the other hand, takes up the Christologically suggestive trade of carpentry and otherwise "imitates the Nazarene." Another Faulkner character, Joe Christmas in *Light in August,* is even more explicitly a Christlike scapegoat.

Though Pilate is necessary to Morrison's hint of a messianic theme, the author has no interest in making Pilate herself a Christ-figure, however redemptive her suffering. Pilate functions rather as a kind of proleptic moral vessel. She represents, as such, an improvement over the myth of Solomon that, however exciting, remains morally inchoate or even retrograde to the extent that it seems to endorse an abdication of responsibility. (Solomon simply abandons Ryna and their children, and the book suggests that no imperative—not even freedom—should be pursued at the expense of one's family.) Solomon, then, embodies a myth of masculine insouciance and irresponsibility that Pilate's selfless example challenges. The narrative seems to reach its apogee with the recovery of the Solomon story, which is to say the rediscovery of a quasi-divine sky-figure, antetype of the masculine sky-god typified by Zeus, Apollo, and their Olympian brothers. But older than the gods of classical antiquity, as Robert Graves has argued, older than a pantheon dominated by male gods, is the Great Mother, one with the Earth, older than the sky. Graves's White Goddess becomes Morrison's black goddess, an all-nurturing mother whose name puns on *pilot,* i.e., one who flies or one who guides through dangerous waters—the waters, for example, of the life-voyage. She represents something older and finer than Solomon, as Milkman seems to recognize as he holds her body at the end.

Yet the biblical Solomon, whose name in Hebrew, Shelomo, means *peaceable,* is the inheritor of David and thus a type of the Christ as well as the messiah's ancestor in the supreme family romance. He also lends his name to that splendid compilation of love verses in the Bible wherein the beloved says, "I am black, but comely" (Song of Solomon 1:5). The Song of Solomon gives the novel its title and, obliquely, its underlying theme: "Many waters cannot quench love, neither can the floods drown it" (8:7). Born into the House of Solomon, which is to say the House of David, Pilate enjoys a special spiritual distinction. Her smooth stomach hints at an awful mystery. The reader associates it with her ability to survive against great odds, always a gift for those whose lives the oppressor holds cheap, but it also reveals her identity as a kind of primal mother, an Eve (who "had no navel," says Stephen Dedalus)[16] guiltless of the world's sin. "There must be another one like you" (336), Milkman cries as he cradles her body. He prays, in effect, for the new Eve, the one blessed among women who will bear the messiah to lead the oppressed out of bondage.

But Morrison's adumbration of messianic yearnings functions, as I have attempted to show, within a larger pattern of affinities with a literary tradition represented here by Faulkner and Joyce. Whether hinting at millenarian desire, probing history and identity, or exploiting the symbolism of flight, Morrison handles her themes in such a way as to provide testimony of her maturity as an artist. The individual talent, says Eliot, at once extends and modifies an inherited literary tradition, and Morrison reveals her power as she integrates her precursors—their subjects, their themes, sometimes even their language—into a fiction of universal humanity and moral authority. The presence of her precursors does not qualify her originality and artistic autonomy—it merely guarantees that she will produce not black literature but literature.

NOTES

1. Her insistence that the myth of an airborne Solomon reflects the myth of the Flying African and only incidentally that of Daedalus and Icarus reflects an oft-iterated wish to be perceived as uncontaminated with sources and myths and stories outside the Afro-American spectrum. Speaking of "the flying myth in *Song of Solomon*," she declares, "if it means Icarus to some readers, fine; I want to take credit for that. But my meaning is specific. It is about black people who could fly. That was part of the folklore of my life; flying was one of our gifts." Thomas LeClair, "The Language Must Not Sweat: A Conversation with Toni Morrison," *New Republic*, March 21, 1981, p. 27.

2. I was reminded of this formulation from the Epilogue to *Invisible Man*,

in Alan Nadel's "Reading the Body: Alice Walker's *Meridian* and the Archeology of the Self," *Modern Fiction Studies*, 34 (1988): 55.

3. Nellie McKay, "An Interview with Toni Morrison," *Contemporary Literature*, 24 (1983): 426.

4. Bessie W. Jones and Audrey L. Vinson, "An Interview with Toni Morrison," in their *The World of Toni Morrison* (Dubuque, Iowa: Kendall/Hunt, 1985), p. 131.

5. Morrison's remarks to the contrary notwithstanding, scholarly critics have previously been content with little more than passing references to the Faulknerian features of her work. In a review of *Sula*, for example, Anthony Thwait notes the presence of "Faulknerisms" in *Song of Solomon* ("Borders of Fantasy," *Observer*, November 23, 1980, p. 28). Audry L. Vinson, by the same token, briefly suggests that Morrison's handling of multiple points of view owes something to Faulkner ("Pilate Dead: Conjuress," in Vinson and Jones, *The World of Toni Morrison*, p. 63). Other critics have as briefly noted the Faulknerian overtones of the hunt that Milkman goes on late in the novel.

6. For the relevance of the name-theme to the conventional theme of black invisibility, see Cynthia A. Davis, "Self, Society, and Myth in Toni Morrison's Fiction," *Contemporary Literature*, 23 (1982): 323–4, 326. For the significance of Biblical names, see Cynthia Dubin Edelberg, "Morrison's Voices: Formal Education, the Work Ethic, and the Bible," *American Literature*, 58 (1986): 228–30. See also Ruth Rosenberg, "'And the Children Shall Know Their Names': Toni Morrison's *Song of Solomon*," *Literary Onomastics Studies*, 8 (1981): 195–219.

7. *Song of Solomon* (New York: Knopf, 1977), pp. 17–18. All parenthetically cited page numbers refer to this text.

8. Charles Ruas, *Conversations with American Writers* (New York: Knopf, 1985), p. 230.

9. For the interesting suggestion that the reader encounters an artist-figure in Pilate, see Bessie W. Jones, "Pilate Dead: A Symbol of the Creative Imagination," in Jones and Vinson, *World of Toni Morrison*, pp. 81–6.

10. *A Portrait of the Artist as a Young Man,* Definitive Text, edited by Richard Ellmann (New York: Viking, 1964), p. 253. For a discussion of Ellison's allusions to this novel, see Ellin Horowitz, "The Rebirth of the Artist," in *On Contemporary Literature*, edited by Richard Kostelanetz, 2nd ed. (New York: Avon, 1969), pp. 330–46.

11. Joyce, p. 221.

12. This according to Morrison's own testimony in Kay Bonetti, *Toni Morrison Interview*, Columbia, MO: American Audio Prose Library, May 1983.

13. It will be obvious that I do not agree with the assertion in Marilyn Judith Atlas, "The Darker Side of Toni Morrison's *Song of Solomon*," *Society for the Study of Midwestern Literature Newsletter*, 10 (1980), 1–13, that Morrison refuses to judge Guitar.

14. Brenda Marshall shows how in the police station scene Pilate's Aunt Jemima act is tempered with ironic touches known only to her and the reader. "But if the cops are amused, they are also mocked; so is Milkman, who learns something about shame," "The Gospel According to Pilate," *American Literature*, 57 (1985): 487.

15. Joyce, p. 194.

16. *Ulysses*, Corrected Text, edited by Hans Walter Gabler with Wolfhard Steppe and Claus Melchoir (New York: Random House, 1986), p. 32.

Civilizations Underneath: African Heritage as Cultural Discourse in Toni Morrison's *Song of Solomon*

Gay Wilentz

In each of her acclaimed novels, Toni Morrison writes what she calls "village literature, fiction that is really for the village, for the tribe" (LeClair, 26). Yet Morrison has been hailed as one of the greatest writers (I will do away with any of the qualifiers) of the twentieth century. She has been compared to Faulkner and Marquez in her use of stream of consciousness and magic realism, but we need to look a little closer at Morrison's own comments and her historical roots to explore the rich complexity of her written work. Although she wrote her master's thesis on Faulkner and has acknowledged influence by Marquez and other Latin American writers, Morrison's writings are deeply entrenched in her own black folk roots and the community in which she grew up. Moreover, her text is informed by her mother's stories, her tribe, and her ancestors—African and African American. In "Rootedness: The Ancestor as Foundation," Morrison yearns for a closer identification of the black American artist with her community:

> There must have been a time when an artist could be genuinely representative of the tribe and in it; when an artist could have a tribal or racial sensibility and an individual expression of it. There were spaces and places in which a single person could enter and behave as an individual within the context of the community. (339)

The relationship between the artist and the community that Morrison describes is an Afrocentric one, the discourse based in an African orature whose artists are both participants in and representatives of the community.[1] Morrison hopes to recreate this participatory experience in her fiction.

Although she does not discuss Morrison, Catherine Belsey, in *Critical Practice*, might call a work like *Song of Solomon* an "interrogative" text which "literally invites the reader to produce answers to the questions it implicitly or explicitly raises" (91). Within the context of Afrocentric cultural discourse, the questions raised in the novel are interrogative in the manner of a dilemma tale (Abrahams, 16–17). Certainly, the finale of the novel reflects the openendedness of this West African form of orature. Morrison's use of African modes of storytelling and orature is a way of bridging gaps between the black community's folk roots and the Black American literary tradition. Furthermore, through this dilemma tale, Morrison compels us to question Western concepts of reality and uncover perceptions of reality and ways of interpretation other than those imposed by the dominant culture. By examining *Song of Solomon* as literature beyond the limitations of Euro-American discourse, I focus on Morrison's use of African values, characteristics, and community as an alternative to mainstream assimilation or radical separatism. Furthermore, I center on Morrison's attempt to transform Eurocentric cultural discourse through the acceptance of African heritage, told by generations of women storytellers. In the weaving of this tale, Morrison can be seen as an Afrocentric tale teller who overturns Western Biblical and cultural notions by revealing the legends and folkways of her community. From the double entendre of the title to the mythical, contradictory ending, Morrison bears witness to "that civilization that existed underneath the white civilization" (LeClair, 26), a society in which the fathers soared and the mothers told stories so that the children would know their names.

It may be useful before I examine the novel to define my use of *Afrocentric discourse* and the importance of African cultural traditions to contemporary African American life. My use of the term *Afrocentric* comes from *Toward the Decolonization of African Literature*. *Afrocentric discourse* refers to the connections among those of African descent, and particularly the literary "achievements of the African peoples, in the homeland and in the diaspora" (Chinweizu et al., 3). Molefi Kete Asante further defines *Afrocentricity* as a critical perspective "which means, literally, placing African ideals at the center of any analysis that involves African culture and behavior" (*Afrocentric*, 6). To examine literature in the African diaspora, an Afrocentric approach exposes what has been hidden by dominant discourse. For even in the African American community, attitudes about African heritage have differed. Dialogue on Africa and African heritage has been prominent in the course of African American history. Depending on the historical moment, one side of the conflicting dialectics—the desire to assimilate or to assert one's own ethnic identity—has been stronger. But within communities, African cultural practices have remained even when the historicity of an age has reflected an assimilationist stance. At our historical moment, serious attention has been paid to documenting continuing African cultural practices.[2] Recent studies like *Africanisms in American Culture* examine not only West African but also Central African "cultural carryovers" (Holloway, xiii). According to Asante, "Afrocentricity" pervades every aspect of African American culture (as well as much of dominant Euro-American society). Moreover, he states that "Black Americans retained basic components of the African experience rather than specific artifacts" ("African," 21). So, when Morrison recreates African cultural traditions in *Song of Solomon*, she is formulating her discourse within an Afrocentric world view.

Song of Solomon is a complex novel with an unresolved ending which has been seen as a biblical allegory, a detective novel, and a young man's search for his roots. Some male critics, like Mel Watkins of *The New York Times*, have more closely identified with this novel than with *The Bluest Eye* or *Sula* since it is not about "the insulated, parochial world of black women," but about black men (50). Indeed, the novel includes a prominent male character, Milkman; however, the work is equally concerned with the world of black women that is disparaged by Watkins, and the focal character of the novel is Milkman's aunt, Pilate. In a similar manner, Eurocentric literary critics—more versed in Faulkner than black folk culture, in New Criticism than cultural criticism—initially privileged the influence of written discourse on Morrison's writings rather than her oral antecedents, no matter how many times she explained her sources.[3] A cursory reading of the novel does not expose its oral antecedents as clearly as a first reading of Walker's *The Color Purple*, for example. *Song of Solomon* is dense, filled with visual description and literary devices.[4] Yet Morrison's role as an Afrocentric storyteller is unmistakable, and the orature of her foremothers as well as the oral traditions of the black community is evident in both the language and the structure of the novel. Morrison comments on her own process of recreating the richness of black speech in her writings: ". . . I have to rewrite, discard, and remove the print quality of the language to put back the oral quality, where intonation, volume, gesture are all there" (Tate, 126). The voicings of the stories that were told to her when young and the unique resonances of family and community filter through her characters: "When I think of things my mother or father or aunts used to say, it seems the most absolutely striking thing in the world. That is what I try to get into my fiction" (Watkins, 48).

Morrison's attention to her writings' oral antecedents extends further than her precise recreation of the voicings of her community; her works incorporate the use of African American folktales, folk songs, and legends.[5] *Song of Solomon*, based on a story she learned from her maternal grandparents, is imbued with folk myths and legends from the African diaspora. Most important is the tale of the Flying Africans—who escaped slavery by flying back to Africa. Legends abound throughout the New World about Africans who either flew or jumped off slave ships as well as those who saw the horrors of slavery when they landed in the Americas and, "in their anguish, sought to fly back to Africa."[6] For Morrison, as for Paule Marshall (whose Igbos walk back) and Ishmael Reed (whose slave Quickskill flies Air Canada), the notion of using the supernatural, especially this most exalted form of freedom, to overcome a catastrophe captivated her "I wanted to use black folklore, the magic and superstitious part of it. Black people believe in magic. . . . It's part of our heritage. That's why flying is the central metaphor in *Song* . . ." (Watkins, 50). Although I explore this issue in more detail in relation to the novel's conclusion, clearly one's perception regarding whether the slaves killed themselves or flew back to Africa is culture bound.

From the opening of the novel, when insurance agent/Seven Days member Robert Smith either commits suicide or flies away on his own wings, Morrison questions the imposed values and perceptions of the dominant culture and begins to offer alternative cultural knowledge and belief based on black Americans' African traditions and heritage. Also revealing is the folk song of Sugarman/Solomon's flying away, sung by Pilate at Milkman's birth. The song is the key to Milkman's quest and illustrates the function of the African American woman in passing on stories to future generations. The novel, structured in the manner of a surreal detective story, has a multi-faceted plot, but it is Milkman's relationship with Pilate, his female "ancestor," that transforms his search for gold into an acknowledgment of his heritage. It is Pilate's role as an African woman to be the "custodian of the culture" (Arhin, 92–4). In a quest to learn the complete family history partially related by Pilate, Milkman repeats Pilate's journey to Virginia to find her mother's family and ends up uncovering the legend of his ancestors—that of the Flying Africans.

In *Black Feminist Criticism*, Barbara Christian comments that, "in dramatizing the traditions of her community, Morrison's novels resemble the oral technique of the storyteller" (57). Equally pertinent to this study is the importance of storytelling within the context of the novel itself. In the manner of an African woman storyteller, Morrison tells the tale of the Flying Africans to keep her traditions and culture alive on paper. Within the discourse of the novel, her characters voice the stories of family and ancestral life, although some "informants" are more reliable than others. Joseph Skerrett, in "Recitations to the Griot," points out the importance of Morrison's transformation of the orature: "Milkman's parents, Macon and Ruth, are not effective informants for Milkman. Their narration of their own parts of the mystery of his heritage is partial, egocentric, defensive . . . . It is only Pilate for whom storytelling is not self-dramatization, self-justification, or ego-action" (194–95). Although Pilate is unmistakably Morrison's preferred storyteller, the other stories and the differing voices further emphasize the oral quality of the novel. For it is the sum of the stories, told by this community of voices in the Midwest, Northeast, and South, and Milkman's ability to select among them, which gives us a greater sense of the workings of the oral tradition. With that sense comes the realization that, when a tale is "not actually being told, all that exists of it is the potential in certain human beings to tell it" (Ong, 11). It is this apprehension of the possible loss of the orature and cultural history hat informs this novel and most of Morrison's works. Milkman Dead, the recipient of these stories, has an overachieving, dominant, "Black white man" for a father and a beaten-down, faded rose for a mother, and is—at thirty years old—bored. Only his rapport with Pilate, whose scent is of African ginger, has kept Milkman alive (both literally and metaphorically). Not only does she save him (as a fetus) from his father's aggression, but it is her sensory world of African smells, tastes, and visions which both engages his curiosity and enlivens his recursive memory. Moreover, Milkman's unraveling of his family history hinges on the decoding of the folk song Pilate sings at his birth.

In the dedication of *Song of Solomon*, Morrison writes, "The fathers may soar/ And the children may know their names." But there is a group missing from the dedication whose presence is overpowering in the novel itself—the mothers (grandmother, aunt, older sibling, female ancestor). When the father soars off, there must be someone left to teach the children their names. Although I discuss the importance of naming and the woman blues of "you can't fly off and leave a body" later, it is evident that the tales of the Flying Africans and the stories of endurance and strength in the face of slavery and oppression, as well as the values of the African communities from whence they came, have been encapsulated in the orature of the women—left behind not only to sing the blues but to sing of home. Within an African context, the role of the woman has been that of educator of the children into the culture. Ada Mere, Igbo sociologist, comments on the role of women as tale tellers and instructors. Women, she writes, "are the most primary and constant agents of child socialization" (3); furthermore, as agents of this education, women "are the mainstay of the oral tradition" (15). As Filomina Steady and others contend, the black woman through Africa and the diaspora "represents the ultimate value in life, namely the continuation of the group" (32). It can be argued that part of the cultural achievement of Africans in the Americas has come from the diaspora women who "mothered" African American culture into being (Reagon, 177). For Morrison and other contemporary black women writers, the attention to the role of women in passing on the traditions comes directly from their African and African American foremothers. Morrison, in her role as storyteller, creates an environment within the context of the novel for the stories of women, especially Pilate's, to be recognized and privileged—Macon's stories direct Milkman to unrewarding ends; it is Pilate's rendition of their past which helps Milkman grow. Moreover, the stories of his sister Lena, his mother Ruth, and his distant cousin Susan Byrd, along with Pilate, help Milkman learn how to be "a single, separate Afro-American person . . . while also connected to a family, a community, and a culture" (Skerrett, 200).

Morrison's attention to storytelling traditions reflects specific aspects of women's role in African culture; *Song of Solomon* employs other African artistic traditions as well. By leaving out the "mothers" in her dedication, Morrison has not necessarily forgotten them; rather, it is up to us through our reading of the book—and our own understanding of how women are often left out of recorded history—to fill in what is missing. Morrison comments:

> My writing expects, demands participatory reading, and that I think is what literature is supposed to do. It's not just about telling the story; it's about involving the reader. . . . My language has to have holes and spaces so the reader can come into it. . . . Then we [you, the reader, and I, the author] come together to make this book, to feel this experience. (Tate, 125)

As Morrison's community of readers, we are constantly called to question values as well as supply information—in short, to read with an Afrocentric approach. Morrison's engagement with her readers (community) in this interrogative text may very well be based on the concept of the artist's role and responsibility in African societies: The "artist in the traditional African milieu spoke for and to his [or her] community" (Chinweizu, 241). Certain genres of African orature, particularly the dilemma tales, have unresolved endings which call for community response; moreover, the participation of the community/audience is often insured by a "chorus" designed to engage them. In writing village literature, Morrison emphasizes the use of a chorus in making the "story appear oral, meandering, effortless, spoken. . . . The real presence of a chorus. *Meaning the community or the reader at large, commenting on the action as it goes ahead* " ("Rootedness," 341; emphasis added).

One of the questions raised in *Song of Solomon* has plagued African Americans since emancipation—that of one's place in American society.

From Du Bois's "double self" to Ralph Ellison's "invisible man," the question of identity in a hostile and antagonistic world has been paramount. Often, this search for identity has led to one of two opposite approaches: mainstream assimilation/accommodation or radical separatism. Two characters in the novel illustrate these warring factions: Macon Dead, Milkman's father (assimilation), and Guitar Bains, Milkman's friend (separatism). In addition, Milkman's mother, Ruth, appears to symbolize the death of the genteel, bourgeois, light-skinned black who is isolated from her community. Through the characterization of Pilate, a female ancestor, Morrison emphasizes the dead-end of both mainstream assimilation and radical separatism by offering an alternative—perhaps not a reconciliation but a more clearly articulated dialectic of the double self by the acceptance of one's African values and cultural heritage.

African values and African culture, exemplified in Pilate, are privileged in the text. Like the woman in yellow in *Tar Baby*, Pilate has all the qualities Morrison associates with an ideal African woman: She has stature, strength, presence. Pilate is tall, as tall as her brother Macon, with black skin and wine-colored lips; moreover, she constantly has a "chewing stick" between her lips, much like a West African market woman. And even if those images are missed by the casual reader, one easily notes Macon's statement to his son: "'If you ever have a doubt we from Africa, look at Pilate'" (54). Pilate also has mystical powers. She is born without a navel, which allows her special privileges as a conjure woman, even though it separates her—like any religious figure—from her community. Pilate's house resembles one in a traditional African village compound; she has forgone gas and electricity by using candles and kerosene, and she cooks over a three-stone fireplace.[7] Pilate lives "pretty much as though progress was a word that meant walking a little farther down the road" (27).

When Milkman and Guitar try to rob Pilate of what they think is the gold, they encounter in the ginger-smelling air a surreal middle passage back to the western coast of Africa from whence their ancestors were stolen:

Breathing the air that could have come straight from a marketplace in Accra, they stood for what seemed to them a very long time. Although they had stood deliberately in the dark of the pine trees, they were unprepared for the deeper darkness that met them there in that room. Neither had seen that kind of blackness, not even behind their own eyes. (186)

Pilate's house reflects her African heritage in other ways. Her house appears to her in-law Ruth as "an inn, a safe harbor" (135), and "true to the palm oil that flowed in her veins," Pilate offers both food and hospitality to all who enter (150). Even Macon, who deserted his sister, sees the house as a place of music, warmth, and caring, not realizing that he has destroyed the music in his own house. The two houses stand in stark contrast. In the Deads' house, built by Ruth's acerbic and bourgeois father, the women cower and Milkman is bored. Ruth suffers under Macon's rule, her creativity stunted, her flowers dying. The two daughters, Magdalene called Lena and First Corinthians, pine for lack of love and life, since no man in the community is good enough for Macon Dead's daughters. In contrast to this "dead" house, three generations' worth of women in Pilate's house can live and breathe and sing in harmony (28). There is deep consanguineous bonding between grandmother Pilate, mother Reba, and daughter Hagar. The grandmother, as sociologists Wilhemina Manns and Niara Sudarkasa note, has had a profound influence on the socialization of children in both African and African American cultures, based on African family organization.[8] Grandmother Pilate is certainly the head of this household. Ironically, Milkman, brought into existence through Pilate's powers, practically destroys the foundation of these women's lives.

Pilate has been called a "primal mother goddess" (Lee, 347), and her role as conjurer is well documented throughout the book. Revealingly, she is also the one who attempts to rebuild her extended family as well as pass on the knowledge of her heritage to her nephew/son so that he can recover their roots. I have noted the importance of women in transmitting the stories of the past to maintain the culture within an Afrocentric world view; here generational continuity (passing on the stories of the family) becomes cultural continuity as well. Much of the focus of generational continuity, especially for contemporary writers, has centered on the (grand)mother-daughter relationship so it is interesting, in light of this context, that Morrison chooses the son to make the search rather than any of the daughters of the novel. Perhaps it is because Morrison herself has two sons, but this choice may also illustrate the dominant role the female ancestor/mother plays in passing on cultural knowledge and values to both male and female children in the family. Pilate, in this case, also reflects practices in many West African cultures, where the education of the children—until the boys' initiation—is done by the women of the compound (Nwoga). Pilate seems to understand the necessity of Milkman's life before he is born. Returning to find her brother a "hard man" and her sister-in-law dying from lack of love, she gives Ruth a greenish-gray powder to put in Macon's food so as to revive their sex lives (131). When Pilate finds out later that Macon is trying to abort the child conceived in deception, she reminds him of her obeah powers: She puts a male doll with a chicken bone stuck between its legs in his office. After that, Macon leaves Ruth alone (132).

As one in touch with the continuum of ancestors/descendants, Pilate holds posthumous conversations with her own father and has an uncanny knowledge of events she has not witnessed. She knows her mother's history and the color of her mother's hair ribbons even though her mother died with Pilate's birth. Moreover, after Milkman and Guitar steal the bones they believe to be gold, Pilate goes to the police station and weaves a "sambo" story to save them, incorporating knowledge to which she should not have been privileged. Later, Macon remarks to Milkman: "Who knows what Pilate knows" (207). To get her bag of bones back, Pilate takes on the changeable characteristics of Legba, the African deity worshipped throughout the Caribbean and parts of the South.[9] Almost the height of Macon, she shrinks herself in front of the police, turning her strong powerful African presence into a stereotypic imitation of Aunt Jemima (208).

Pilate is omnipresent in the novel, and many of her values and powers are passed on to her daughter and granddaughter. Reba, for example, wins every contest she enters in spite of her lack of interest in the prizes. The image of the three generations of women living in harmony, plaiting hair, and singing songs, revisions an ideal African village compound, yet the realities of African American life and its constraints shatter this image. For all her powers, Pilate is unable to bring her extended family back together as a force to confront racial oppression, nor is she able to save Hagar from the imposition of the white dominant culture's definition of beauty after Hagar and Milkman's incestuous relationship ends in disaster.

Exogamy, in most African societies, insures that the children from an upcoming marriage will be healthy, productive members of society. According to sociologist Kamene Okonjo, it is one of the most important considerations in mate selection and helps justify the involvement of the extended family in that selection, since the elders would know who was a relative (8). The sexual relationship between Milkman and his cousin Hagar is doomed at the start since it breaks this African cultural practice. Our perceptions of this relationship that destroys Hagar and Pilate's dream of an extended family are shaped by this taboo in many African cultures; it is that reality which determines the breakdown. Pilate foreshadows the disastrous end to their relationship by referring to Milkman as Hagar's brother rather than cousin. When both Reba and Hagar correct her, Pilate questions the difference between the two words: "I mean what's the difference in the way you act towards 'em? Don't you have to act the same way to both? . . . Then why they got two words for it 'stead of one, if they ain't no difference?" (44). Moreover, when Hagar sets out to kill Milkman after being humiliated and dropped by him, the community comments that he's getting what he deserves for "messing with his own cousin" (129).

Another African practice, prolonged breast-feeding, functions antithetically in the novel. In Western medical practice, breast-feeding is recommended up to six months whereas, within traditional communities, it can extend up to two years or more. (It is interesting that contemporary Western women's groups like the La Leche League are now suggesting that women breast-feed as long as they like.) In the novel, Ruth's breast-feeding is a source of embarrassment for both Milkman and Macon and shows her intense loneliness and apparent uselessness. But Milkman's prolonged breast-feeding also highlights the conflict of values in the novel. When the yardman Freddie witnesses one of Milkman's afternoon sucklings, his comments reflect both the knowledge of this traditional practice and the dominant culture's view that the experience is somehow obscene: "I be damn, Miss Rufie. . . . I don't even know the last time I seen that. I mean, ain't nothing wrong with it. I mean, old folks swear by it" (14).

This African practice connects with another as Freddie dubs the young Macon a "milk man." Freddie's renaming of Milkman represents a major occurrence in Milkman's life, and it sticks. Melville Herskovits, in *The Myth of the Negro Past*, focuses on the importance of naming in African American culture. He associates this naming practice with that of their African forebears and comments:

> Names are of great importance in West Africa . . . . That is why, among Africans, a person's name may in so many instances change with time, a new designation being assumed on the occasion of some striking occurrence in his life, or when he goes through one of the rites marking a new stage in his development. (191)

The significance of names and naming in the novel is itself the subject for a separate essay, but naming as a method of resisting the hegemony of white society through African cultural practices is of primary concern here. The power of a name is so strong in much of Africa and the diaspora that often people kept a secret name so that an enemy could not use it for evil intent. In the New World, a name could also be employed in opposition to the oppressor, as slaves were wont to do. The biblical names used in the novel present a "secret" name since they rarely fit the person named, thus transforming the Old Testament (Pilate, of course, is the most obvious example). Morrison comments: "I used the Biblical names to show the impact of the Bible on the lives of black people, their awe and respect for it coupled with their ability *to distort it for their own purposes*" (LeClair, 28; emphasis added). From Sing Dead's insistence that her husband Jake should keep the misguided name he was given by an illiterate white man to Pilate's wearing of her name in her ear, a constant process of oppositional naming and renaming occurs in the novel. In this context, it is evident that naming can be a method of regaining control of one's life. Moreover, this process demonstrates the pattern of passing on the unique cultural traits of Africa within the context of the African American community. In line with Asante's comment about black Americans retaining "the basic components of the African experience" ("African,"

21), I would further suggest that, in reference to Morrison's dedication, it may not be necessary to learn one's original African name; it is the *process* of naming which must survive.

Explicit aspects of African cultural heritage in *Song of Solomon* are the supernatural occurrences throughout the novel. Morrison's attention to the "discredited" knowledge of African Americans and to the African notion of reincarnation both attest to the alternate reality presented in the cultural discourse of the novel. The acceptance of the supernatural is treated, for the most part, very differently in African and Western cultures. Morrison emphasizes this aspect of black Americans' African heritage in comments about *Song of Solomon*:

> [With that novel], I could blend the acceptance of the supernatural and a profound rootedness in the real world at the same time with neither taking precedence over the other. It is indicative of the cosmology, the way in which Black people looked at the world. We are very practical people . . . but within that practicality we also accepted what I suppose could be called superstition and magic, which is another way of knowing things. . . . And some of those things were "discredited knowledge" that Black people had; discredited only because Black people were discredited therefore what they *knew* was "discredited. . . ." That knowledge has a very strong place in my work. ("Rootedness," 342)

It is this special, "discredited" knowledge that Pilate has. Macon tells Milkman to stay away from Pilate because she is a "snake" and explains the way of the world to him in hard-core materialist terms: "After school come to my office; work a couple of hours there and learn what's real. Pilate can't teach you a thing you can use in this world. *Maybe the next, but not this one*" (55; emphasis added). Macon makes a sharp division between the material and spiritual world, privileging the material, but there are other characters, deeply rooted in the African American tradition, who have a more integrated world view. These people, mostly women, extend their knowledge of African American life to include an Afrocentric perspective in which there is dialogue with the ancestors, extended longevity, and perceptions of "things" outside a narrow, literalist vision. Paul

Carter Harrison points out that this is not surrealism within a modernist context:

> Dialogue between living and dead members of the community should not be misconstrued as surrealism: What is important to the mode here is simply the materialization of the ancestral spirit so that one is able to identify the precise source of a particular piece of wisdom. (19)

Therefore, the presence of an ancestor (alive or dead) and the wisdom one receives from that source are seen within the context of the African continuum.

Both of Milkman's "mothers" (Ruth and Pilate) speak with their dead fathers. Ruth, who was "pressed small" by a society which would not allow her to grow, believed her father to be the only friend that she had (124). Unfortunately, her father added to Ruth's "smallness" and alienation so that her love for him has become distorted with profanity. Still, her trips to his grave to "speak" with him reflect the ongoing continuum from the ancestors to the descendants. Pilate's relationship with her dead father is clearly more sustaining than Ruth's. Unlike Ruth's father, Jake (the first Macon Dead) is a proud and connected member of his community. Before his murder, he was a successful farmer, but he did not set himself apart from others in the community; moreover, in death, he still directs Pilate and helps her to understand her life and her heritage. She explains to Ruth: "He's helpful to me, real helpful. Tells me things I need to know. . . . It's a good feeling to know he's around. I tell you he's a person I can always rely on" (141). Through the words and actions of her father and the prenatal knowledge she gains from her mother, Pilate begins to unravel the family history which she passes on to the next generation through Milkman.

Milkman is comfortable with waking dreams, ghosts, and supernatural occurrences, for he states: "Pilate did not have a navel. Since that was true, anything could be, and why not ghosts as well?" (294). It is this ability which separates him from the stark materialism of his father and allows him to understand and respect Pilate's powers. And although it takes him almost twenty years to truly comprehend the importance of what she says, his initial meeting with Pilate and her daughters was "the first time in his life that he remembered being completely happy" (47). The relationship between Pilate and Milkman is the focal one of the novel, and Milkman's beginnings reveal further evidence of the supernatural as part of Morrison's cultural discourse. As noted earlier, Pilate prepares a potion for Macon so that he will sleep with his wife. But Pilate is not only thinking of solving the loneliness of Ruth; she is also worried that the family males may end with the alienated Macon. She tells Ruth: "[Macon's] as good as anybody. . . . Besides you'll get pregnant and your baby ought to be his. He ought to have a son. Otherwise this be the end of us" (125). Pilate's interest in the continuation of her family is typical of most human yearnings, but in another way Pilate seems to prophesy Milkman's becoming not only as a repository for the family's history but also a reincarnation of his great-grandfather Solomon, the Flying African. Pilate's statement to Ruth might appear idle guessing, but since Pilate's powers are well documented in the novel, it seems as if she willed Milkman to come or at least acted as the liaison between the ancestors and the unborn. In *Beloved*, Morrison returns to this theme. The daughter "Beloved," throat slashed by fugitive slave mother, is "reincarnated" as a young woman who reenters her mother's post-slavery life.

Reincarnation, as it functions in the diaspora, remains a powerful concept within an Afrocentric world view. African scholar Donatus Nwoga comments that, although this concept, as "rationally valid acceptable knowledge," is yet to be analyzed, both traditional religion and contemporary literature explore reincarnation in the black world.[10] By the end of the novel, Milkman's flight, which mirrors his great-grandfather's, appears predestined. Milkman, who is born under the blue satin wings of Robert Smith's suicide/flight, is imprinted with the desire to fly: "Mr. Smith's blue silk wings must have left their mark, because when the little boy discovered, at four, the same thing that Mr. Smith had learned earlier—that only birds and airplanes could fly—he lost all interest in himself" (9). Morrison gives us the flight of Robert Smith as the reason Milkman wants so desperately to fly. But later in this detective-like, interrogative novel, it is evident that Smith's "blue wings" are only one small part of the story. By the end of the novel, Milkman's yearning for flight is intricately connected with the history of his great-grandfather. If indeed he is the reincarnation of this African, the desire to fly would have been there whether he felt the prenatal flapping of his mother's stomach or not. I am not suggesting that Robert Smith, the insurance agent who may also have been flying to escape his form of slavery, is not at all connected with Milkman's propensity for flight or the alternative reality of the novel; rather, Smith's takeoff from Mercy Hospital appears to echo the flight of Solomon (Shalimar) and this collective myth of freedom throughout the African diaspora.

Milkman's penchant for flight leads him to seek the gold his father wants retrieved. Macon sends his son because he still thinks the gold is in the cave in which Pilate and he hid after their father was killed. Milkman's own search, however, reaches beyond the gold which is the final aim for both his father and Guitar. On the airplane, he thinks: "In the air, away from real life, he felt free, but on the ground . . . the wings of all those other people's nightmares flapped in his face and constrained him" (222). Milkman envisions this trip back east as an escape from the drudgery of his life, but through the remembered instructions of Pilate, the search for gold becomes a greater search for family history and African heritage. Milkman's search takes him further than his grandfather's farm in Pennsylvania; he returns to the world the slaves made--the South.

The American South, in spite of its iniquitous history of racial segregation and slavery, has become for many African American writers a source of heritage, one's familial home. This may seem, and perhaps is, ironic, but the fact remains that this is where Afro-America began and where the relationship to one's African roots is the strongest. From Harrison's *The Great MacDaddy* (in *Kuntu Drama*), in which the protagonist travels from Los Angeles to the Sea Islands in South Carolina to find the "source," to the work of contemporary women writers such as Bambara, Marshall, and Naylor, who center healing experiences and awareness of one's heritage in Southern coastal regions, movement south reaffirms a connection to the African diaspora. Morrison is no exception, and Milkman's trip south—this time to Virginia—finally leads him to an understanding of himself, his family, and his culture. Milkman's growing comprehension that rural life differs extensively from the life he has known in the city starts when he visits his grandfather's community in Pennsylvania. As he hears stories about his family heritage, he realizes a strength in his culture that he had paid little attention to in the past: "It was a good feeling to come into a strange town and find a stranger who knew your people. All his life he'd heard the tremor in the word. . . . But he hadn't known what it meant: links" (231). Milkman's appreciation that people may be more important than material goods, that family and community are strengths, and that knowing one's heritage is a power separate from the power of money affects him in both conscious and subconscious ways. To search for the gold surreptitiously, Milkman makes up a story that he is going to look for his grandfather's remains (251). Yet it is the search for his ancestors, not necessarily for the remains but for the remainder of the story, that directs Milkman to Virginia. He follows not the gold of his father but the song and story of his aunt: "Macon didn't even try to get to Virginia. Pilate headed straight for it" (297).

Milkman's journey south is a learning experience for him as he pieces together the different stories and lore of his family. There are aspects of his culture of which he, from an isolated, assimilated family, knows nothing. What little he has gleaned comes from the presence of his Aunt Pilate. He notices that the women do not carry purses and their walk and carriage reflect a personal strength that the overly made-up city women have lost. He thinks: "That's the way Pilate must have looked as a girl, looked even now. . . . Wide sleepy eyes that tilted up at the corners, high cheekbones, full lips blacker than their skin, berry-stained, and long, long necks" (266). In addition to the slow pace and sense of community that he finds in Shalimar (pronounced Shallimone/Solomon—another renaming), he realizes that he is unlearned in rural customs. He alienates the men around him by his garish display of money. Before they accept him, he has to go through an initiation consisting of hunting and fighting. Moreover, he has to reconnect with the natural world before he can clearly see what is right in front of him.

Milkman's awareness of the community, the culture, and the natural world around him leads him to reassess his family as well as his own selfishness. He sees all of his extended family in a different light and is sympathetic to both his father's distorted ambition and his mother's pathetic helplessness. His understanding encompasses both those he hurt and ignored and those who were out to "kill" him. However, his perception centers on his two "mothers," who never wanted to take his life, but had given it to him—one physically, the other spiritually: "The two exceptions were both women, both black, both old. From the beginning, his mother and Pilate had fought for his life and he had never so much as made either of them a cup of tea" (335).

In "Rootedness," Morrison states that Pilate functions as the ancestor for Milkman, and it is under her guidance that he becomes responsible and humane (343–44). Moreover, it is her stories and songs, passed on to all of her children, which not only lead him to unravel his family history but implant in him the desire to know. Although she cannot save her own granddaughter from the imposing environment which inevitably destroys Hagar, she manages to protect both Ruth and Milkman. In the end, she bequeaths to Milkman not only his birthright but a legacy which allows him, too, to fly: "She had told him stories, sang him songs, fed him bananas and cornbread, and on the first cold day of the year, hot nut soup" (211). More than the traditional West African peanut soup fed to him, Pilate gives Milkman back his heritage through her African-based orature, although it takes him years to understand the true value of the tales and songs. Most importantly, the children's song, turned into a woman's blues by Pilate, is what leads Milkman to the legacy of his great-grandfather and the Flying Africans.

From the homophone of Pilate's name to Robert Smith's flying on his own wings and the Shalimar children's rendition of the folk song with the sounds of an airplane, the desire to fly and its execution, much discussed by critics, is a major motif in *Song of Solomon*. This motif markedly augments the alternative reality of an Afrocentric world view presented in the novel. This song from Pilate's voice that accompanies Milkman's birth and which he hears throughout his life helps Milkman to realize that he is descended from the Flying Africans who refused to exist under the confines and humiliation of slavery. As Milkman listens to the ancient words of the song sung by children who do not even understand the African words like *yaruba* (possibly *Yoruba*), he begins to piece together his family history as told to him by Pilate, Circe, and his Grandmother Sing's niece, Susan Byrd, a Native American. Byrd (her name a further configuration of the flying motif) not only confirms Milkman's thoughts about the song but tells him about the flying. Milkman asks her incredulously, "Why did you call Solomon a flying African?" She answers: "Some of those Africans they brought over here as slaves . . . flew back to Africa. The one around here who did was this same Solomon" (326). When Milkman returns to his lover Sweet, with whom sex is also a dream of flying (302), he is vibrant as he tells her what he has always felt but never before known—that somewhere in his ancestry, someone could fly: "No more cotton! No more bales! No more orders! No more shit! He flew, baby. Lifted his beautiful black ass up in the sky and flew on home" (331–32).

Our enjoyment as readers at Milkman's elation is marred by the death of Hagar (chapter 13), sandwiched in between the two chapters on Milkman's comprehension and acceptance of his birthright. Evidently, Morrison is quick to remind us that the man flying away leaves people behind, most often women and their children. Both Ryna, Solomon's wife, and Hagar, Milkman's spurned lover and cousin, cannot function after being left and basically die of broken hearts. Hagar unfortunately has been passed on the weakness of her great-grandmother, and this trait is further exacerbated by the imposition of the dominant culture, the lack of a truly extended family, and Milkman's selfishness. But there is another female tradition that is exhibited in the myth of the Flying Africans—the tradition of women left to tell the tale. These women pass on the stories so that the children will know their names. In this context, Morrison states: "There is a price to pay and the price is the children. . . . All the men have left someone, and it is the children who remember it, sing about it, make it a part of their family history" (Watkins, 50).

As illustrated in the novel, it is the women who have kept track of the names and stories so that the men could soar and the children could learn and remember. Pilate hears the words from her father, "You just can't fly off and leave a body," and she lives her life that way—a lament for those who left and a commitment, from the bones of her father to the name that is pierced in her ear, to bear witness. Pilate tells the tale to the young ones who would not even have guessed without her. Indeed, the men who fly off have a price to pay for disappearing without a thought to the women and children left behind. The novel reveals, however, that not all women are destroyed by an oppressive system's dissolution of their family (for the men would not have had to fly away if they were not subject to slavery). Just as the spirituals transformed the slaves' misery into music,

Pilate and the other women storytellers turn their "plea into a note" (321) and pass on the memory of the names that were stolen and the stories suppressed.

Germane to this transformational aspect of the storytelling which uncovers the words hidden by the dominant culture is Morrison's statement: "If you come from Africa, your name is gone. It is particularly problematic because it is not just your name but your family, your tribe. When you die how can you connect with your ancestors if you have lost your name?" (LeClair, 28). The concept of knowing one's name, tribe, and cultural heritage is paramount to the novel, but Morrison takes it one step further. She shows the necessity of stripping off the layers of hegemonic discourse that have hidden both the names and values of "that civilization which exists underneath." Morrison catches us in our own Eurocentric assumptions to expose one of that civilization's legends. Most readers even vaguely familiar with the Bible will immediately assume the title of the novel relates in some way to the song in the Old Testament, but as the plot unravels, we realize the song is about the Flying African Solomon. As in the earlier examples of the use of naming, Morrison emphasizes the ability of black people to subvert images of dominant white Christian values to expose underlying cosmologies while taking on some of the characteristics of the original.

Not only does Morrison demonstrate the ability black people have in turning around the mythologies of the West, but closing her novel in the form of an African dilemma tale's participatory ending compels us to focus on another hegemonic Western notion—science as the sole explanation of the universe. The end of *Song of Solomon* has evoked much critical discussion about what happens to Milkman at Solomon's Leap. After witnessing Pilate's murder by Guitar, Milkman offers his life to his friend and leaps: "As fleet and bright as a lodestar, he wheeled toward Guitar and it did not matter which one of them would give up his ghost in the killing arms of his brother. For now he knew what Shalimar knew: If you surrendered to the air, you could *ride* it" (341). One question which has been raised is whether Milkman lives or dies. Reynolds Price, in a *New York Times* review, asks, "Does Milkman survive to use his new knowledge, or does he die at the hands of a hateful friend?" (48). The ending of the novel is unresolved, but the question the reader should ponder in this interrogative text is not whether Milkman lives or dies, but whether Milkman dies or flies! Which perception of reality are we to believe?

As evidenced by slavers' reports, many slaves committed suicide by jumping overboard during the Middle Passage. Yet in the southern United States and throughout the Caribbean, legends abound that tell us the slaves flew back to Africa. If Morrison is ending this novel in the style of an African dilemma tale, there is both a question and a caveat for the reader: In a multicultural society, there may be other perceptions of reality, other values, and other ways of interpretation than the ones ordained by the dominant culture. In this case, Morrison exposes the conflict of Western and African cultural perceptions, revealing the importance of African heritage and values for black Americans. In the reincarnation of his great-grandfather and through the instructions of his female ancestor and aunt, Milkman flies as his ancestors flew, leaving a legacy for women's tales and children's songs.

In "Towards Dialectical Criticism," Fredric Jameson states, "The process of criticism is not so much an interpretation of content as it is a revealing of it, a laying bare, a restoration of the original message, the original experience beneath the distortions of the various kinds of censorship that have been at work on it" (404). *Song of Solomon* is a text that lends itself to precisely this kind of critical methodology. And Morrison has lent us guideposts along the way, at least for readers who also strip bare their Eurocentric perceptions. In so visibly layering her novel, she directs us to the original message that has been censored, almost effaced, by the language of slavery, oppression, and hegemonic discourse. But the novel makes it clear that we must do the work to uncover the civilizations underneath. Morrison, in the manner of African women storytellers, weaves a tale to confound our notions of reality and leaves us with a dilemma that, in finishing the novel, we have to solve. Her aim, of course, is to catch us (whatever our ethnic background) in our easy acceptance of Euro-American cultural hegemony; her discourse is based in the values and traditions of an African heritage that informs the African American community and its writers.

NOTES

1. Most African writers and critics (as well as other African artists) refer to the participatory nature of their art. See, for example, Achebe, "The Writer," and Soyinka.

2. In addition to Holloway's *Africanisms in American Culture*, see Van Sertima's *They Came Before Columbus* and Magubane's *The Ties That Bind*. Literary criticism like Henry Louis Gates, Jr.'s *The Signifying Monkey* and conferences such as "The Black Woman and the Diaspora," held at Michigan State University in 1986—and the ensuing conference proceedings in the Mar/Apr 1986 *Black Scholar*—also reflect this trend.

3. See, for example, Jean Strouse, "Toni Morrison's Black Magic," *Newsweek*, March 30, 1981: 52. Fortunately, the privileging of Western culture and written text over African cultural traditions and orature has begun to change since black feminist and cultural critics have been exploring these works.

4. There is evidence that the novel has its development in orature as well as in literature. Chinweizu et al. argue that the modern African novel has evolved from the African epic in terms of structure, content, and the world it creates. Moreover, Russian theorist M.M. Bakhtin, in *The Dialogic Imagination*, persuasively states that even the traditional European novel incorporated its oral antecedents.

5. Most essays dealing with folklore in *Song of Solomon* do not examine the African basis of those folk traditions. One article that does specifically is Susan L. Blake's "Folklore and Community in *Song of Solomon*." In addition to the studies cited in the text, works which address myth/folk heritage and, to some extent, African carryovers include DeWeever, Samuels, and Harris. See also Samuels and Hudson-Weems and Smith.

6. Caribbean writer and scholar Wilson Harris referred to the extensiveness of this phenomenon throughout the New World in a seminar at the University of Texas, Spring 1983. Most African American folktale collections include tales of flying Africans. References to this legend are found in *Drums and Shadows* and in Caribbean studies like Monica Schuler's *Alas, Alas, Congo*. For a more developed study of the flying Africans in literature, see my article "If You Surrender to the Air: Folk Legends of Flight and Resistance in African American Literature," *MELUS*, 16 (1989–90): 21–32.

7. The three-stone fireplace is a direct carryover from the Bakongo peoples in Central Africa. The stones not only are practical in terms of designing the fire, but they also have religious significance. I am grateful to C. Daniel Dawson, Director of Special Projects at the Caribbean Culture Center, NYC, for bringing this to my attention.

8. For discussion of the role of the grandmother in African American society and its connections to African family organization, see Manns and Sudarkasa.

9. For a fuller examination of Eshu Elegba, see Consentino.

10. Discussion with African critic and philosopher Donatus Nwoga, University of Nigeria, Nsukka, February 1983. At the time, Dr. Nwoga was working on an article seriously appraising the concept of reincarnation within the context of modern African society. In addition to *Beloved*, Buchi Emecheta's *The Joys of Motherhood* and John Edgar Wideman's *Damballah* offer examples of contemporary African and African American novels that incorporate reincarnation.

WORKS CITED

Abrahams, Roger. *Folktales*. New York: Pantheon, 1983.

Achebe, Chinua. *Morning Yet on Creation Day*. London: Heinemann, 1972.

———. "The Writer and His Community." *Hopes and Impediments*. New York: Doubleday, 1988. 47–61.

Arhin, Kwame. "The Political and Military Role of Akan Women." *Female and Male in West Africa*. Edited by Christine Oppong. London: George Allen, 1983. 92–98.

Asante, Molefi Kete. "African Elements in African American English." In Joseph Holloway, pp. 19–33.

———. *The Afrocentric Idea*. Philadelphia: Temple University Press, 1987.

Bakhtin, Mikhail M. *The Dialogic Imagination: Four Essays*. Edited by Caryl Emerson and Michael Holquist. Trans. Michael Holquist. Austin: University of Texas Press, 1981.

Bambara, Toni Cade. *The Salt Eaters*. New York: Random, 1980.

Belsey, Catherine. *Critical Practice*. London: Methuen, 1980.

Blake, Susan L. "Folklore and Community in *Song of Solomon*." *MELUS* 7 (1980): 77–82.

Chinweizu, Onwuchekwa Jemie, and Ihechukwu Maduibuike. *Toward the Decolonization of African Literature*. Washington: Howard University Press, 1983.

Christian, Barbara. *Black Feminist Criticism*. New York: Pergamon, 1985.

Consentino, Donald. "Who Is that Fellow in the Many-Colored Cap? Transformations of Eshu in Old and New World Mythologies." *Journal of American Folklore* 100 (1987): 261–75.

DeWeever, Jacqueline. "Toni Morrison's Use of Fairy Tale, Folk Tale, and Myth in *Song of Solomon*." *Southern Folklore Quarterly* 44 (1980): 131–44.

Emecheta, Buchi. *The Joys of Motherhood*. New York: Braziller, 1979.

Evans, Mari. *Black Women Writers (1950–1980)*. New York: Doubleday, 1984.

Gates, Henry Louis, Jr. *The Signifying Monkey*. New York: Oxford University Press, 1988.

Harris, Leslie A. "Myth as Structure in Toni Morrison's *Song of Solomon*." *MELUS* 7.3 (1980): 69–76.

Harrison, Paul Carter, ed. *Kuntu Drama: Plays of the African Continuum*. New York: Grove, 1974.

Herskovits, Melville. *The Myth of the Negro Past*. Boston: Beacon, 1941.

Holloway, Joseph E., ed. *Africanisms in American Culture*. Bloomington: Indiana University Press, 1990.

Jameson, Fredric. *Marxism and Form*. Princeton: Princeton University Press, 1971.

LeClair, Thomas. "The Language Must Not Sweat." *New Republic* March 21, 1981: 25–32.

Lee, Dorothy, H. "The Quest for Self: Triumph and Failure in the Works of Toni Morrison." In Mari Evans, pp. 346–50.

Magubane, Bernard Makhosezwe. *The Ties That Bind: African-American Consciousness of Africa*. Trenton: Africa World Press, 1987.

Manns, Wilhemina. "Support Systems of Significant Others in Black Families." In Hariette McAdoo, pp. 237–49.

Marshall, Paule. *Praisesong for the Widow*. New York: Putnam's, 1983.

McAdoo, Hariette. *Black Families*. Beverly Hills: Sage, 1981.

Mere, Ada. "The Unique Role of Women in Nation Building." Unpublished paper. University of Nigeria, 1984.

Morrison, Toni. *Beloved*. New York: Knopf, 1986.

———. "Rootedness: The Ancestor as Foundation." In Mari Evans, pp. 339–45.

———. *Song of Solomon*. New York: Knopf, 1977.

———. *Tar Baby*. New York: Knopf, 1981.

Naylor, Gloria. *Mama Day*. New York: Ticknor, 1988.

Nwoga, Donatus. Personal Interview. March 1983.

Okonjo, Kamene. "Aspects of Continuity and Change in Mate Selection among the Igbo West of the River Niger." Unpublished paper, University of Nigeria, 1978.

Ong, Walter J. *Orality and Literacy*. London: Methuen, 1982.

Price, Reynolds. Review of *Song of Solomon*. *New York Times Book Review*. September 11, 1977: 48–50.

Reagon, Bernice Johnson. "African Diaspora Women: The Making of Cultural Workers." *Women in Africa and the Diaspora*. Edited by Rosalyn Terborg-Penn, Sharon Harley, and Andrea Benton Rushing. Washington: Howard University Press, 1987. 167–80.

Reed, Ishmael. *Flight to Canada*. New York: Random, 1976.

Samuels, Wilfred D. "Liminality and the Search for Self in Toni Morrison's *Song of Solomon*." *Minority Voices* (Spring/Fall 1981): 59–68.

Samuels, Wilfred D., and Clenora Hudson-Weems, eds. *Toni Morrison*. Boston: Twayne, 1990.

Savannah Unit, Georgia's Writers Project. *Drums and Shadows: Survival Studies among the Georgia Coastal Negroes*. Athens: Georgia University Press, 1940.

Schuler, Monica. *Alas, Alas, Congo: A Social History of Indentured Africans in Jamaka*. Baltimore: Johns Hopkins University Press, 1980.

Skerrett, Joseph T. "Recitations to the Griot: Storytelling and Learning in Toni

Morrison's *Song of Solomon.*" *Conjuring: Black Women, Fiction, and the Literary Tradition*. Edited by Marjorie Pryse and Hortense Spillers. Bloomington: Indiana University Press, 1985. 192–202.

Smith, Valerie A. *Self-Discovery and Authority in Afro-American Narrative*. Cambridge: Harvard University Press, 1987.

Soyinka, Wole. *Myth, Literature and the African World View*. Cambridge: Cambridge University Press, 1979.

Steady, Filomina Chioma, ed. *The Black Woman Cross-Culturally*. Boston: Schenkman, 1981.

Sudarkasa, Niara. "Interpreting the African Heritage in Afro-American Family Organization." In Hariette McAdoo, pp. 38–50.

Tate, Claudia. "Toni Morrison." *Black Women Writers at Work*. Edited by Claudia Tate. New York: Continuum, 1983, 117–31.

Van Sertima, Ivan. *They Came Before Columbus*. New York: Random, 1976.

Watkins, Mel. "Talk with Toni Morrison." *New York Times Book Review*. September 11, 1977: 48, 50.

Wideman, John Edgar. *Damballah*. New York: Avon, 1981.

"Rememory": Primal Scenes and Constructions in Toni Morrison's Novels

Ashraf H. A. Rushdy

Somewhere between Wordsworth and Freud, between extremes of the relationship of forgetting to memory, lies another understanding of how adult recollection faithfully reflects or neurotically constructs childhood activity. "The Child is father of the Man," sang Wordsworth. "Analytic experience has convinced us," wrote Freud, "that the child is psychologically father to the adult" ("Outline," 187). For both thinkers, what made childhood consequential for adulthood was that it existed only as an anamnesis, only as a "recollection." The difference between the two thinkers lies in what recollection means, whether a genuine act of self-presencing (however possible), or a neurotic act. For Wordsworth, what "nature yet remembers" is the "primal sympathy" whose original existence assures its perpetual existence—which "having been must ever be" (lines 131, 181–2). For Wordsworth, remembering the heaven lying about us in infancy both defers an ultimate heaven and confers on present nature a substitute glory. "The shadowy recollections, . . . be they what they may," answer the human desire for eternal significance (lines 149–56). For Wordsworth, though birth and childhood are the forgetting of a prenatal divinity, memory is yet an agency for revival and rehabilitation. For Freud, on the other hand, because childhood is a period of latency and ennui, memory is an agency for constructing fantasies from a phylogenetic plane in order to rid oneself of the residual neuroses of an imagined distress. Wordsworth's "primal sympathies" become Freud's "primal scenes," which, in time, become Freud's "primal phantasies." Because Freud's fluid thoughts on the subject of the reality of primal scenes are important to this study, I will briefly trace his development in the two critical decades of denunciation and dogma.

In 1917, Freud argued that what children remember are "primal scenes," naming three: observation of parental intercourse, seduction by an adult, and the threat of being castrated (*Introductory Lectures,* 369). But already in 1917, he had begun to foster doubts about the reality of the remembered events, which he now judged to be "not real as often as seemed at first to be shown by the findings of analysis." Nonetheless his skepticism was still not thoroughgoing; he cautioned that "so often they are not phantasies but real memories" (370).[1] By the next year, 1918, Freud still concluded his discussion "of the reality of the primal scene" with "a *non liquet*" ("From the History," 295). Although ascribing to the "primal phantasies" an existence in the Jungian collective unconscious— "unquestionably an inherited endowment, a phylogenetic heritage"— Freud nonetheless did not preclude the possibility of their being "primal scenes": "they may just as easily be acquired by personal experience" (337).[2] Wistfully he adds, "I should myself be glad to know whether the primal scene in my patient's case was a phantasy or a real experience."

By 1925, Freud conceded the predominant occurrence of "primal phantasies" over the rare event of "primal scenes." By 1933, he asserted that, in the case of daughters' claiming that their fathers seduced them, the "hysterical symptoms are derived from phantasies and not from real occurrences" ("Some Psychical Consequences," 250; *New Introductory Lectures*, 154). Primal scenes gave way to primal fantasies. By denying any original empirical event, by arguing that a "phylogenetic endowment" replaces a personal experience, Freud implicitly argues that memory loses its individual validity as an act of "deferred understanding of the impressions" of an experienced event and becomes instead a mendacious agency of self-denial and self-misconstrual. Memory of a self that was could not be, for memory did not remember.

Wordsworth's "recollections" lead him to remember his "past years," his childhood, giving him a "primal sympathy," leading him to remember his celestial origins, and therefore his heavenly destination. Whatever element of Wordsworthian romanticism about an original ontic state of real being remained in the architectonics of Freud's thought was minuscule. For origins were, in the words of one of Freud's modern commentators, "rigorously undecidable" and terminations equally indeterminate: "No demand for closure, regardless of the personal or collective forces that inform it, can overcome the radical problematization of the origin and the bases of explanation that Freud has put into effect through his notion of the differential pathway, the temporal spacing, that always characterizes the joint work of memory and unconscious phantasy" (Lukacher, 140–1). Without an original event, without an anticipated destination, what is left to anchor the desires governing human experience? Primal scenes, though perhaps pathogens, at least allow the belief in a presence, a self, a subject. It is questions of this sort, questions about desire and despair, about subject and object, about the possibility for self-knowledge, about, finally, memory and being, that Toni Morrison's novels ask. And they ask. For Toni Morrison, as much as Milan Kundera, seems to take for granted that the novel does not answer questions. "The questions are already an answer in themselves, for as Heidegger put it: the essence of man has the form of a question" (Kundera, vii).[3]

The question Morrison poses in her narratives concerns the role of recollected being in present activity, the question of "primal scenes." Here I should wish to offer a redefinition of primal scenes, answering Ned Lukacher's recent attempt. For Lukacher a primal scene is "a circumstantial construction that is predicated when there is a need to interpret but at the same time a fundamental concealment or absence of the sort of evidence that could definitively substantiate a particular interpretation" (330). The primal scene Lukacher has in mind is not solely the province of the patient's experience or imagination but rather the context of the patient-analyst's fabrications. As he argues earlier in his book, "the primal scene comes to signify an ontologically undecidable intertextual event that is situated in the differential space between historical memory and imaginative construction between interpretive free play" (24). The primal scene, then, is the space between the couch and the chair, between the neurosis and the cure. But this strikes me as a cruel dispossession, this taking from the neurotic human her or his memory and claiming it as the property, rather than the basis, of the analysis. And what is more cruel, more reductive, is the excision of experience in the exercise of expression, the denial of being in the claim that the "primal scene is always the primal scene of words. At its most elemental the primal scene becomes the primal *seme"* (68).

In Lukacher's terms, there is no participant in the primal scene; there is only the verbal construct of the disremembered, ontically displaced individual. Without returning quite to Freud, I wish to redefine the primal scene as the critical event (or events) whose significance to the narrated life becomes manifest only at a secondary critical event, when by a pre-conscious association the primal scene is recalled. However, *pace* Freud, I wish to argue that the primal scene need not be sexual; it need only be of such significance that an individual would recollect that episode, and not another, at the crucial moment when driven to re-evaluate her or his life. A primal scene is, then, an opportunity and affective agency for self-discovery through memory and through what Morrison felicitously calls "rememory."

Morrison's "rememory" is a nice addition to the vocabularies of both psychology and narratology—psychology because anamnesis becomes accessible to rediscovery as well as discovery, narratology because the word suggests the process by which narrative worlds are increations as much as re-creations, as much remimesis as mimesis. We are familiar with those devices, in both literary and film art, wherein a memorable sentence or action is delivered or done at the beginning of the work in order that it may be reiterated at a critical juncture later in the narrative, demonstrating either ironic or empathetic development. This folding back on itself gives the work of any narrative its own mimetic quality, a remimesis. Morrison's novels, studies in the process of rememory in characters' lives, are especially concerned with how anamnesis serves and conserves a sense of self.

In Morrison's most recent novel, *Beloved*, the mother Sethe is talking to her daughter Denver:

> I was talking about time. It's so hard for me to believe in it. Some things go. Pass on. Some things just stay. I used to think it was my rememory. You know. Some things you forget. Other things you never do. But it's not. Places, places are still there. If a house burns down, it's gone, but the place—the picture of it—stays, and not just in my rememory, but out there, in the world. What I remember

is a picture floating around out there outside my head. I mean, even if I don't think it, even if I die, the picture of what I did, or knew, or saw is still out there. Right in the place where it happened. (35–6)

These "rememories" not only exist outside the agent's mind but are available to anyone who enters the sphere of the action: "Someday you be walking down the road and you hear something or see something going on. So clear. And you think it's you thinking it up. A thought picture. But no. It's when you bump into a rememory that belongs to somebody else" (36). The term "rememory," signifying a magical anamnesis available to one not involved in the originary act, a Kantian noumenon substantiated into what Freud calls "psychical reality," is new in Morrison's writing (new, indeed, to the language). But the idea of rememory, the concept of mental recollection, both anamnesis and construction, that is never only personal but always interpersonal, has been an important theme in all her novels.

Now, Morrison, it seems to me, presents primal scenes, not primal fantasies. Each primal scene has an actual existence in the experience of the individual involved, presented dramatically to the reader in *Sula* and *Song of Solomon,* represented narratively to the reader in *Beloved.* But that is not to deny the role of imaginative re-creation in the remembering of these scenes. In fact, it is precisely the space between recollection and reconstruction, the place between what, in *Sula,* Morrison calls the "cave mouths of memory" (10) and what, in *The Bluest Eye* she calls the "glare of the lover's inward eye" (160) that Morrison's narratives find their urgency. Whereas in Freud we discover a progressive ambivalence in differentiating "primal scenes" from "primal phantasies," we find in Morrison a committed duality to asserting both constructed and remembered events. In *The Bluest Eye,* Claudia intones, "We remembered . . .We remembered . . .Or maybe we didn't remember; we just knew" (148–9). Or, more tellingly, in *Song of Solomon,* as Milkman walks the street he "remembered something. Or believed he remembered something. Maybe he'd dreamed it and it was the dream he remembered" (77). With a dialogical imagination, subtle almost to a fault, making of nonassertion almost an ideology, Toni Morrison has artfully delineated the pain and necessity of remembering primal scenes in each of her novels. Tracing the use of primal scenes and their recollections in the second, third, and fifth of these novels will allow us to see how Morrison has developed this theme in her art. Such a survey will also demonstrate how primal scenes are never just individual events or independent memories of those events. In Morrison's novels, understanding self and past is always a project of community, memory always situated within a context of rememory. In *Sula* the context of rememory is that of female friendships, in *Song of Solomon* of familial relations, in *Beloved* of a subjugated culture of slaves.

SULA

Sula is the story of two girls growing up in Medallion, each requiring an element the other possesses for her completeness. At one crucial point in the story, on a hot July day in 1922, Sula overhears her mother saying, "I love Sula. I just don't like her." The words send Sula into an abyss of "dark thoughts," from which only the call of Nel raises her. The two girls go play by a river, performing a ritual act of stripping two twigs of their bark, digging two holes until they become one large hole, and burying in this hole various bits of debris littering the banks. A little boy much younger than they, Chicken Little, comes to the riverbank. Playing with him, Sula swings him around and around. He slips from her hands and sails into the water, never to resurface. Although Sula is not malicious in her actions, she makes no attempt to rescue Chicken Little. Nel thinks that somebody has seen them (the only stated worry), and Sula goes to investigate the only house in the vicinity, that of the town's resident madman, Shadrack. He smiles at the girl and "as though answering a question" says, "Always" (57–63). "Sula covered her mouth as they walked down the hill. Always. He had answered a question she had not asked, and its promise licked at her feet."

This one episode in Sula's life, overhearing her mother admit that she does not "like" her, is arguably her primal scene. Critics have already attempted to forestall the sort of reading proposed here. Robert Grant argues that "too often Hannah's comment is interpreted as a 'determining' factor in Sula's personality formation, as if this one remark betokened a socio-behavioral pattern and 'key'—that is, maternal neglect or insensitivity" (98). Or, as Hortense J. Spillers argues, to "pin the entire revelation of the source of Sula's later character development on this single episode would be a fallacy of over-determination" (201). To argue that this episode is somehow responsible for Sula's personality on the basis of its importance as an event in a predetermined psychological or sociological paradigm would indeed be such a fallacy. But to argue that it is so responsible on the basis of its importance in the character's individual psychic life, especially her recollected life, is not fallacious. When Sula attempts in 1939 to trace to some primary event her present state, she remembers that hot day in July 1922: "As willing to feel pain as to give pain, to feel pleasure as to give pleasure, hers was an experimental life— ever since her mother's remarks sent her flying up those stairs, ever since her one major feeling of responsibility had been exorcised on the bank of a river with a closed place in the middle. The first experience taught her that there was no other that you could count on; the second that there was no self to count on either" (118–19). Or the next year, 1940, as Sula lies dying, she remembers the critical word on which her life has been based: "Always. Who said that? She tried hard to think. Who was it that had promised her a sleep of water always?" She does not remember, because the "effort to recall was too great" (149).

Quoting with misleading selectivity, Grant argues that Sula remembers the episode in order "to clarify an independence." It is not independence that Sula is clarifying, but rather instability: "no other that you *could* count on." Grant wishes to posit Sula as an intractable enigma. Were there a "key" that does define her character, her unabsent self, that key must be denied, unprivileged. But his denial is contrived; his reading posing its own privileging gestures: "Why wouldn't a mother. . . like her own daughter? Hannah, we may infer, has intimations of Sula's unresolved 'difference'" (98). A reading that did not privilege a certain textual moment at the cost of another, however, would discover that Hannah is not alone in sensing this "difference," nor Sula alone in possessing it. Patsy and Valentine, whom she is addressing when she makes her comments, also assert that their children, Hester and Rudy, are different.

> "Well, Hester grown now and I can't say love is exactly what
> I feel."

"Sure you do. You love her, like I love Sula. I just don't like her. That's the difference."

"Guess so. Likin' them is another thing."

"Sure. They different people, you know. . . ." (57)

Neither Rudy nor Hester kills anyone, so far as we are told; neither Rudy nor Hester hears his or her mother exclaim that she does not like him or her. Despite a concerted determination to argue that Sula's character is an intractable enigma, her role in the novel part of a program of "calculated indeterminacies," and her being an "unresolved 'difference,'" Grant's case fails because, paradoxically, he both privileges and denies privileging of the text. He privileges Hannah's comment while ignoring (placing on a lower level of significance) Patsy's and Valentine's. And he willfully denies the character's privileging of that crucial moment in her own estimation of its significance. But it is significant and indeed more significant than other moments in her life.

Consider the episode on which Spillers and Grant argue; we do injustice to place too great a burden of etiological significance. That scene becomes the object of Sula's memory at two crucial episodes: the first as Sula attempts to understand her fragmented life, having caused Nel's estrangement from her husband by seducing him into an act of infidelity; the second as Sula dies her articulate death. The episode where Sula's mother openly states her inability to like her daughter does not stand as a primal scene by virtue of its importance in itself; it is a primal scene because it is the object of recollection, of anamnesis at critical stages in the character's life.

The other girl, Nel, has her own primal scene. She and her mother, Helene, set out to travel by train back to New Orleans to visit Nel's dying great-grandmother in November 1920. As they walk through the train to the "colored only" car, a white conductor insults Helene. She replies to the affront with an "eagerness to please and an apology for living" in her voice. The conductor pursues his insult further. Helene's response initiates Nel's primal scene: "Then, for no earthly reason, at least no reason that anybody could understand, certainly no reason that Nel understood then or later, [Helene] smiled. Like a street pup that wags its tail at the very doorjamb of the butcher shop he has been kicked away from only moments before, Helene smiled." All those who watched the scene with their "midnight eyes" bubbled with hatred for Helene, a hatred that "had not been there in the beginning but had been born with the dazzling smile." The scene affects Nel profoundly: "It was on that train, shuffling toward Cincinnati, that she resolved to be on guard—always. She wanted to make certain that no man ever looked at her that way. That no midnight eyes or marbled flesh would ever accost her and turn her into jelly" (21–2). Nel, then, has her primal scene and draws from it a resolution by which to conduct her life.

As Nel remembers, in a soliloquized narrative in 1937, how she had caught Sula and Jude, Nel's husband, in the very act of adultery, her primal scene comes back to haunt her. Addressing an imaginary Jude, she laments, "if only you had not looked at me the way the soldiers did on the train." She states her fear at seeing her husband's eyes looking at her "like the soldiers' that time on the train when my mother turned to custard" (105–6). At the crucial moment in the life of the domestic Nel, she remembers the primal scene that had initiated her life's course.

So much, then, for memory. Each character has a primal scene that is recollected at a crucial moment in her life. The context of this novel, I have suggested, is the rememory between the two women, that participation of one character in another's primal scene.

In 1965, Nel goes to visit Eva, Sula's grandmother and the matriarch who plays God in the novel, whom Sula had placed in a nursing home in April 1937 (see Stepto, 218; Parker, 255). Eva remembers Nel but confuses Nel and Sula:

> "Tell me how you killed that little boy."
>
> "What? What little boy?"
>
> "The one you threw into the water. I got oranges. How did you get him to go in the water?"
>
> "I didn't throw no little boy in the river. That was Sula."
>
> "You. Sula. What's the difference? You was there. You watched, didn't you? Me, I never would've watched." (168)

Nel leaves Eva and the nursing home, and suddenly "a bright space opened in her head and memory seeped into it" (169). As Nel remembers the scene of Chicken Little's murder she attempts to determine how Eva could accuse her of Sula's crime: "What did Eva mean by you *watched?* How could she help seeing it? She was right there. But Eva didn't say *see,* she said *watched.* ' I did not watch it. I just saw it.' But it was there anyway, as it had always been, the old feeling and the old question. The good feeling she had had when Chicken's hands slipped." For Nel, the recollection of the resolved action of Sula's primal scene forces her to renew that meditation on the good feeling she had experienced and to question the interpretation she had always put on that feeling: "Now it seemed that what she had thought was maturity, serenity and compassion was only the tranquillity that follows a joyful stimulation. Just as the water closed peacefully over the turbulence of Chicken Little's body, so had contentment washed over her enjoyment." The image of the water closing peacefully over a turbulent life reminds us of Sula's recollection of her final moments of life: "Who was it that had promised her a sleep of water always?"

Shadrack's answer to an unasked question, his immaculate "Always," has connected the two women on two separate planes. Nel, at her primal scene, "resolved to be on guard—always." Sula at her primal scene heard from Shadrack the word by which she would live her life. For Shadrack, who represents "a form of madness that was clear and compact to bounce off of Sula's strangeness," the meeting with Sula on that July day in 1922 was also his primal scene (Stepto, 223).

In 1941, on National Suicide Day, a holiday instituted by Shadrack in 1920, as a way of "making a place for fear as a way of controlling it" (14), Shadrack recalls the episode that altered his life, in July 1922: "Shadrack remembered the scene clearly" (156). Sula had been the first and only person to enter his house, and he had seen fear in her tearful face: "He tried to think of something to say to comfort her, something to stop the hurt from spilling out of her eyes. So he had said 'always,' so she would not have to be afraid of the change—the falling away of skin, the drip and slide of blood, and the exposure of bone underneath. He had said 'always' to convince her, assure her, of permanency" (157). In 1941 he sees the dead body of Sula Peace and realizes that "he had been wrong. Terribly wrong. No 'always' at all."

The "always" binds Nel and Sula together on a second plane. Nel remembers, in that pained moment of recollecting the scene of adultery, that Sula had once said to her that the "real hell of Hell is that it is forever" (107). Nel, at that moment, realizes that Sula was wrong: "Hell ain't things lasting forever. Hell is change" (108). Sula lived her experimental life believing in a hell where stability debilitated; Nel lived her responsible life believing in a Heraclitean hell where flux and change were the painful constants. But the moment of hell for each was the primal scene with her mother, when Sula realizes that her mother is not interested in her as a human being, when Nel realizes that her mother prefers rejection by the white world over acceptance by the black.

This story is about two solitary girls who first meet in a dream, a dream "that always included a presence, a someone, who, quite like the dreamer, shared the delight of the dream." As Nel sits on her front porch, "surrounded by the high silence of her mother's incredibly orderly house," she dreams of a "fiery prince" who approaches but never arrives. "But always, watching the dream along with her, were some smiling sympathetic eyes" (51). Sula, also an only child, residing in a "household of throbbing disorder constantly awry," spends her hours "galloping through her own mind on a gray-and-white horse tasting sugar and smelling roses in full view of a someone who shared both the taste and the speed" (51–2).[4]

These two daughters of distant mothers each believe that hell was what the other had to abide: Nel's orderly house would be Sula's hell, and Sula's disorderly one would be Nel's. The "always" of permanence and the "always" of change are inscribed into the two girls from their mothers. Nel's imagination is domesticated by her mother's calming influence (18). Sula's sexual imagination was bequeathed to her from her mother through her grandmother: "The Peace women simply loved maleness, for its own sake" (41). Sula only once found her mother in bed with a lover, and it is noteworthy that she never remembers this particular scene, which would, under an older definition of "primal scenes," have proved pivotal to her life. The "al-ways" of Sula's sexual imagination, with its appetite for variety, is not so different from the "always" of Nel's domestic imagination, believing that marriage is a thing forever: "All those days and years, Jude, you *knew* me" (104). Sula's sexual engagements could well be solitary, for the thing she desires is "the postcoital privateness in which she met herself, welcomed herself, and joined herself in matchless harmony" (123).

Shadrack and Nel pass each other on the final day of the story, just after Nel has visited Eva. He stops and tries to remember where he has seen her before, but the "effort of recollection was too much for him" (173). Just as Sula had found the effort to recollect who had said "always" too great, so Shadrack finds the effort to recollect the face of the other face of the girl who had visited him, and to whom he had said "always," "too great."[5] Nel and Shadrack "moved in opposite directions, each thinking separate thoughts about the past. The distance between them increased as they both remembered gone things" (174).

The one gone thing Nel remembers is Sula, as she comes to realize that she has been mistaken in thinking she has been missing Jude for the past twenty-eight years. What triggers the final movement of Nel's knowledge is her recollection, not of her own, but of Sula's primal scene. This is not memory but rememory. The rememory of Sula's primal scene gives Nel the opportunity to understand anew, with refreshed vigor, the meaning of the loss of Sula: "'O Lord, Sula,' she cried, 'girl, girl, girlgirlgirl.' It was a fine cry—loud and long—but it had no bottom and it had no top, just circles and circles of sorrow." Nel realizes now the validity of Sula's final question to her: what made Nel think she was the "good" girl of the two (146)? Nel realizes, with a sorrow that is not polarized, having neither top nor bottom, that she and Sula were not so different from each other (Grant, 99). And she knows now what Sula knew just before she died: that they shared another hell, not of immutability or of eternal flux, but the hell of being an individual, knowing that completeness is not in self but in other, and also knowing that other is not self (119). Their hell was in being girls who were close enough to dream together but not close enough for even their most earnest yearning for "matchless harmony," for involvement of an intensity strong enough to dismantle the boundaries of self and other, to achieve the peace they sought.

SONG OF SOLOMON

In *Sula*, Morrison presents the story of two daughters who lose faith in their mothers—one because her mother did not care, the other because her mother sold out to a dominating culture. In *Song of Solomon,* Morrison presents the story of two sons who lose faith in their families—one in both mother and father because they use him as a ground for their struggle, the other in his mother because she sold out to the dominant culture.

The older of the two boys, Guitar, has lost his father to an accident in the mill. For the loss of her husband's life, the mill owner gave Guitar's mother forty dollars, which she used to buy candy for her children. Guitar ever after felt nauseated at the taste of sugar. Just after being released from jail only because the person whose house he had broken into was willing to degrade herself before the white police, Guitar "remembered anew how his mother smiled when the white man handed her the four ten-dollar bills. More than gratitude was showing in her eyes. More than that. Not love, but a willingness to love" (226). Like Nel, whose mother's smile gave birth to Nel's selfhood, Guitar is the one person in this friendship who has a definite self. Like Sula, Macon Dead III, known to the world as Milkman, must confront the question of whether his mother "likes" him or not: he "had always known that she had loved him . . . He wondered if there was anyone in the world who liked him. Liked him for himself alone" (79). And, like Sula, Milkman attempts to formulate a theory of his "self—the cocoon that was 'personality'" (280).

Considering these similarities, it is worth noting that the working title of this novel was *Milkman Dead* (Stepto, 229). Perhaps the reason Morrison altered the title is that she also altered the context of rememory. Rather than naming her novel after one of the two friends, as she had done in *Sula,* she names it after the family patriarch, Shalimar, which everyone "pronounced *Shalleemone"* (305). For it is only superficially that *Song of Solomon* parallels *Sula* in presenting "two friends, each of whom finds the completing aspect of his self in the other. Indeed, while Guitar's primal scene is important in demonstrating the continuity from *Sula* to *Song of Solomon*, it is negligible demonstrating the development within *Song of Solomon*. For this novel, ultimately, does not treat the theme of friendship as profoundly as it does the theme of family.

This novel is about Milkman's struggle at self-definition through understanding the three primal scenes that constitute his family history. The context of rememory in this novel is the family unit. Of the three primal scenes that play crucial roles in Milkman's odyssey, he is a participant in only one; the other two are related to him, one by both his father and his mother, the other by both his father and his aunt. Milkman's attempt to discover himself follows an uneven path because of his contrary desires. He has a desire to know his origins, both of his name and of his family. But he has a conflicting desire to remain ignorant, to rest secure in unknowingness. The first desire requires memory, the second forgetfulness. In a mood of "lazy righteousness," Milkman feels an eagerness for death, desiring "to escape what he knew, escape the implications of what he had been told" (120). Death, for Milkman, held the promise of renewed ignorance: "there would be no remembrance of who he was or where" (126). As she had done in *Sula,* but with greater and more intricate complexity, Morrison presents us with a series of primal scenes in which a remembered past forms the future. Milkman spends his life looking backward: "It was becoming a habit—this concentration on things behind him. Almost as though there were no future to be had" (35). The lesson Milkman must learn is that to see the future, he must see, remember, and reconcile himself to the past. It is only after his first act of any moment, at age twenty-two hitting his father after his father hit his mother, that Milkman begins tentatively to look forward, "like a man peeping around a corner or someplace he is not supposed to be, trying to make up his mind whether to go forward or to turn back" (70, cf. Bruck, 290–1).

It is after and because of his action that Milkman first hears related the first of the series of familial primal scenes, the one concerning Ruth Dead's (née Foster's) relationship with her father. Macon Dead II, Milkman's father, relates the story. After Dr. Foster died, Macon entered the bedroom in which the corpse lay and saw Ruth with her dead father "In the bed. That's where she was when I opened the door. Laying next to him. Naked as a yard dog, kissing him. Him dead and white and puffy and skinny, and she had his fingers in her mouth" (73). Macon then rehearses his suspicions of the incestuous relationship that might have occurred between Ruth and her father. This discovery affects Milkman in two important ways. First of all, he begins to consider his mother as "a separate individual, with a life apart from allowing or interfering with his own." But he grants her personality only that he may have something substantial to distrust. Secondly, it initiates the remembrance of the second primal scene, the one concerning his relationship with his mother:

. . . He had remembered something. Or believed he remembered something. Maybe he'd dreamed it and it was the dream he remembered. The picture was developing, of the two men in the bed with his mother, each nibbling on a breast, but the picture cracked and in the crack another picture emerged. There was this green room, a very small green room, and his mother was sitting in the green room and her breasts were uncovered and somebody as sucking them and the somebody was himself. So? So what? My mother nursed me. Mothers nurse babies. Why the sweat? . . . He tried to see more of the picture, but couldn't. Then he heard something he knew was related to the picture. Laughter. Somebody he couldn't see, in the room laughing . . . at him and at his mother, and his mother is ashamed. She lowers her eyes and won't look at him. "Look at me, Mama. Look at me." . . .

. . . My mother nursed me when I was old enough to talk, stand up, and wear knickers, and somebody saw it and laughed and— and that is why they call me Milkman and that is why my father never does and that is why my mother never does, but everybody else does. And how did I forget that? And why? And if she did that to me when there was no reason for it, when I also drank milk and Ovaltine and everything else from a glass, then maybe she did other things with her father? (77–8)

Immediately Milkman begins to doubt his father, his mother, himself. He tells Guitar his father's story about Ruth and her father's corpse; Guitar advises him to "forget it." As to the origin of Milkman's name, Guitar remarks, "Niggers get their names the way they get everything else—the best way they can" (88).

Later in the story, Milkman follows his mother to an out-of-town cemetery, discovers her piously mourning at her father's tomb, and determines beyond "any doubts, that all his father had told him was true" (123). He confronts his mother in order to verify the facts about the two primal scenes:

"Were you in bed with your father when he was dead? Naked?"

"No. But I did kneel there in my slip at his bedside and kiss his beautiful fingers. They were the only part of him that wasn't . . ."

"You nursed me."

"Yes."

"Until I was . . . old. Too old."

Ruth turned toward her son. She lifted her head and looked deep into his eyes. "And I also prayed for you. Every single night and every single day. On my knees. Now you tell me. What harm did I do you on my knees?" (126)

The breast-feeding episode is presented dramatically early in the novel (13–15), and Milkman's memory of it is true to the event.

The primal scene with Ruth and her father exists only in the minds of Ruth and Macon. And Macon, we are told, early in the novel, has reconstructed the event in his febrile mind: "Once he believed that the sight of her mouth on the dead man's fingers would be the thing he would remember always. He was wrong. Little by little he remembered fewer and fewer of the details, until finally he had to imagine them even fabricate them, guess what they must have been. The image left him, but the odiousness never did" (16). But Macon is not consciously lying to Milkman when he tells him that he discovered Ruth naked in bed with her father. He is confusing and fusing the two memories that occupy his mind: "For the nourishment of his outrage he depended on the memory of her underwear." The "underwear" is a metonymy for his own lovemaking to his wife: "Ruth wore lovely complicated underwear that he deliberately took a long time to undo [until] . . . Ruth was naked." The association of the underwear with the primal scene of Ruth and her father has caused Macon to implicate nakedness where there was none.

The interview with his mother leaves Milkman doubting both his parents: "He'd always believed his childhood was sterile, but the knowledge Macon and Ruth had given him wrapped his memory of it in septic sheets, heavy with the odor of illness, misery, and unforgiving hearts" (181). The recollection of the two primal scenes drives Milkman to that state of desiring death as a way of eradicating memory. It takes the third primal scene, that concerning the murder of his grandfather, to set him on the path of discovery, both of self and of family origin.

Milkman begins to remember what he had not experienced when he hears his aunt, Pilate, tell about the murder of her father, enigmatically linking his murder with Macon's murder of another man in Pennsylvania (141, 148). Milkman then hears the story more fully from his father. Macon tells Milkman how Macon I had been murdered, how his "body had twitched and danced for whole minutes in the dirt." As Macon II and Pilate set out for Virginia, they are haunted/attended by their father's ghost. In a cave, where the ghost leads them, they discover a "very old, very white" man, whom Macon "stabbed . . . again and again until he stopped moving his mouth, stopped trying to talk, and stopped jumping and twitching on the ground" (170–71). Following this arbitrary and ritualistic murder, justifying his father's, Macon discovers a bag of gold that commences a fight between Pilate and Macon. Milkman begins his odyssey putatively in search of this bag of gold, but this gold has been transmuted. What Milkman seeks is family knowledge. Significantly, the bag he steals from Pilate's house, which he believes contains gold, turns out to contain the bones of his grandfather. Without consciously realizing that his object of desire must be reoriented, Milkman begins to feel a new sense of identity: "He felt a self inside himself emerge, a clean-lined definite self" (184).

The second part of the novel traces Milkman's travels, geographically, to Pennsylvania and Virginia, autobiographically, to his family. In Shalimar, Virginia, hearing the children sing the song of Solomon, Milkman justifies for himself his mother's actions in the two primal scenes of his mother's narration—Ruth's relationship with her father, and Ruth's relationship with her son:

The best years of her life, from age twenty to forty, had been celibate, and aside from the consummation that began his own life, the rest of her life had been the same. He hadn't thought much of it when she'd told him, but now it seemed to him that such sexual deprivation would affect her, hurt her. . . . His mother had been able to live through that by a long nursing of her son, some occasional visits to a graveyard. What might she have been like had her husband loved her? (303–4)

Likewise, hearing the Song of Solomon, Milkman uses his knowledge of the two primal scenes of his father's narration, that of Ruth and her father, and that of his father's murder, to justify to himself his father's cupidity:

And his father. An old man now, who acquired things and used people to acquire more things. As the son of Macon Dead the first, he paid homage to his own father's life and death by loving what that father had loved: property, good solid property, the bountifulness of life. He loved these things to excess. Owning, building, acquiring—that was his life, his future, his present, and all the history he knew. That he distorted life, bent it, for the sake of gain, was a measure of his loss at his father's death. (304)

And so the three primal scenes come together and give the youngest generation an understanding of the dynamics of his family's history, its present eccentricities, and its emotional failings. All that remains now of Milkman's self-discovery is to remember to remember his name: Milkman Dead.

Onymity plays a significant part in this novel. Names are acquired, as Guitar says, by any means available. He, Guitar, for example, is so called because he once desired to own a guitar. Yearning is a signifying, a nominating, aspect of life. The Deads are so named by a "literal slip of the pen" of a drunken Yankee soldier, who had, when registering the patriarch of the family, put down Macon (the place of birth) as the first name, and Dead (the fate of the patriarch's father) as the last (18, 53). Ever since, the family gave to each member, save the eldest male, an arbitrarily selected name from the Bible (18). Names were the products of "yearnings, gestures, flaws, events, mistakes, weaknesses." These were the real names of people, subsisting beneath their recorded names. The lesson Milkman learns is that "when you know your name, you should hang on to it, for unless it is noted down and remembered, it will die when you do" (333). Remembered. Milkman must remember how his name came to be, must remember how his grandfather came to fulfill his name, Macon Dead, and, most importantly, must decipher the song of Solomon in order to discover the names of the mythical matriarch and patriarch of the family, Ryna and Solomon, and the real names of Macon Dead I and his wife, Jake and Sing. The relationships between Milkman's father and mother, or his father and aunt, are not ameliorated in any way by these discoveries (338–9). Milkman, though, is reconciled to his name, to his self, to his family and their failings. In the end he is able to live and die with the knowledge that he is, really and in spite of records to the contrary, Milkman Dead: "Milkman" as a testimony to his mother's need for love after the loss of her father, "Dead" as a testimony to his father's need for possessions after the loss of his father. Milkman learns that he must look backward in order to look forward, that he must remember the past in order to know the future, and that only by accepting this Janus-like attitude to the world can he fly: "For now he knew what Shalimar knew: If you surrendered to the air, you could *ride* it" (341).

BELOVED

Morrison's latest work demonstrates yet again how she has developed the idea of rememory in a further unexplored context. In *Beloved*, the context of rememory is neither close friendship, nor family, but a subjugated culture. The story, I wish to argue, traces the merging lives of Sethe and Paul D, the last two living ex-slaves from Sweet Home. The action is set in a house in Ohio, a house called "124." Each of the three parts of the novel begins with a reference to the mood of the house: "124 was spiteful"; "124 was loud"; "124 was quiet" (3,169,239). Each of these moods is related to the state of existence of Beloved, the baby who haunts the story in three forms: first as spiritual ghost, then as incarnated ghost, and finally as disremembered ghost.

Beloved is many things. She is Sethe's baby daughter whom she murdered at age two in order to save from a life of slavery. Beloved is also the medium of a story that was best left untold, unrecollected. "It was not a story to pass on. . . . Remembering seemed unwise" (274). Beloved is, moreover, a quality that is both called and unnamed: "Everybody knew what she was called, but nobody anywhere knew her name." For Beloved is finally what must be "disremembered," what must be "deliberately" forgotten by everyone involved. Once again, Morrison has presented us with a story in which memory is the crucial device of being, in which primal scenes are not personal but rather interpersonal. In this novel, the interpersonal primal scenes belong to Sethe, the ex-slave woman, and Paul D, the ex-slave man, and Beloved is the story that stops haunting when told, and stops being when disremembered, but must be remembered to be told, and must be told to be disremembered.

Sethe, like Milkman, lives her life trying to avoid confronting the past: "she worked hard to remember as close to nothing as was safe" (6). "To Sethe, the future was a matter of keeping the past at bay" (42). But her "devious brain," devious because it would not grant her forgetfulness, can be corrected only by reliving that past in order to enter the future. Coming home one day, she sees "Paul D, the last of the Sweet Home men." He comes "as if to punish her further for her terrible memory" (6). In fact, Paul D shall prove to be the anodyne for her memory. For Paul D's appearance signals to Sethe that it is now possible to "trust things and remember things because the last of the Sweet Home men was there to catch her if she sank" (18). Paul D drives the spiritual, spiteful ghost out of the house. Beloved, the incarnation, arrives immediately thereafter. Slowly, Sethe begins to realize that Beloved is the daughter she murdered come back from the dead. Hearing Beloved hum a song Sethe had made up for her children, Sethe "recalled the click—the settling of pieces into places designed and made especially for them" (175). Beloved's incarnation draws no amazed response from Sethe because "a miracle that is truly miraculous [is so] because the magic lies in the fact that you knew it was there for you all along" (176). A miracle, that is to say, is an anamnesis, not a novel revelation. And with this click, that marks the rememoried miraculous, Sethe realizes that "she would not have to remember now" (182). Likewise, Paul D, who did not know Beloved when she was a baby, finds her presence disturbing: "She reminds me of something. Something, look like, I'm supposed to remember" (234). Paul D is supposed to remember Beloved, even though he had no encounter with her before, because Paul D's and Sethe's individual primal scenes are joined by rememory. In *Beloved*, Morrison attempts her most ambitious intervolvement of primal scenes, one that accentuates the deferral of narrative origins further and further back, until only slavery stands alone as cause and curse.

Sethe's primal scene is murdering her baby, an act that is never narrated because its subject does not conform to the linearity of narrative. She tells Paul D about the fateful day:

> Sethe knew that the circle she was making around the room, him, the subject would remain one. That she could never close in, pin it down for anybody who had to ask. If they didn't get it right off—she could never explain. Because the truth was simple, not a long-drawn-out record. . . . Simple: she was squatting in the garden and when she saw them [the slave owners from whom she had escaped] coming and recognized Schoolteacher's hat, she heard wings. Little hummingbirds stuck their needle beaks right through her head-cloth into her hair and beat their wings. And if she thought anything, it was No. No. Nono. Nonono. Simple. She just flew. Collected every bit of life she had made, all the parts of her that were precious and fine and beautiful and carried, pushed, dragged them through the veil, out, away, over there where no one could hurt them. Over there. Outside this place, where they would be safe. (163; cf. 148–49)

Over there is beyond the pale of life, the place Beloved visually remembers in her soliloquy in the fourth chapter of the second part: "how can I say things that are pictures" (210–13).

Sethe kills her baby because she sees the slave owners, especially the coolly malign "Schoolteacher," whose purpose in life is to demonstrate the subhumanity of blacks. In her soliloquy in the second chapter of the second part, Sethe states her desire to explain to Beloved the reason she killed her: "if I hadn't killed her she would have died and that is something I could not bear to happen to her" (200). She then recalls another primal scene antedating the murder of the baby, the time Schoolteacher's nephews raped her and stole her breast milk from her, "like I was the cow." Sethe had already remembered this scene of the rape at the beginning of the novel, which is also the beginning of the interdependency of Sethe's and Paul's stories.

On the day Paul came to 124, Sethe told him about the rape (16–17). Later, Paul tells Sethe about her primal scene, about how Halle, her husband, had seen the rape:

> "He saw?"
> "He saw."
> "He told you?"
> "You told me."
> "What?"
> "The day I came in here. You said they stole your milk. I never knew that it was that messed him up. That was it, I guess. All I knew was that something broke him. . . .
> "It broke him, Sethe." Paul D looked up at her and sighed. "You may as well know it all. Last time I saw him he was sitting by the churn. He had butter all over his face." (68–9)

Paul infers that the setting of his primal scene, seeing Halle at the churn, is related to Sethe's by constructing a joint narrative in which her rape acts as the cause of Halle's actions at the churn. The discrete primal scenes become a sequence in a unified narrative.

Sethe, unable to "picture what Paul D said," asks him what he said to Halle, in response to which Paul tells about his primal scene.

> "Did you speak to him? Didn't you say anything to him? Something!"
> "I couldn't, Sethe. I just . . . couldn't."
> "Why!"
> "I had a bit in my mouth." (69)

Sethe now forms the serial narrative pictures in *her* mind, a continuity born of two separate visions, separated by eighteen years. She remembers the two nephews sucking on her breasts, the schoolteacher noting it down as a scientific experiment, her husband "squatting by the churn smearing the butter as well as the clabber all over his face because the milk they took is on his mind," and Paul D looking on with an iron bit in his mouth (70). The two individual experiences, of Sethe and of Paul D, join to form one single narrative, forged in the interpersonal primal scenes each remembers for the other.

When Sethe tells Paul the scene of murdering her daughter, called the "crawling-already? baby," Paul responds, mentally, by thinking that this Sethe "didn't know where the world stopped and she began" and verbally by telling her, "You got two feet, Sethe, not four" (164–5). That enigmatic reference reminds us that she was treated like a cow, and he like a wild horse, she milked, he put in halter and bit.

Sethe is the first to realize that Paul's life and her life are inextricably bound: "she knew that Paul D was adding something to her life . . . : new pictures and old rememories" (95). She knows that their lives are part of one linear narrative: "Her story was bearable because it was his as well—to tell, to refine and tell again. The things neither knew about the other—the things neither had word-shapes for—well it would come in time: where they led him off to sucking iron; the perfect death of her crawling-already? baby" (99). But when she tells him about the "perfect death" of her daughter, Paul leaves. It takes him time to digest the possible motivations for such an act; it takes the dissipation of Beloved (literally), to allow him to come to the border of Sethe's life; and it takes a rememory to let him cross that threshold. "There are too many things to feel about this woman. His head hurts. Suddenly he remembers Sixo [another Sweet Home man] trying to describe what he felt about the Thirty-Mile Woman. 'She is a friend of my mind. She gather me, man. The pieces I am, she gather them and give them back to me in all the right order. It's good, you know, when you got a woman who is a friend of your mind'" (272–3). Paul remembers how Sethe had allowed him to retain his manhood by not referring to the neck shackles he was forced to wear after his attempted escape from Sweet Home and decides that he "wants to put his story next to hers": "'Sethe,' he says, 'me and you, we got more yesterday than anybody. We need some kind of tomorrow.'"

Sethe's primal scene is deferred from the "perfect death" of her daughter, to the causative entrance of Schoolteacher, to her rape at the hands and mouths of his nephews, to the belief Schoolteacher teaches his nephews, that blacks are not humans but animals. It is this basic denial of humanity, that is slavery, that is the original cause. Baby Suggs, the matriarch of this novel, whose son, Halle, bought her freedom by selling his life over again, states the truth basic to this subjugated culture: "Those white things have taken all I had or dreamed . . . and broke my heartstrings too. There is no bad luck in the world but whitefolks" (89; cf. 104). Baby Suggs is the one who knows that "death was anything but forgetfulness" (4), the one whose heart starts beating the minute she crosses the Ohio River, escaping slavery (147), the one who recognizes that retaliation is futile: "Lay down your sword. This ain't a battle; it's a rout" (244). And she is the one who possesses sadness at her center, "the desolated center where the self that was no self made its home." Baby Suggs, like all slaves, has never been given the "map to discover what she was like" (140). The map of self-discovery belongs only to those whose shared narratives give them memory and rememory. Paul, at the reconciliation scene, finds Sethe in Baby Suggs's bed. "He is nervous. This reminds him of something" (271). He is reminded of how Baby Suggs died, how she chose no longer to live, simply letting her "big old heart" quit. What is noteworthy is that Paul D entered 124 nine years after Baby Suggs died. He is not reminded; he has a rememory. It is Sethe who witnessed the demise of Baby Suggs, but Paul who rememories it. And that sums up the context of this novel's rememory: Sethe and Paul, the last of the Sweet Home slaves.

Beloved, then, traces the involvement of Sethe's and Paul's primal scenes, "rememoried," each by the other, until they form one story: discrete scenes become a coherent whole in this interpersonal anamnesis. The origin of the pain is the dominating culture's unwillingness to allow the subjugated culture the right to self-definition, self-discovery, and, when they deem it necessary, self. That is the yesterday both Paul and Sethe must remember, Paul in order to open the rusty lid of the tobacco tin buried in his chest where a red heart used to be (72–3), Sethe in order to quiet that spite haunting her mind, in order to make a future that is not haunted by the past. Their tomorrow is what they will have when they forget Beloved, the girl who was killed so she would not have to die, the story that is told so that it may be disremembered: "This is not a story to pass on."[6]

Memory, a modern heir of Descartes tells us, is always present: "When I remember something I had previously experienced, I am merely having a new present experience. I do not re-experience the prior experience; I have a quite different experience which I claim is a replication, a copy, of the earlier one. So remembering the past is exactly like perceiving the external world" (Allan, 29). Because it is persistently present, memory is liable to all the problems of Cartesian phenomenology, the problems, in Santayana's phrase, of the "solipsism of the present moment."

In the world of Morrison's novels, however, memory is neither as stable nor as intensely personal a thing as is perception. For memory exists as a communal property of friends, of family, of a people. The magic of memory is that it is interpersonal, that it is the basis for constructing relationships with the other who also remembers the reality of memory is that it must be experienced individually, first, before it becomes communal property. In individual experience, memory is painful, as Milkman and Sethe discover. In shared experience, memory is healing, as everyone in Morrison's narratives discovers.

NOTES

1. On the current debate concerning Freud's integrity in the suppression of the evidence for the seduction theory, see Masson and Malcolm; for an incisive review of the debate, see Crews, chapters two and three.

2. We must remember that though this case study was written the same year as the secession of Jung, Freud made this addition just before publication, the painful event of four years past perhaps less poignantly disabling him from appreciating the direction of Jung's thought.

3. Compare Morrison, "Rootedness," 341: a novel, she states, "suggests what the conflicts are, what the problems are. But it need not solve those problems because it is not a case study, it is not a recipe."

4. Barbara Smith argues (175–81), citing the full passage from which I have selectively quoted, that *Sula* is "an exceedingly lesbian novel in the emotions expressed, in the definition of female character, and in the way that the politics of heterosexuality are portrayed" (180–1). Smith's case is interesting and informed, not least of all for her revisionary definition of the constitution of lesbian literature. Her reading, however, ignores certain forms of heterosexual fulfillment that Morrison inscribes, including Hannah's "manlove," an endowment from her mother, Eva, who also "simply loved maleness for its own sake" (41–2). More importantly, Smith reduces the profundity of Sula's affection for Ajax to an ephemeral thing: "the closest Sula comes to actually loving a man." Interestingly,

Morrison has recently "rejected the suggestion that *Sula* is a lesbian novel" (Russell 45–6): "What was valued was their friendship . . . it was spiritual, of first order priority." For support of Smith's reading, see Holloway and Demetrakopoulos, 147.

5. Morrison herself suggests that Nel and Sula are "like a Janus head" (Parker, 53). It is also worth noting that Morrison uses the exact same sentence, "The effort to recall was too great," in *The Bluest Eye* (144).

6. In discussing this novel, Toni Morrison, with "hushed intensity," said to Sandi Russell: "The story has lots of questions in it for me. The novel is an attempt to deal with those questions. It was an era I didn't want to get into—going back into and through grief" (Russell, 45). For Morrison's sources for and attitude toward the story of *Beloved,* see Naylor and Morrison.

WORKS CITED

Allan, George. *The Importances of the Past. A Meditation on the Authority of Tradition.* Albany: State University of New York Press, 1986.

Bruck, Peter. "Returning to One's Roots: The Motif of Searching and Flying in Toni Morrison's *Song of Solomon." The Afro-American Novel Since 1960.* Edited by Peter Bruck and Wolfgang Karrer. Amsterdam: Gruner, 1982.

Crews, Frederick. *Skeptical Engagements.* New York: Oxford University Press, 1986.

Fabre, Genevieve. "Genealogical Archeology, or the Quest for Legacy in Toni Morrison's *Song of Solomon."* In Nellie McKay, pp. 105–14.

Freud, Sigmund. "From the History of an Infantile Neurosis." 1918. *Case Histories* II. Trans. James Strachey. Harmondsworth, Eng.: Penguin, 1979.

———. *Introductory Lectures on Psychoanalysis. The Standard Edition of the Complete Psychological Works of Sigmund Freud. Vols.* 15–16. Ed . James Strachey. London: Hogarth, 1969. 24 vols. 1952–74.

———. *New Introductory Lectures on Psychoanalysis.* 1933. Trans. James Strachey. Harmondsworth, Eng.: Penguin, 1973.

———. "Outline of Psychoanalysis." *The Standard Edition of the Complete Psychological Works of Sigmund Freud.* Vol. 23. Ed. James Strachey. London: Hogarth, 1969. 139–207. 24 vols. 1952–74.

———. "Some Psychical Consequences of the Anatomical Distinction Between The Sexes." *The Standard Edition of the Complete Psychological Works of Sigmund Freud.* Vol. 19. Ed. James Strachey. London: Hogarth, 1969. 241–58. 24 vols. 1952–74.

Grant, Robert. "Absence into Presence: The Thematics of Memory and the 'Missing' Subjects in Toni Morrison's *Sula."* In Nellie McKay, pp. 90–103.

Holloway, Karla F. C., and Stephanie A. Demetrakopoulos. *New Dimensions of Spirituality: A Biracial and Bicultural Reading of the Novels of Toni Morrison.* New York: Greenwood, 1987.

Kundera, Milan. *Life Is Elsewhere.* Trans. Peter Kussi. New York: Penguin, 1987.

Lukacher, Ned. *Primal Scenes: Literature, Philosophy, Psychoanalysis.* Ithaca: Cornell University Press, 1986.

Malcolm, Janet. *In the Freud Archives.* New York: Knopf, 1984.

Masson, Jeffrey Moussaieff. *The Assault on Truth: Freud's Suppression of the Seduction Theory.* New York: Farrar, 1984.

McKay, Nellie, ed. *Critical Essays on Toni Morrison.* Boston: Hall, 1988.

Morrison, Toni. *Beloved.* New York: New American Library, 1987.

——. *The Bluest Eye.* New York: Washington Square, 1970.

——. "Rootedness: The Ancestor as Foundation." *Black Women Writers (1950–1980): A Critical Evaluation.* Edited by Mari Evans. New York: Doubleday, 1984.

——. *Song of Solomon.* New York: New American Library, 1977.

——. *Sula.* New York: New American Library, 1973.

Naylor, Gloria, and Toni Morrison. "A Conversation." *Southern Review* 21 (1985): 567–93.

Parker, Bettye J. "Complexity: Toni Morrison's Women—An Interview Essay." *Sturdy Black Bridges: Visions of Black Women in Literature.* Edited by Roseann P. Bell, Bettye J. Parker, and Beverly Guy-Sheftall. New York: Doubleday, 1979.

Russell, Sandi. "'It's OK to Say OK.'" In Nellie McKay, pp. 43–7.

Smith, Barbara. "Toward a Black Feminist Criticism." *The New Feminist Criticism: Essays on Women, Literature, and Theory.* Edited by Elaine Showalter. London: Virago, 1986.

Spillers, Hortense J. "A Hateful Passion, A Lost Love." *Feminist Issues in Literary Scholarship.* Edited by Shari Benstock. Bloomington: Indiana University Press, 1987.

Stepto, Robert. "'Intimate Things in Place': A Conversation with Toni Morrison." *Chant of Saints: A Gathering of Afro-American Literature, Art, and Scholarship.* Edited by Michael S. Harper and Robert B. Stepto. Urbana: University of Illinois Press, 1979.

Wordsworth, William. "Ode: Intimations of Immortality." *Norton Anthology of English Literature.* 4th ed. Vol. 2. Edited by M.H. Abrams et al. New York: Norton, 1979. 213–17. 2 vols.

PART 4
Tar Baby

Paradise Lost and Found: Dualism and Edenic Myth in Toni Morrison's *Tar Baby*

Lauren Lepow

Toni Morrison's fiction embodies a powerful critique of dualistic thinking. Dualism—any system of thought that polarizes what we perceive—is a narrowing world view, for it inevitably cuts the individual off from the "other," the not-I or the not-good or the not-ordered. Dualism creates warring antitheses: the "other" is an enemy to strive with and, ideally, to dominate. Feminist theologian Rosemary Radford Ruether suggests that Christianity, as "the heir of both classical Neo-Platonism and apocalyptic Judaism" embodies a dualistic world view that leads to authoritarianism and sexism:

> All the basic dualities—the alienation of the mind from the body; the alienation of the subjective self from the objective world; the subjective retreat of the individual, alienated from the social community; the domination or rejection of nature by spirit—these all have roots in the apocalyptic-Platonic religious heritage of classical Christianity. But the alienation of the masculine from the feminine is the primary sexual symbolism that sums up all these alienations. The psychic traits of intellectuality, transcendent spirit, and autonomous will that were identified with the male left the woman with the contrary traits of bodiliness, sensuality, and subjugation. (44)

Ruether argues that male subjugation of the female is "the primary psychic model for . . . oppressor-oppressed relationships between social classes, races and nations" (46). Similarly, Mary Daly asserts that "the projection of 'the other'— easily adaptable to national, racial and class differences—has basically and primordially been directed against women. Even the rhetoric of racism finds its model in sexism" (61).[1]

In her novels, Morrison continually requires us to confront the quite literally self-defeating and self-destructive qualities of dualistic thinking, demonstrating that half a reality is insufficient for anyone. Confronting her readers with the dangers of our customary way of perceiving the world, Morrison also suggests that transcending dualism is one ideal, imaginable route beyond our culturally ingrained and religiously sanctioned sexism, racism, and other self-narrowing dogmas. She knows, however, that we are all so mired in dualism that she must shake the world, mix it, and stand it on end before we can have even a glimmering of what a non-dualistic existence might be.

It is in *Tar Baby* that Morrison's critique of dualism—sexism, primarily, but also racism and class distinction—finds fullest realization; however, for her characters, dualistic thinking has long been the enemy. In Morrison's first novel, *The Bluest Eye,* Pecola defines her world in terms of antitheses: there is the perfect, blond, blue-eyed, much-beloved Shirley Temple; then there is Pecola herself, all that is left over. The hatred and violence in her world, she is certain, emerge from the distance between her ideal and her actual, antithetical self. Nel's tragedy, in *Sula,* is also a product of her determinedly dualistic world view. When she discovers her husband Jude's infidelity with her best friend, Sula, Nel for the first time is forced to define a self apart from Sula. She falls into the trap of believing that the separate selves must be antithetical, representatives of simply defined polarities of good and evil. Only near the end of the novel is she required to question her tidy morality and finally to recognize all that she has deprived herself of by choosing not to be Nel but rather not-Sula.

Song of Solomon further advances Morrison's challenge to dualistic thinking. In her presentation of Milkman Dead's quest, she begins to suggest that the trap of dualism is not inescapable. Milkman begins his life and indeed spends the first thirty years of it in a pat, moral universe like Nel's. His mother is good and his father evil—or, easily, the reverse. His father is order; Pilate is disorder: Milkman tries to choose and never can, because the disjunction he insists on is false. Only as he labors in his quest does he gradually come to realize that the lines he has so darkly drawn between perceived dualities have not helped but hindered him in his search for identity. In the novel's final paragraph, when Milkman and Guitar, life and death, victory and surrender all merge, Milkman truly triumphs.

In *Tar Baby* Morrison stands the world on end remorselessly, attacking dualism on every front. One of her most effective techniques involves her telling us a story we already know very well indeed, the myth of Eden. As John Irving asserts, this is "a novel deeply perceptive of the black's desire to create a mythology of his own to replace the stereotypes and myths the white man has constructed for him" (31). Morrison recasts the Genesis story in such a way that its dualism is upset and its moral absolutes evaporate. She also merges the Genesis story with the tar baby folk tale that gives the novel its name. In the convergence of these retold stories, Morrison defines a world where our customary definitions do not stick, where human potential is enhanced precisely to the degree that dualism is transcended. How far can dualism be transcended? The novel leaves that question open, but the possibility of self-redemption flavors its conclusion.

The tar baby story and the myth of Eden are both stories of creation, the creation of human beings, or what passes for them, from such unpromising material as clay or tar. They are also stories about temptation and entrapment, the fall from grace, and redemption. Morrison's interest in these two overlapping stories lies in part in their adaptability to her critique of dualism. The version of the Genesis story she invokes most sharply is Milton's, and this adds an edge of ironic humor to the novel. By drawing misogynist Milton into the service of this work, Morrison finds yet another way, a delightfully amusing one, of reminding us that nothing need be what it seems. In fact, all things can be their "opposites": no territory is forbidden to the self in the act of self-creation.

Tar Baby echoes Milton's subject at every turning. The novel's setting is fully a character, and it is a character, like the others, that shimmers with its abilities to be both A and not-A. The Isle des Chevaliers disturbs protagonist Jadine with its excess: "The island exaggerated everything. Too much light. Too much shadow. Too much rain. Too much foliage and much too much sleep" (57). By endowing her island with such excess, Morrison can easily make of it both Eden and hell. The first glimpse Morrison gives us of her island puts trees and snakes in the foreground: "Only the champion daisy trees were serene. After all, they were part of a rain forest already two thousand years old and scheduled for eternity, so they ignored the men and continued to rock the diamondbacks that slept in their arms" (7). The Isle des Chevaliers certainly a tropical paradise, like Milton's, a "happy Isle" (II, 410), with its "hills and vales so bountiful it made visitors tired to look at them: bougainvillea, avocado, poinsettia, lime, banana, coconut and the last of the rain forest's champion trees" (8). Yet the island is not all paradise: beneath the hills lies the swamp, Sein de Vieilles: "And witch's tit it was: a shriveled fog bound oval seeping with a thick black substance that even mosquitoes could not live near" (8). In this pitchy lake, Jadine will later nearly sink, thinking that "perhaps she was supposed to lie horizontally" (156). The image recalls to the reader that of Milton's Satan "rolling in the fiery Gulf" (I, 52). Her "burning" legs (158) also enhance that parallel, while at the same time the episode makes of Jadine the tar baby Son will later tell her she is. "Jesus, what *is* that stuff," another character asks. "It looks like pitch" (158).

The swamp is a product of the diverting of the river, a human interference with natural process. Morrison's critique of dualism is operating here, for, as Ruether argues, dualistic thinking—the alienation of consciousness from nature—has resulted in "religious sanction for modern technological exploitation of the earth" (49). At the Isle des Chevaliers, men had

folded the earth where there had been no fold and hollowed her where there had been no hollow, which explains what happened to the river. It crested, then lost its course, and finally, its head. Evicted from the place where it had lived, and forced into unknown turf, it could not form its pools or waterfalls, and ran every which way. The clouds gathered together, stood still and watched the river scuttle around the forest floor, crash headlong into the haunches of hills with no notion of where it was going, until exhausted, ill and

grieving, it slowed to a stop just twenty leagues short of the sea.
(7)

The description invites comparison with Milton's in Book I of *Paradise Lost:* the fallen angels' rape of the infernal landscape in preparation for constructing Pandemonium. Like the developers at Isle des Chevaliers, those spirits "Ransack'd the Center, and with impious hands / Rifl'd the bowels of thir mother Earth / For Treasures better hid" (I, 686–88).

For Morrison's developers, the treasures are the building lots themselves, where luxury estates will be built. Chief among these is Valerian Street's l'Arbe de la Croix, the house wherein most of the novel's action takes place. The name is a tease: "Arbe" is not quite "arbre," yet we think of tree, increasingly, in this context, of the primeval tree of Paradise. The "Croix" foreshadows the agony that the house's inhabitants will experience and the redemption they may or may not attain to. But the tree and the cross are also apparent polarities that, upon closer examination, merge: medieval tradition has it that the cross on which Jesus was crucified was constructed from the Tree of Knowledge.

L'Arbe de la Croix, like both Satan's Pandemonium and God's Heaven, is a magnificent, elaborately constructed mansion. Valerian Street's house, like Satan's, is the product of first-rate craftsmanship and the object of enthusiastic praise. Yet the house's most remarkable feature is its natural quality: it is gardenlike in being "wide, breezy and full of light" (8), in not "looking 'designed'" (8–9); and its greenhouse seems to some critics to be *de trop.* But even Pandemonium rivaled nature with its lamps that "yielded light / As from a sky" (I, 729–30). A house is not, after all, a garden, and the greenhouse serves as a reminder of how easily the apparent polarities, artifice and nature can overlap and merge. It is as much the heavenly mansion Milton describes in Book III of his epic as it is either Satan's palace or Adam's first home.

Morrison's richly allusive prose effects the superimposition of one half of our dualistic world view upon the other. Thus, we begin to achieve an integrated perspective, not only of setting but also of characters. At first seeming a godlike controller of others' destinies, Valerian Street, the wealthy, white owner, presides over his "paradise." Sitting in his greenhouse among "the peonies, the anemones and all their kind" (9), he evokes

Milton's Satan's image of a God who "Lordly sits / Our envied Sovran, and his Altar breathes / Ambrosial Odors and Ambrosial Flowers, / Our servile offerings" (II, 243–6). Sydney, his butler asserts, "I've known him practically all his life and I'll tell you this: he gets his way" (31). He is a creator not only in his "creation" of the setting but also in his making Margaret, Sydney, Ondine, and Jade much of what they are. Jade is, at least in Son's view, the "tar baby" of Valerian's creation, and Morrison slyly lets us know that the candy magnate has appropriate credentials to undertake such an act of creation: "Valerians," the candy named for him, and which his company continues to produce—"made from the syrup sludge left over from their main confection" (42)—are tar babies, too.

Valerian directs his creatures' lives, and he seems a largely benevolent deity. Of his servants Sydney and Ondine, for example, he says with considerable justification, "I have always taken care of them" (25). But he is also capricious, and his petty attacks on Margaret are detestable, though she sees him as "some lord or priest who doubted her confession" (73) when he is at his most unkind. Perhaps he is, more than anything else, the image of a white man's god, that is, the white man *as* God, unquestionable especially by the likes of his black servants and the black outsider, Son. He is therefore a seriously flawed God, given the totality of Judeo-Christian belief. His emperor's name and his "head-of-a-coin profile" are contrasted with the novel's conspicuous emperor butterflies, who have true dominion on the island, while Valerian is merely the false coinage of an emperor. Indeed, the Roman Emperor Valerian (253 C.E.), although famous for his campaigns against the Persians, was eventually surrounded and captured by enemy horsemen and held prisoner for the rest of his life. Valerian Street may initially dominate the Isle of the Horsemen, but he certainly ends his days in apparent captivity. The name, the profile, Valerian's belief in "industry" (opposed to Son's in "fraternity")— all these qualities suggest that what is due Valerian is what was rendered unto Caesar, that spiritual currency has some other source and destination.

Valerian may have godlike powers over his creatures, but even he acknowledges that there are things outside his control, things for which he "can't be responsible" (60). This notion of responsibility is at the heart of the terrible innocence that prevents him from seeing or foreseeing the effects of their exercise. He cannot see what will happen when he uproots Margaret and brings her into his world; he does not foresee the disastrous results of his whim to share his holiday dinner with Son and the servants as well as with Jade and Margaret. On that occasion, "nobody was in his proper place" (167) in Valerian's rigid hierarchy, and by the end of the evening he realizes that "he had played a silly game, and everyone was out of place" (179). He has long permitted arbitrary roles and values to blind him and must at last convict himself of being "guilty . . . of innocence" (209).

Valerian can be culpably innocent because his view of sin is too simplistic. He is mired in the traditional view of original sin: for him, it is disobedience to higher authority. As Sydney puts it, "'What he wants is for people to do what he says do'" (139–40). Since Valerian is the highest authority in his world, he feels justified in all he does, including his remaining aloof from those he ought to know and understand. Morrison restages Adam and Eve's fall, using relatively minor characters, to enable us to question the tradition. Gideon is, like Adam, a gardener in paradise (94); Thérèse has a "craving for apples" (93) and an equal craving for such knowledge as she is not already master of (128–30). When Gideon and Thérèse steal his apples, Valerian judges them and exiles them from Eden.

But knowledge cannot be sin, in Morrison's world view: the theft catalyzes the release of much long-hidden knowledge, and it is therefore not a culpable action. Valerian's treatment of Gideon and Thérèse, Son believes, "would outrage Satan himself" (174). Son's rage at Valerian comes from his perception of a larger picture in which it is Valerian who is guilty (both of excess and of innocence), while Gideon and Thérèse are entitled to what they have appropriated. For Morrison, the fall is a falling away from nature, one's human nature as well as the natural world. The real original sin, Morrison seems to say, is dualism, the either-or vision that deprives us of knowledge as it fragments and distorts the world.

Theologian Valerie Saiving calls for theology to "redefine its categories of sin and redemption" (41). Morrison has forged such a theology. To move us toward knowledge of what sin is, she defines what it is not. Just so, in redefining redemption, she begins by undefining it. Redemption cannot come from Valerian for more reasons than one. Granted, he has married Margaret, who is endowed with some Marian attributes: her cross (58–9), her simplicity and humble origins, her beauty so stunning that "the moment he saw her something inside him knelt down" (13). But there are many ways in which she is antithetical to the Christian Virgin, and the island's "Marys," including Thérèse of the magic breasts, are reminders of that ironic distance. Margaret is a very far from perfect mother, and the Marys may be judging her, among others, by their refusal to enter l'Arbe de la Croix (34). Margaret nevertheless bears Valerian's only-begotten son, Michael, and she sees him as Christlike. She speaks of her view

> that he loved people, was not selfish, was actually self-sacrificing, committed that he could have lived practically any kind of life he chose, could be dissolute, reckless, trivial, greedy. But he wasn't. He had not turned out that way. He could have been president of the candy company if he had wanted, but he wanted value in his life, not money. He had turned out fine, just fine. (171)

But Michael, whom the reader never meets in the novel's present, may not have turned out so fine. Margaret's physical abuse has damaged him, perhaps irreparably, and Michael's conspicuous absence throughout the novel's action is an emblem of failed redemption. Of course Michael is "sacrificed," too, as a direct result of Valerian's culpable innocence, his uprooting of Margaret, and his failure to help her become rooted in the alien soil in which he so shallowly transplants her. We are invited to contrast his irresponsibility toward Margaret with all his careful work in the greenhouse: he will transplant hydrangeas from Philadelphia to the Caribbean and see that they grow, but he will not begin to do the same for his wife. When Valerian finally is robbed of his innocence and given the knowledge that Margaret abused Michael, indeed his world is *un*created. He imagines his tiny son thinking that

> no world in the world would be imagined, thought up, or even accidentally formed not to say say say say *created* that would permit such a thing to happen. And he is right. No world in the world would allow it. So this is not the world at all. It must be something

else. I have lived in it and I will die out of it but it is not the world. This is not life. This is some other thing. (202)

Valerian, the traditional God, is dethroned, and his world is uncreated. Meanwhile, Son's role in the novel undergoes a startling metamorphosis. The name "Son" is the most overt of Morrison's Miltonic allusions in the novel, and the character is the most spectacular demonstration of the limitations of dualistic thinking. When we first see Son at Isle des Chevaliers, he is clearly satanic, an intruder in Eden, a terrifying, threatening figure, a man with "hair like snakes" (149). His attachment to his "original dime" may initially be puzzling, but the phrase suggests some connection with "original sin," and he is certainly a temptation to Jadine. Even his belief in fraternity connects him with Satan, for Milton tells us that "Devil with Devil damn'd / Firm concord holds, men only disagree / Of Creatures rational" (II, 496–98). Star imagery associates Son with Lucifer: Son is "as silent as a star" (89), and Jadine will find it "so very hard to forget the man who fucked like a star" (251).

Son strongly evokes the traditional Satan: like Milton's, he brings out the intrinsic "evil" in others. But, as Gideon's and Thérèse's theft demonstrates, traditional "evil" is actually no more than the challenge to authority and the liberation of knowledge. Morrison underlines this imagistically when Ondine, in the act of revealing her long-suppressed knowledge of Margaret's guilt, has "her diadem braids turned into horns" (180). Son too is Satan-like (or "Satan Hero"-like) in catalyzing the release of knowledge, in challenging Valerian's authority, feeling justified in so doing because he knows his own worth and he knows it is independent of Valerian's actions or assessments. He tempts away Valerian's prize "creature," though not without himself being tempted.

Quickly transformed by a shower, new clothes, and Paco Rabanne into a man "so beautiful" (112) that even Margaret and Jadine are dazzled, Son upsets the system we were encouraged to lock him into. Indeed, light images characterize him from the outset, even setting the scene for Margaret's discovery of him in her closet when she is thinking about the poetic line, "And he glittered when he walked" (73). Transformed from serpent to spirit of light, he becomes plausible as a redeemer who may rescue Jadine from Valerian's world. The very actions that initially evoked the satanic now require us to see Son as its opposite. It is, after all, Son's intrusion into Valerian's troubled Eden that ultimately precipitates everyone's return to his or her true self. By the novel's conclusion, Margaret, Sydney, Ondine, Jade, even Valerian himself are liberated from the false and stressful positions they occupied in Valerian's hollow hierarchy. Son is no tidy evil opposite some absolute good embodied in Valerian. On the contrary, he appears at first as a power untrammeled by dualistic limitations, a power that surpasses even Valerian's "Christian," white, male, capitalist supremacy. Morrison underlines this still further by alluding to another mythic system. Son is always the "chocolate eater" to prophetic Thérèse: Morrison may be invoking the Aztec veneration of a chocolate drink they believed to be the gods' food.

But Son is flawed, like Valerian, by a crucial lack of knowledge. Pearl K. Bell argues that "Only a man like Son, in sure possession of ancestral values, can redeem Jadine, who has sacrificed her tribal soul to 'white' sophistication and learning" (57). But Bell's view suffers from the limitations of dualistic thinking, and, finally, so does Son's. Paradoxically, though he can be both A and not-A, his world view is narrowed by both sexism and racism. Son fails to understand that Jadine is his equal, another imbiber of chocolate (31, 71), who is as much a tempter and savior as he. Son perceives her as a tar baby (232–3), a white man's creation that tempts and entraps him, but if a tar baby has been created at all, Son has been the creator, when, watching Jade sleep, he labored "to breathe into her the smell of tar and its shiny consistency" (102).

Son's friend Soldier is closer to the truth when he tells Jadine that Son "wouldn't know a good woman from a snake" (219). That is, Jadine is satanic in very much the same way Son is. Trapped in the pitchy swamp, she evokes Milton's Satan, and she tempts Son not because she is Valerian's creation, but because she is her own. It is she who gives Son back his "original dime" (234) and lets him know that it is not the emblem of personal achievement he had always taken it to be, but rather a seal of his existence as a "Mama-spoiled black man" (232). When he tempts her away, "He saw it all as a rescue: first tearing her mind away from that blinding awe. Then the physical escape from the plantation" (189). But Son cannot see that she is as much his potential savior as he is hers:

She thought she was rescuing him from the night women who wanted him for themselves, wanted him feeling superior in a cradle, deferring to him; wanted her to settle for wifely competence when she could be almighty, to settle for fertility rather than originality, nurturing instead of building. He thought he was rescuing her from Valerian, meaning *them*, the aliens, the people who in a mere three hundred years had killed a world millions of years old. . . . Each was pulling the other away from the maw of hell—its very ridge top. Each knew the world as it was meant or ought to be. (231–2)

In fact, neither can finally save the other. Each has a personal vision of paradise that is remote from the other's, and Son's separatist ideology (181) is as far from realization as is Jadine's dream of a world in which no lines need be drawn. New York City may be for Jade a "happy Isle"—indeed, it "made her feel like giggling" (190)—but it is not in the city that Jadine and Son find their paradise. For them the phenomena of the external world vanish altogether: "Vaguely aware of such things when they were apart, together they could not concentrate on the given world. They reinvented it, remembered it through the other" (198). And Eloe is not Eden, either, though we may be lulled briefly into making the too-simple connection. Even Son ceases to see Eloe as paradisal after he has lost Jade, when he looks at photographs she took on their trip and finds their radiance gone: "It all looked miserable in the photographs, sad, poor and even poor-spirited" (254).

What then is redemption in this novel's world and whence can it come? If original sin is not disobedience to an arbitrarily "higher" authority, but rather a falling away from—or failure ever to discover—one's own true nature, then redemption must be the reclaiming of that nature, that self. Redemption must involve the discovery or rediscovery that, to be truly meaningful, the voice of authority must come from within; it must not arise from some arbitrary system. Jadine is the novel's hero because she is from the beginning insistent on not being limited by dualism. Carol P. Christ's description of women's spiritual quest applies well to Jadine: "Women's new naming of self and world often reflects wholeness, a movement toward overcoming the dualisms of self and world, body and soul, nature and spirit, rational and emotional, which have plagued Western consciousness" (13–14).

Jadine refuses to choose between the apparent opposites offered her— "blackening up or universaling out" (54); that is, she refuses to internalize an external image—either black or white—as a definition of self. "I belong to me" (101), Jadine tells Son, and she becomes most outraged at him in their initial encounter when he tries to impose a dualistic, defining vision on her:

> as soon as you let me loose I am going to kill you. For that alone. Just for that. For pulling that black-woman-white-woman shit on me. Never mind the rest. What you said before, that was nasty and mean, but if you think you can get away with telling me what a black woman is or ought to be. . . (104)

She seems to know what Cynthia A. Davis asserts in her analysis of Morrison's earlier novels:

> The problem with such internalization is . . . that it is life-denying, eliminating "the dreadful funkiness of passion, the funkiness of nature, the funkiness of the wide range of human emotions" (*[The Bluest] Eye,* 48, 64). One who really accepts the external definition of the self gives up spontaneous feeling and choice. (326)

Jadine is determined to be "only the person inside—not American—not black—just me" (40), and the enormity of her ambition can be assessed in terms of the traditional view of evil, of Satan's fall. Jade wants to do what Milton's Mammon counsels his fellow fallen angels to do, to

> . . . seek
> Our own good from ourselves, and from our own
> Live to ourselves, though in this vast recess,
> Free, and to none accountable. (II, 252–55)

Indeed, whatever help she has received from Valerian, her patron, and her aunt and uncle, Ondine and Sydney, it is not they but she who has established a career and earned a doctorate.

Yet Jadine is problematic as a hero. Part of the problem is that she defies our stereotype of the black woman as hero. We are accustomed to the heroic black woman who is deprived, downtrodden, who triumphs against enormous odds. The marvelous Celie in Alice Walker's *The Color Purple* fits the image; Jadine does not:

> If you had just been chosen for the cover of *Elle*, and there were three count three gorgeous and raucous men to telephone you or screech up to your door in Yugoslavian touring cars with Bordeaux Blanc and sandwiches and a little *C*, and when you have a letter from a charming old man saying your orals were satisfactory to the committee— (37)

you are Jadine Childs, a very different sort of black female hero from the norm but not a new one to Morrison's fictional world. In many ways Jade is the descendant of Sula, who knows well before her short life ends that she has "sung all the songs there are" *(Sula,* 137). Jadine strikes many readers as spoiled and pampered, not heroic nor even likable. But embracing that assessment may reveal a strain of both racism and sexism. Why are readers not comfortable with Jadine? Why can't a black woman "have it all"—on her own terms—and ask for more?

Like other Morrison characters, Jadine is questing for and creating self (Lee, 355). But because it is in many ways easier for her to know who she is not than who she is, the dangers of dualistic thinking beset her. Susan Willis is one of a group of critics who feel that Jade's failure to embrace a maternal role detracts seriously from her integrity. Calling Jade a cultural exile, Willis continues:

> As the individual whose cultural exile is the most profound, Jadine is haunted by waking visions, born out of guilt and fear. In her most terrifying vision, a mob of black women—some familiar, some only known by their names—crowds into her room. Revealing, then waving their breasts at her, they condemn Jadine for having abandoned the traditional, maternal role of black women. (37)

But if Jadine's "rejection of traditional cultural roles" (Willis, 37) cannot be disputed, she still merits the label Morrison gives her, "culture-bearing black woman" (232); she never finally embraces dualistic thinking. Son jabs at her by wondering *whose* culture she is bearing, but to ask that question is to succumb to the either-or vision the novel has presented as pernicious. The African "woman in yellow," whose apparent contempt for Jadine so unsettles her in Paris, is really, with her "skin like tar" (38), a tar baby to Jade: a dazzling temptation but actually a trap, an illusion, not a valid object of desire or emulation. Peter B. Erickson notes the connection between the African woman and the swamp (18); however, he concludes that "the novel will not allow her [Jadine's] avoidance of motherhood to be perceived sympathetically" (29). But surely a non-maternal Jadine is more attractive and laudable than the swamp women who, in all their "exceptional femaleness" (157), would gladly watch Jade sink in the slime. Sein de Vieilles does not nourish her; it attempts to destroy her.

In rejecting the breasts and eggs of the night women (225–6), Jadine need not be cutting herself off completely from her "ancient properties." At twenty-five, she has many roles open to her and many discoveries yet to make about herself. While she refuses to define herself in maternal terms alone, as the night women seem to do, she is interested in nurturing both herself and others. One of the earliest images we are given of her shows her shopping for exotic ingredients to prepare a lavish meal for "all the people she loved and some she did not" (37). Although Thérèse insists to Son that Jade has "forgotten her ancient properties" (263), we need not trust Thérèse, who "love[s] lies" (130), with the final word. Dorothy H. Lee validly points out that the book is dedicated to women who "knew their true and ancient properties" (358), but Lee feels Jade must be excluded from their number. On the contrary, Jade may also know her true properties—or come to know them—but she refuses to be limited by anyone else's definition of what they are. She must walk away from Ondine's accusation that she is an inadequate daughter and woman (242–3), for she has fully accepted her responsibility to mother herself.

Both Jade and Son know, long before they know one another, that the individual's only possible redeemer is self. They lose their grasp on the knowledge when they try to become one another's Messiahs. But if their time together is in one sense a fall, it is also potentially part of their separate personal redemptions. In one another's company, although they cannot stay there, they have experienced a world without the boundaries of dualism, each experiencing and perceiving "through the other" (198). At the novel's end, Son seems to be absorbed into a mythic world, as he joins the blind horsemen of the island's interior. But has Son thereby transcended conventional limitations? Lee associates the "Lickety-split. Looking neither to the left nor to the right" of his flight with the tar baby story: "Son, like and yet unhappily unlike Brer Rabbit, is to be seen at the end of the book running 'lickety-split' down the road but *toward* the source of his entrapment, alienated from his home and still 'stuck on' Jade" (356). Son's situation also echoes that which he decried in the New York City men who "were looking neither to the right nor to the left" (185).[2] Then, in New York, Son was able to look "first to the right and then to the left" (186), seeing polarities, except in his moments of transcendence with Jade. Now he has not abandoned dualistic thinking: "It was all mixed up. He had it straight before: the pie ladies and the six-string banjo and then he was seduced, corrupted by cloisonné and raw silk the color of honey and he was willing to change, to love the cloisonné, to abandon the pie ladies" (257). But he has added to his dualism a single-mindedness that we feel—and Thérèse prophesies—to be doomed.

In contrast, Jade has—literally—embraced the extremes of traditional, patriarchal good and evil and found them one. It is Jade, newly aware of the many choices open to her, who shows potential for continued development and eventual self-redemption. She has chosen to leave Son's paradise as well as Valerian's, for neither holds her salvation:

> She would go back to Paris and begin at Go. Let loose the dogs, tangle with the woman in yellow, with her and with all the night women who had *looked* at her. No more shoulders and limitless chests. No more dreams of safety. No more. Perhaps that was the thing—the thing Ondine was saying. A grown woman did not need safety or its dreams. She *was* the safety she longed for. (250)

The final image we are given of Jade, in which Morrison likens her to a soldier ant queen (250–1), is a deliberately anti- romantic image of solitary fecundity designed to reinforce our knowledge that Jade must be alone in her act of self-redemption. Sex and romance are a very small part of what both the ants and Jadine are about: self-creation and self-perpetuation against the odds of the dualistic world.

Self-creation is hard work, and it is an artist's work. Sula, Morrison tells us, was an "artist with no art form" *(Sula,* 121), and Jadine "loved to paint and draw so it was unfair not to be good at it" (155). But both find their artistic medium in self-creation. In art and in self-creation alike, conscious creativity is to be valued above adherence to tradition and authority. As Jadine asserts the superiority of Picasso's painting over the Itumba masks that inspired him, so Morrison has found *Paradise Lost* more useful to her purpose than Genesis unadorned. Like Milton in his epic, Morrison has set out to reinterpret myth. But while Milton sought to "justify the ways of God to men" (I, 26), Morrison's purpose has been to urge us to transcend dualism and external authority, to be our own justification. Like the "colored girls" of Ntozake Shange's choreopoem, who are "movin to the ends of their own rainbows" (67), Morrison's Jadine marks the path of personal spiritual quest. Ideally, Jadine—and the reader who follows her—will some day echo the words of Shange's Lady in Red:

i found god in myself
& i loved her / i loved her fiercely. (67)

NOTES

1. For further discussion of dualism in modern Western religion and culture, see Rita Nakashima Brock, "The Feminist Redemption of Christ," in *Christian Feminism: Visions of a New Humanity,* ed. Judith L. Weidman (San Francisco: Harper & Row, 1984), 58, 60–61. In *Womanspirit Rising: A Feminist Reader in Religion,* ed. Carol P. Christ and Judith Plaskow (San Francisco: Harper & Row, 1979), see Elisabeth Schussler Fiorenza, "Women in the Early Christian Movement," 86, and "Feminist Spirituality, Christian Identity, and Catholic Vision," 141–3; and Eleanor L. McLaughlin, "The Christian Past: Does It Hold a Future for Women?" 94.

2.   For this observation, I am indebted to Laraine Yaeger, my former student at the University of Missouri-St. Louis, She and her classmates who studied *Tar Baby* with me in the fall of 1984 stimulated many of the thoughts developed here.

WORKS CITED

Bell, Pearl K. "Self-Seekers." *Commentary* 72.2 (1981): 56–60.

Christ, Carol P. *Diving Deep and Surfacing. Women Writers on Spiritual Quest.* Boston: Beacon, 1980.

Daly, Mary. "After the Death of God the Father." *Womanspirit Rising: A Feminist Reader in Religion.* Edited by Carol P. Christ and Judith Plaskow. San Francisco: Harper & Row, 1979. 53–62.

Davis, Cynthia . "Self, Society, and Myth in Toni Morrison's Fiction." *Contemporary Literature* 23 (1982): 323–42.

Erickson, Peter B. "Images of Nurturance in Toni Morrison's *Tar Baby.*" *College Language Association Journal* 28 (1984): 11–32.

Irving, John. "Morrison's Black Fable." *The New York Times Book Review.* March 29, 1981: 1, 30–1.

Lee, Dorothy H. "The Quest for Self: Triumph and Failure in the Works of Toni Morrison." *Black Women Writers (1950–1980). A Critical Evaluation.* Edited by Mari Evans. Garden City, NY:Anchor Press/Doubleday, 1984. 346–60.

Milton, John. *Paradise Lost. John Milton. Complete Poems and Major Prose.* Edited by Merritt Y. Hughes. Indianapolis: Odyssey, 1957. 207–469.

Morrison, Toni. *The Bluest Eye.* 1970. New York: Pocket Books, 1972.

———. *Song of Solomon.* 1977. New York: New American Library, 1978.

———. *Sula.* 1973. New York: New American Library, 1982.

———. *Tar Baby.* 1981. New York: New American Library, 1983.

Ruether, Rosemary Radford. "Motherearth and the Megamachine." *Womanspirit Rising: A Feminist Reader in Religion.* Edited by Carol P. Christ and Judith Plaskow. San Francisco: Harper & Row, 1979. 43–52.

Saiving, Valerie. "The Human Situation: A Feminine View." *Womanspirit Rising: A Feminist Reader in Religion.* Edited by Carol P. Christ and Judith Plaskow. San Francisco: Harper & Row, 1979. 25–42.

Shange, Ntozake. *for colored girls who have considered suicide/when the rainbow is enuf.* 1977. New York: Bantam Books, 1980.

Walker, Alice. *The Color Purple.* 1982. New York: Pocket Books, 1983.

Willis, Susan. "Eruptions of Funk: Historicizing Toni Morrison." *Black American Literature Forum* 16 (1982): 34–42.

The Ancestor as Foundation in *Their Eyes Were Watching God* and *Tar Baby*

Sandra Pouchet Paquet

The restorative power of folklore is a recurring theme in African American literature. In novels like James Weldon Johnson's *The Autobiography of an Ex-Colored Man* (1912), Jean Toomer's *Cane* (1923), and Ralph Ellison's *Invisible Man* (1952), folklore is a powerful spiritual and artistic resource. Conversely, cultural orphanage is associated with spiritual malaise, a loss of creativity, and a variety of psychic disorders. It is the price African Americans pay for upward social mobility in a racist society. In novels like Toni Morrison's *Song of Solomon* (1977), Toni Cade Bambara's *The Salt-Eaters* (1980), and Paule Marshall's *Praisesong for the Widow* (1983), folklore is perceived as the repository of a complex culture of survival. Reconnection with folk culture is the key to psychological and spiritual reconstruction in a hostile and culturally alienating environment.

In "The Art of Fiction," Ralph Ellison speaks explicitly to the importance of folklore to an ever-expanding African American literary tradition. Ellison looks to folklore to discover "what in our background is worth preserving or abandoning":

> The clue to this can be found in folklore, which offers the first drawings of any group's character. It preserves mainly those situations which have repeated themselves again and again in the history of any given group. It describes those rites, manners, customs

and so forth, which insure the good life, or destroy it; and it describes those boundaries of feeling, thought and action which that particular group has found to be the limitation of the human condition. It projects this wisdom in symbols which express the group's will to survive; it embodies those values by which the group lives and dies. (172)

In "Rootedness: The Ancestor as Foundation," Toni Morrison goes a step further. She identifies a link between folklore as a repository of ancestral wisdom and values and the use of an ancestral figure as a barometer of cultural integrity in contemporary African American literature:

What struck me in looking at some contemporary fiction was that whether the novel took place in the city or in the country, the presence or absence of that figure determined the success or the happiness of the character. It was the absence of an ancestor that was frightening, that was threatening, and it caused huge destruction and disarray in the work itself. (343)

She explains that "these ancestors are not just parents, they are a sort of timeless people whose relationships to the characters are benevolent, instructive, and protective, and they provide a certain kind of wisdom" (343) and concludes: "When you kill the ancestor you kill yourself" (344).

In novels like *Song of Solomon, The Salt-Eaters,* and *Praisesong for the Widow,* the restorative power of African American folklore is invested unequivocally in ancestral figures like Pilate, Minnie Ransom, and Aunt Cuney in the United States, and Lebert Joseph in the Caribbean. However, as Morrison points out, some writers, notably Richard Wright and James Baldwin, have great difficulty with ancestors ("Rootedness," 343). These writers resist the valorization of the ancestor as an unqualified source of good for later times. Toni Morrison's own *Tar Baby* (1981) is particularly instructive in this regard. *Tar Baby* not only raises troubling questions about the ancestor as foundation and the divorce from ancestral roots that accompanies conventional notions of success, it repeats and revises key tropes and rhetorical strategies used by Zora Neale Hurston in her "paradigmatic signifying text" (Gates, 290) on cultural rootedness, *Their*

Eyes Were Watching God (1937). Both *Tar Baby* and *Their Eyes Were Watching God* lend themselves to a Morrison-style evaluation on the basis "of what the writer does with the presence of an ancestor" ("Rootedness," 343). Both make statements about a roots-directed redefinition of self as a means to psychic wholeness, and both make guarded statements about the role of the ancestor in this process.

In *Their Eyes Were Watching God,* the heroine, Janie Crawford, eventually reconnects with her ancestral roots through the pursuit of romantic love and personal freedom. In this novel, the benevolent, instructive, protective, and wise ancestor is reconceived as Vergible "Tea Cake" Woods, one of Morrison's "timeless people." He is the iconoclastic folk hero who takes Janie home to the folk as his bride. But Janie's relationship with Tea Cake is short lived and ends after only a year and a half with his untimely death. In this novel, reconnection with the folk as a lived reality is not envisioned as a permanent condition and neither is romantic love. They are a means to an end, in this case the heroine's self-fulfillment. In *Tar Baby,* a roots-directed redefinition of self as a means of achieving psychic wholeness is not possible for Janie's namesake, Jadine Childs. The arguments for reconnection with ancestral roots change significantly when the heroine's disconnection from ancestral roots is accompanied by an explicit disaffection with women's role and status in the folk community, and the ancestral figure is the iconoclastic folk hero as lover who wants to take her home to the folk as his bride.

The parodic/polemic elements (Gates, 296) in *Tar Baby* are even more specific to *Their Eyes Were Watching God* than this suggests. A pattern of repetition and revision is readily discernible in the formal structure of the novels. To begin with, the heroines are both orphans and alienated from their African American roots by the circumstances of their upbringing. Janie Crawford is raised in the yard of the white Washburn family by a grandmother who is Nanny in that household. Jadine Childs is sent away to posh schools by her aunt and uncle with financial help from Valerian Street, the white industrialist for whom they work as cook and butler/manservant, respectively. Both Janie and Jadine are raised to be separate from black folk life and culture with economic security and social advancement as a core value in their upbringing. Both heroines experience a crisis of identity as a result of their upbringing. As a child of six Janie is unable to identify herself as the dark child in a group photo of the Washburn children. Much later in her life, as an accomplished and successful young woman in Paris, Jadine does not know what category of woman she is or wants to be, pulled as she is in different directions by a dream of hats, the vision of an African woman in yellow, and her white boyfriend's expectations of her. Both heroines are financially independent at critical points in their lives. Janie inherits her second husband's wealth after his death, and Jadine's beauty and education are readily marketable commodities, which gives them both a rare freedom as women in African American literature. Both heroines are racially mixed, and both novels make their mulatto status an issue affecting their relations with others. Both Janie and Jadine repudiate the values of their surrogate parents in their conscious quest for selfhood.

Beyond this both novels explore the conflicts of their heroines' alienation from ancestral roots in intimate relations with men who embody core aspects of folk life and culture. Both use all-black communities in rural Florida to explore issues of black nationalism. Both novels end with extraordinary statements of self-sufficiency and independence of men, family, and community from their heroines. In both novels the men that attend the heroines are cut loose with remarkable ease; whether it is Logan Killicks, Joe Starks, or Vergible Woods in *Their Eyes Were Watching God,* or Ryk or Son in *Tar Baby.*

Within these readily discernible formal relationships, Toni Morrison's *Tar Baby* charts new territory structurally and thematically. The novels embody two different reflections of reality in radically different narrative strategies. In *Their Eyes Were Watching God* the problems of ancestry and cultural identity are explored and resolved as one woman's story, Janie Crawford's. Despite the community chorus that begins and interrupts the narrative periodically and brief verbal exchanges with Phoeby, the narrative is structured around Janie's authoritative assumption of voice. Janie emerges as the final authority in this rite of passage chronotope. She talks to Phoeby not as an equal but as an initiate to a novice. At the end of the novel Janie's education seems complete. She is not only the positive heroine but a model for others like Phoeby to emulate. The difference between Janie and everyone else, perhaps with the exception of Tea Cake, is so pronounced that Janie's story assumes something of the quality of the "how I got over—look at me—alone—let me show you how I did it" kind of contemporary autobiography that Morrison describes in "Rootedness" (339–40). In *Tar Baby* Janie's authoritative voice is replaced by voices in conflict. At the end of this novel, the main characters, Son and Jadine, are represented as young and still evolving, rather than complete. The conflict between Son and Jadine assumes the nature of an unfinished dialogue. The novel offers no solutions. Instead it maps, through its myriad characters, the ongoing interaction of conflicting ideologies which, though unresolved, continually present opportunities for metamorphosis in individuals and in the society at large.[1] In place of the organizing unity of one woman's achievement of inner calm and unity of being in *Their Eyes Were Watching God,* the dialogic structure of *Tar Baby* focuses on the unresolved conflict between characters whose values appear to be irreconcilable within the African American community. In *Their Eyes Were Watching God,* Janie's new-found harmony of being acts as an effective buffer against the alienation from community that characterizes her return to Eatonville. In *Tar Baby,* selfhood is not conceived as a stable plateau of being separate from the world around; it is conceived as an evolving state of consciousness that is simultaneous with the interaction of conflicting values in that world.

In *Their Eyes Were Watching God,* alienation from self and community is a core theme; at times they are separate and distinct and at others closely interconnected. Alienation from community is a class issue when Janie returns to Eatonville at the beginning of the novel. "Why don't she stay in her class?" (10) the women of Eatonville ask each other, relishing the sight of the former mayor's wife apparently abandoned by her lover and reduced to wearing overalls. Janie is equally contemptuous: "If God don't think no mo' 'bout 'em then Ah do, they's a lost ball in de high grass" (16). Janie is in fact alone as the novel begins and ends, except for Phoeby; she is, however, fulfilled and at peace with herself. The net result of her adventures with Tea Cake and her immersion experience in the Everglades is neither adulation of the folk nor adoption of their way of life but rather self-realization and self-containment. Janie is self-satisfied to the point of smugness when she returns home to Eatonville.

Of course he wasn't dead. He could never be dead until she had finished feeling and thinking. The kiss of his memory made pictures of love and light against the wall. Here was peace. She pulled in her horizon like a great fish-net. Pulled it from around the waist of the world and draped it over her shoulder. So much of life in its meshes! She called in her soul to come and see. (286)

Tea Cake is dead at her hands, but her memories of their good times together are alive and well and sufficient to her needs.

As Janie's story unfolds in a mixture of first-person and third-person narration, alienation from community acquires a different value; it is also alienation from race and self. Abandoned by her mother as an infant and raised by her grandmother with the Washburn grandchildren, at the age of six Janie is still quite unconscious of her racial identity: "Ah wuz wid dem white chillum so much till Ah didn't know Ah wuzn't white" (21). She calls her "Grandma nothin' but Nanny, 'cause dat's what everybody on de place called her" (20). And Janie herself is called "Alphabet 'cause so many people done named me different names" (21). In school, Janie is rejected by the other black children because of her looks and because she dresses better in Washburn cast-off clothing than they do. As Houston A. Baker, Jr. points out, Janie "offers a striking narrative instance of a black person's encounter with the 'zero image'" (152).

As Janie's story unfolds it becomes clear that her alienation from self and community as a child is Nanny's doing. Nanny's concern is with security first, and she gets this through the patronage of the Washburn family, "good white people" (36) with whom Nanny feels safe and secure. But Nanny is also status conscious. At first she lives with Janie in the Washburns' backyard but, when this proves an embarrassment to Janie at school, she buys her own property with the Washburns' help. Security and status are again Nanny's concerns when she pressures sixteen-year-old Janie to marry Logan Killicks, an old man, or so he seems to Janie, a widower and successful black farmer, "honest and hard workin'" (53), with "a house bought and paid for and sixty acres uh land right on de big road" (41).

As an African American who matured sexually, emotionally, and politically under slavery, bearing a child for her master and abused for this by her mistress, experience has taught Nanny that black women are vulnerable and in need of protection from the abuse of "menfolks black or white" (37). She tells Janie: "De nigger woman is de mule uh de world so fur as Ah can see. Ah been prayin' fuh it tuh be different wid yuh" (29). The root cause of Janie's alienation is Nanny's resolve to change Janie's status as a black woman, to provide her with different options: "Ah didn't want to be used for a work-ox and a brood sow and Ah didn't want mah daughter used that way neither" (31). Nanny's politics are clear; Janie's marriage to Logan Killicks is a means to an end. She entirely rejects romantic love as a goal worth pursuing:

> Dat's se very prong all us black women gits hung on. Dis love! Dat's just whut's got us uh pullin' and uh haulin' and sweatin' and doin' from can't see in de mornin' till can't see at night. (41)

Nanny wants to remove the element of risk and chance from Janie's life and, with this, romance and the far horizon. Janie is in fact orphaned twice under Nanny's direction; from knowing herself racially and knowing herself sexually. In her exclusive concern to make life safe for Janie, Nanny has lost touch with her ancestral roots in the African American community. She is compared with "the standing roots of some old tree that had been torn away by the storm. Foundation of ancient power that no longer mattered" (26). In Nanny an ancestral trust is abandoned, and Janie is left to find her own way. "You know, honey," she tells Janie, "us colored folks is branches without roots and that makes things come round in queer ways. You in particular" (31).

Two marriages later, with great rancor and bitterness, Janie discovers that she hates her "benevolent, instructive, protective" grandmother and why:

> She had been getting ready for her great journey to the horizons in search of *people;* . . . But she had been whipped like a cur dog, and run off down a back road after *things.* (138)

Nanny had taken the far horizon "and pinched it in to such a little bit of a thing that she could tie it about her granddaughter's neck tight enough to choke her" (138). No longer burdened by Nanny's dreams of "whut a woman oughta be and to do" (310), Janie perceives her grandmother in the odious terms of the slave trade:

> She had found a jewel down inside herself and she had wanted to walk where people could see her and gleam it around. But she had been set in the market-place to sell. Been set for still-bait. (138)

For Janie the process of psychological and emotional reconstruction begins with the recognition that she must find her own way.

It is interesting to note that Janie's initial conflict with Nanny over her marriage to Logan Killicks is not about taking "a stand on high ground" (32) as Nanny wishes, but about her awakening sexuality. Self-definition begins here for Janie. Her "conscious life" (23), she decides, begins at Nanny's gate in the springtime, after three days of sensuous reverie under a blossoming pear tree, when Johnny Taylor kisses her. Nanny perceives a real menace in "shiftless Johnny Taylor, tall and lean" (25) and his sex appeal. But this is Janie's life line; it will lead her much later to love another such man in Tea Cake and the healing of psychic wounds engendered by Nanny's misapplied love and Janie's two unhappy marriages.

When Janie abandons Logan Killicks and his farm, her restlessness and frustration are partly sexual frustration and partly her own attachment to Nanny's ideal of "sittin' on porches lak de white madam" (172). Janie wants romance *and* a high chair. Logan's belated attempt to make Janie a working partner in the care of the farm is entirely unacceptable to Janie; she is unable to make that kind of commitment without sexual passion. Partnership on those terms will be Tea Cake's prerogative.

Janie's second husband, Joe Starks, is a young, more glamorous version of Logan Killicks. He reminds her of Mr. Washburn, which would please Nanny no end. Moreover, Joe Starks echoes Nanny's aspirations of privilege and safety in a high place: "a pretty doll-baby lak you is made to sit on de front porch and rock and fan yo'self and eat p'taters dat other folks plant special just for you" (19). Janie takes a calculated risk in running off with Joe Starks: "he did not represent sun-up and pollen and blooming trees, but he spoke for far horizon. He spoke for change and chance" (50). Joe accomplishes all he said he would and Janie discovers the isolation of the high chair on the front porch. She grows to resent her indenture to Joe as prized possession and occasional store clerk. She is alienated twice in this marriage: by her husband's attitude to women— "Somebody got to think for women and chillun and chickens and cows" (10)—and by her status as Mrs. Mayor Starks, for Joe has forbidden her to join in the spirit-renewing rituals of folk life on the store's front porch.

Janie's perception of folk culture as engendering a creativity and vitality absent in her own life and her longing for reconnection with those cultural roots coalesce here with the failure of her marriage and her isolation from a community life she witnesses on a daily basis. Janie grows detached and cultivates a double life: "She had an inside and an outside now and suddenly she knew how not to mix them" (112–13). She assumes the survival mask of the slave until Joe humiliates her publicly by announcing that he no longer finds her sexually attractive. The sexual insult is returned in kind, when Janie tells everyone that Joe is impotent.[2] This is a turning point for Janie; a victory from which she does not retreat. Their marriage is a failure in public as well as private, and Joe dies sadly and emptily in the hands of a dishonest root-doctor.

Joe's death leaves Janie financially independent and very free; free of Joe and free of Nanny and free to explore the far horizon that Tea Cake represents. Spiritual and psychological reconstruction begins in earnest when Janie falls in love with Tea Cake. He is king of the road, itinerant farm worker, gambler, music-maker, sweet-talker, a marvelous lover, and, sometimes, a wife-beater. In the tradition of wandering American heroes, rootless and unattached to work as a means of self-definition and to conventional notions of success and security, Tea Cake combines a spirit of adventure with sexual power. What Morrison calls "the traveling Ulysses scene"; black men on the move, leaving home, going from place to place, and spreading "their seed all over the world" ("Intimate," 226–7). To Janie, he is sun-up and pollen and blooming pear trees; he is a way of life she has been longing to explore. He is the folk, and when Janie returns his love with her own commitment, she has a place in the heart of the folk community, a place to recover herself in racial and sexual terms. We are told: "She felt a self-crushing love. So her soul crawled out of its hiding place" (192).

When Janie moves on to the Everglades with Tea Cake in pursuit of "money and fun and foolishness" (192), Hurston has Janie leave her money behind, thus freeing their relationship from the taint of a business proposition and freeing Janie from the class distinctions that her money would bring. In the Everglades with Tea Cake, Janie's recovery of self in racial terms appears complete through immersion in the black community there:[3]

> The men held big arguments here like they used to do on the store porch. Only here she could listen and laugh and even talk herself if she wanted. She got so she could tell big stories herself from listening to the rest. (200)

Janie is happy with her new identity, but the novel does not end with Tea Cake and Janie contentedly picking beans together in the Everglades. Hurston is careful to establish that their relationship is vulnerable and that Janie's place among the farm workers is precarious without Tea Cake's protection.

First Janie worries about competition from Nunkie, a "little chunky girl" (203) who teases Tea Cake sexually in the fields and in the quarters. But sexual jealousy also surfaces with Tea Cake, and here it is less easily resolved. He starts dropping in on her at odd hours during the day: "Come to see 'bout you. De boogerman liable tuh tote yuh off whilst Ah'm gone" (198).[4] He explains that he misses her when he is working in the fields and wants her working along with him, not for the money, but to ease his lonesomeness. As it turns out, he is unnerved by Janie's tolerance of Mrs. Turner's negrophobia and is jealous of Mrs. Turner's brother. He feels threatened and slaps Janie around: "Not because her behavior justified his jealousy, but it relieved that awful fear inside him. Being able to whip her reassured him in possession" (218). Later, when Tea Cake is fatally ill and deranged from the bite he receives from a rabid dog, he is driven not by simple jealousy but by his jealousy of Mrs. Turner's brother.

In his crazed state, Tea Cake, once a "benevolent, instructive, and protective" ancestral presence, is suddenly menacing. In an extraordinary scene, Hurston has Janie shoot Tea Cake in self-defense. What is even more extraordinary is the swiftness with which Hurston has Janie locked in conflict with the black community over Tea Cake's death. She is tried by a white jury and freed, but black men of the Everglades are unconvinced and their mistrust is specific to the stereotype of a mulatto woman: "you know dem white mens wuzn't goin' tuh do nothin' tuh no woman dat look lak her" (280). They contradict Nanny's testimony on the status of black women directly: "Well, you know whut dey say—uh white man and uh nigger woman is freest thing on earth. Dey do as dey please" (280).

Janie makes peace with them in due course; in fact she buys their love and forgiveness with an elaborate and very expensive funeral for Tea Cake. Though she earns her welcome, she does not want life among them on the muck without Tea Cake. She returns to Eatonville, to her house, and to her money in the bank. She tells Phoeby: "Ah'm back home agin and Ah'm satisfied tuh be heah. Ah done been tuh de horizon and back and now Ah kin set heah in mah house and live by comparisons" (204).[5]

Janie emerges as a figure of unmatched strength in the novel. She grows enormously in resolve and independence on the strength of her adventures with Tea Cake in the Everglades. She has changed utterly from the culturally orphaned child who could not recognize herself in the second chapter of the novel and who, years later, is unable to handle a tobacco knife and "cut a little thing like a plug of tobacco" (121). At the end of the novel she is a self-contained and self-sufficient black woman who emerges from her wanderings with Tea Cake quite undaunted by his death at her hands. It is clear that she no longer needs his presence. Her psychological and spiritual reconstruction seems complete. Whatever his shortcomings Tea Cake has helped her to a definition of self that absorbs his male resourcefulness and freedom into herself. He has taught her how to be free of a middle-class preoccupation with security and privilege. He has even taught her mastery of that quintessential symbol of the American folk hero—the gun. Janie's metamorphosis as an African American heroine is both complete and radical.

In Toni Morrison's *Tar Baby*, an ancestral relationship with folk culture is lost to Jadine Childs through the patronage of Valerian Street, through education in select schools through the aspirations of her surrogate parents, Sydney and Ondine, and what Ondine later describes as her own abdication of responsibility: "I never told you anything at all and I take full responsibility for that" (242).

Jadine prefers the "Ave Maria" to Gospel music (62) and Picasso to an Itumba mask. As a student of art history she asserts: "Picasso is better. The fact that he was intrigued by them is proof of his genius, not the mask-makers'" (62). She is ignorant of and uncommitted to the politics of race except in terms of social advancement:

> black people she knew wanted what she wanted—either steadily and carefully like Sydney and Ondine or uproariously and flashily like the theater or media types. But whatever their scam, "making it" was on their minds and they played the game with house cards, each deck issued and dealt by the house. (108)

She fulfills Sydney and Ondine's expectations of her and also Valerian's. She mirrors their shared commitment to social and economic security. "She crowned me," Ondine explains, "that girl did. No matter what went wrong or how tired I was, she was my crown" (166). To Valerian, she is a measure of what he could not accomplish with his own son: "I haven't given you one thousandth of what I gave him, of what I made available to him. And you have fifty times the sense he does" (63).

Jadine defines herself in terms of the community that nurtured her, and that community is the Street household. She tells Son: "I belong to me. But I live here. I work for Margaret Street. She and Valerian are my. . . patrons" (101). She gropes for the right words then, apparently dissatisfied with the result, she explains her status in the household:

> They educated me. Paid for my travel, my lodgings, my clothes, my schools. My mother died when I was twelve; my father when I was two. I'm an orphan. Sydney and Ondine are all the family I have, and Valerian did what no one else even offered to do. (101)

Jadine, like Sydney and Ondine, is a member of the Street household; the press toward upward social mobility consumes all three of them. Sydney and Ondine's commitment to the smooth functioning of the Street household leads to a divorce from their roots in the African American community and this effectively disqualifies them as repositories of ancestral wisdom. After all they see no connection between themselves and Son. Ondine reasons: "The man upstairs wasn't a Negro—meaning one of them. He was a stranger" (87). To Sydney the distinction between them is quite clear; he is "a Phil-a-delphia Negro mentioned in the book of the very same name" (140), while Son is a "stinking ignorant swamp nigger," "a wild-eyed pervert," and a primitive (85–6). Moreover Sydney and Ondine see no connection between themselves and the islanders who work for the Streets under their supervision. To Ondine their way of doing things "gave the place a nasty, common look" (34). No one in the Street household takes the trouble to identify the yardman by his name, or to distinguish the woman who accompanies him from any other "Mary" as Son observes (138). Sydney and Ondine, like their niece after them, have lost touch with their ancestral roots. Without a landscape of their own, they, like Nanny, are rootless; "branches without roots" is Nanny's phrase (31).

Jadine's perception of an ancestral relationship from which she is estranged occurs far away from the Street household, in Paris. The vision in yellow unnerves her utterly, the woman with no eyelashes, too tall, too much hip, too much bust, skin like tar; "that woman's woman—that mother/sister/she; that unphotographable beauty" (39). The image of the black woman as authentic earth mother, a title for which Ondine, Therese, and the women in Eloe are all competing, completely derails Jadine. It triggers an identity crisis at the moment when she ought to have felt most secure as successful model and student—her marketability assured by beauty and education. Toni Morrison explains to Gloria Naylor that Jadine perceives the woman in the supermarket as "the real chic":

> The one is very clear in some deep way about what her womanhood is. And it can happen at any moment and any woman might do it. . . . Still, the memory of that one is somehow a basis for either total repression or a willingness to let one's true self surface. ("Conversation," 572)

After the vision in yellow, Jadine measures herself by different standards, standards that reveal the insecurities of her landless, rootless condition. She questions her plans to marry Ryk, her European boyfriend:

I wonder if the person he wants to marry is me or a black girl? And if it isn't me he wants but any black girl who looks like me, talks and acts like me, what will happen when he finds out that I hate ear hoops, that I don't have to straighten my hair, that Mingus puts me to sleep, that I sometimes want to get out of my skin and be only the person inside—not American—not black—just me? (40)

She returns to the Street household haunted on one hand by the woman in yellow and on the other hand by "a dream of large hats. Large beautiful women's hats like Norma Shearer's and Mae West's and Jeanette McDonald's although the dreamer is too young to have seen their movies or remembered them if she had" (37). She is shamed and repelled by the hats which she fails to identify as the emblems of celebrated sex goddesses of the white world. She frets about the impact of marrying Ryk on the Street household (77). She is uptight about Margaret Street's penchant for "alluding to or ferreting out what she believes to be racial characteristics" (54).

On the Isle de Chevaliers, Sydney and Ondine give her no direction, nothing that will help her to know them and to know herself in ancestral terms. One of the ironies of the Street household is that the ancestral connection is very much alive around them in the island's myths and natives; a reality from which they are cut off by a carefully cultivated attachment to wealth and privilege, Valerian style; a mixture of industrial exploitation of human and natural resources and feudal style patronage. Valerian's wealth is founded explicitly on sugar and the exploitation of black labor and the black consumer. He is tyrant as well as benefactor, as Son explains (174–5).[6] Son is entirely unsympathetic to Valerian's outrage at Gideon and Therese's theft of apples. The two are banished from Valerian's circle of privilege with a swiftness and finality that demonstrates his absolute authority over the household.

It is interesting that the object of Valerian's wrath is the dominant ancestral figure on the Isle de Chevaliers. This crone-like Eve is another version of the washerwoman of his childhood, who is fired for the unorthodox way in which she comforts him when his father dies (121–2). Therese is identified as one of the blind race for whom the island is named; descendent from "slaves who went blind the minute they saw Dominique" (130), whose ship foundered and sank and who swam ashore along with horses and, totally blind escaped recapture. Gideon tells Son:

> They ride those horses all over the hills. They learned to ride through the rain forest avoiding all sorts of trees and things. They race each other, and for sport they sleep with the swamp women in Sein de Vieilles. Just before a storm you can hear them screwing way over there. Sounds like thunder. (131)

The essence of the myth is freedom as phallic power. According to Gideon, the descendants of the blind race also have visionary powers: "they saw with the eye of the mind, and that, of course, was not to be trusted" (131). Therese, he warns Son, is "a mean one and one of the blind race. You can't tell them nothing. They love lies" (130).

It is Therese who identifies Son as one of the blind horsemen and welcomes him as such: "He's a horseman come down here to get her [Jadine]" (91). But Therese is not only characterized as a visionary, she is also the archetypal earth mother by virtue of her "magic breasts." She is the archetypal earth mother as nanny; a wet nurse who earned her living by nursing hundreds of French babies until formula came along. She hates American women for their manipulation of their reproductive function. Therese is an ambiguous figure in the novel. She speaks authoritatively in a "national-historical" context, but her authority beyond this time-space mode is limited. Occupying space-time modes as different as L'Arbe de la Croix and Eloe simultaneously, Son is sympathetic to Therese but not obedient as he skulks around looking for his chance to claim Jadine as his handmaiden.

The task of tearing Jadine away from the Street household and re-storing her to her ancestral roots falls to Son. Duly authenticated by Therese as one of the original horsemen, Son is the embodiment of the folk just as Tea Cake is, with "spaces, mountains, savannas in his eyes" (135); eyes that distract Jadine from the woman in yellow's "original insult" of contempt for her rootlessness (135). He is an extraordinary figure in the way Morrison envelops him in a variety of myths to have him emerge convincingly as the embodiment of phallic power and race consciousness. He is a symbol of the race and of the United States and is both loved and feared. He appears in dreadlocks and Medusa-like immediately transfixes both Margaret and Jadine with fears of sexual aggression. But his dreadlocks also prepare us for his Rastafarian-like division of the world into Babylon and idyllic black pastoral. His appearance is calculated to evoke the primitive, the outlaw, the murderer:

> His hair looked overpowering—physically overpowering, like bundles of long whips or lashes that grab her and beat her to jelly. And would. Wild, aggressive, vicious hair that needed to be put into jail. Uncivilized, reform-school hair. Mau Mau, Attica, chain-gang hair. (97)

Son's jealous attack on his wife recalls Tea Cake's jealousy and, like Tea Cake, he is a music-maker. He is also soldier and seaman. He is *"Americano. Cierto Americano"* (143), according to a Mexican shipmate who recognizes his disposition to violence. Given his disaffection with the status quo, he is identified as the quintessential American article in the tradition of Huck Finns, Nigger Jims, Calibans, Staggerlees, and John Henrys (143). "Anarchic, wandering" (143), he is Toni Morrison's free man in the tradition of Cholly Breedlove and Ajax. He is Ulysses ("Intimate," 226–27) waylaid on his way home by the water-lady (2–3), who, as Circe, Aphrodite, and Erzulie all in one, leads him to the Isle de Chevaliers to fulfill his role as mythic horseman.

Son invades L'Arbe de la Croix, but while the household thrives on Jadine's presence, it cannot accommodate Son and Jadine as polar opposites at the same time. He comes at Christmas time to call the household to a different way of seeing and experiencing the world. He is a disruptive presence and a catalyst for change. He effectively subverts and challenges Valerian's authority with one crude agenda in mind: the appropriation of Jadine. He doesn't succeed finally, but the ensuing conflict prompts radical changes in the structure of power at L'Arbe de la Croix. Valerian goes into decline and his wife Margaret is liberated in the process. Sydney and Ondine find that their security now hinges on their ability to establish a working relationship with Margaret. Their niece has neither the wisdom nor the disposition to free them from the terms of their indenture to a system of patronage that has served her so well.

The conflict of values that Son brings to L'Arbe de la Croix is explicitly and dramatically realized in the sexual passion that consumes Jadine and Son. Though their relationship ends in conflict and separation, the physical and ideological engagement that characterizes their relationship triggers new levels of consciousness in both Son and Jadine. The end of the novel suggests that identity for the African American is a process of becoming that hinges on the continual if spasmodic interaction of individuals who occupy space-time modes as different as the great house on a Caribbean island and an all-black rural community in Florida.

Son's first task is to pry Jadine loose from Valerian's world, from Sydney and Ondine's aspirations; to tear "her mind away from that blinding awe. Then the physical escape from the plantation" (189). When L'Arbe de la Croix is shattered by a carnivalesque reversal of hierarchical distinctions and barriers at Christmas time, Son emerges as Jadine's prop: "She wanted a little human warmth, some unsullied person to be near, someone to be with, so she took his hand without thinking about it and said, 'That was awful!'" (180). She is immediately dependent on those large comfortable hands of his; "large enough to sit down in. Large enough to hold your whole head. Large enough, maybe, to put your whole self into" (182). And Son as her lover assumes the role of ancestor, instructive and protective, voicing his own brand of apartheid; "white folks and black folks should not sit down and eat together" (181). In the aftermath of the Christmas dinner crisis and the splintering of the community that has nurtured her since childhood, Jadine is about as receptive as she ever will be.

At first their love affair appears to provide Jadine with the reassurance she left Paris in search of. In New York with Son she is completely happy. She feels cherished and safe: "he unorphaned her completely. Gave her a brand new childhood" (197). In turn Son is encouraged by her need and by his apparent ability to redefine Jadine culturally and emotionally. His devotion is double-edged. As he struggles to free her from servitude to Valerian, he plans to make her captive to his own dreams of Eloe. He sees Jadine as a defenseless bird for which he must "construct a world of steel and down for her to flourish in" (189). And here Morrison makes a distinction between the liberating, restorative power of their shared intimacy and the constraints of traditional male-female roles.

Son's ancestral voice is nationalistic and separatist, and it also reveals an attitude of containment toward black women that is at the core of Jadine's alienation in racial and sexual terms as it is defined in her relationship with Son. Son's dream of Eloe is of welcoming women, of harem, of fraternity, a separate black world with black men at the center. Susan Willis describes Son's dream of Eloe as "wish-fulfillment, rooted in private nostalgia" (269). His tears at the sight of Gideon's back bent to some gardener's chore at L'Arbe de la Croix suggest that Son is experiencing an identity crisis of his own, consumed as he is with all identity-altering obsession with Jadine, and a longing for reconnection with a world beyond the space-time warp of a plantation-style system of selective patronage and exploitation.

> But now watching Yardman—he was kneeling, chopping at the trunk of a small tree—while he himself was so spanking clean, clean from the roots of his hair to the crevices between his toes, having watched his personal dirt swirl down a drain, while he himself stood wrapped waist-to-thigh in an Easter white towel. Now he was as near to crying as he'd been since he'd fled from home. You would have thought something was leaving him and all he could see was its back. (120)

His preoccupation with his original dime suggests a fear of contamination; a contamination that is already a reality according to the Mexican who identifies him as essentially "American" (175).

In Son's dreams of Eloe, the African American male ego is restored in a community of black men at the center of a black community. But however appreciative Son is of the beauty, the strength, and the toughness of black women, his vision is of male dominion; of the black woman as handmaiden. It is this that terrifies Jadine, that brings her crisis of identity (that is a crisis of racial identification and of gender roles) to a climax. In Eloe the terms of her relationship with Son change completely. As in the Dominique of Gideon and Therese, the rules that govern male-female relationships sacrifice shared intimacy to fraternity. The men are separate and the women in attendance. Jadine finds her sexual freedom curtailed and feels obscene, because within the hierarchy of Eloe, the ancestral role of women as nurturers, as guardians of the hearth and the moral values of the community, is also the preservation of male dominance.

It is no surprise that in Eloe Jadine's sexual fears return with a vengeance in her dream of the night women "taking away her sex like succubi, but not his" (222). While Son thrives in Eloe, it is anathema to her. In Eloe she is Jadine as in Jade, a worthless, disreputable woman, even as she appears to Sydney and Ondine later, when she leaves them to sort out their difficulties with the Streets. In New York City Jadine and Son attack each other with missionary fervor. Jadine appears as committed to rescuing Son from the poverty and dependency that she identifies in Eloe, as he is to rescuing her from servitude to an exploitative capitalist system.

> Each was pulling the other away from the maw of hell—its very ridge top. Each knew the world as it was meant or ought to be. One had a past, the other a future and each one bore the culture to save the race in his hands. (232)

In the battle for absolute control over each other's dreams and aspirations, they drive each other away. When Son retreats to recoup for another round in their ongoing fight, Jadine takes flight as if from death itself and opts for Paris.[7] She feels "lean and male, having left quickly with no peeping back just in case—no explanatory, loophole-laden note. No last supper" (237). Here again Morrison evokes her concept of black men in motion but in female rather than male terms. Jadine dispenses with dependence as a sacred value in women's lives.

> No more shoulders and limitless chests. No more dreams of safety. No more. Perhaps that was the thing—the thing Ondine was saying. A grown woman did not need safety or its dreams. She was the safety she longed for. (250)

Jadine is centered on self and portable property; her emery board and her sealskin coat. Morrison explains to Gloria Naylor that "a person who has all the accouterments of *self-centeredness*, may not be centered at all" ("Conversation," 572). Though uncentered in the traditional sense of what it means to be a woman, Jadine is focused and struggling to define what it means to be a woman with options that were not available to her forebears. As she tells Ondine rather bluntly: "I don't want to learn how to be the kind of woman you're talking about because I don't want to be that kind of woman" (243).

At twenty-five, Jadine is vain, narcissistic, spoiled, but very much about the business of shaping her own identity. Morrison warns that self-reliance in itself is not enough: "Nice things don't always happen to the totally self-reliant if there is no conscious historical connection" ("Rootedness," 344). The conscious historical connection is there for Jadine after Son and Eloe, but without Son's sympathetic attachment to the cultural heartland of poverty, male dominance, and apartheid, Jadine emerges as a heroine in the tradition of black men on the move, and to be in motion in *Tar Baby*, as in *Their Eyes Were Watching God*, is to be about the business of making yourself. Toni Morrison explains this phenomenon at length in her conversation with Robert Stepto as "the traveling Ulysses scene"; "in the process of finding, they are also making themselves" ("Intimate," 226). Jadine takes flight, literal and metaphoric, in a spirit of repudiation, substituting personal freedom, self-reliance, and a "black male" spirit of adventure for rootedness in the ancestral way of black women as nurturers and keepers of hearth and home. Her flight is another version of Milkman's self-centered, self-serving plane flight in *Song of Solomon*, away from his burdensome family, in pursuit of a fortune in gold and the freedom it can buy him.[8] Unlike Milkman, Jadine has already made her pilgrimage to the cultural heartland that is Eloe and, like Sydney and Ondine before her, found it wanting. At the end of *Tar Baby,* Jadine is "on the move," possessed of the problematic but powerful freedom Morrison terms "the Ulysses thing."

Unlike Janie Crawford, Jadine's alienation from self and community is not resolved in ritual immersion and a passionate love affair with a man of the folk. But then Son is not conveniently dead at Jadine's hands in *Tar Baby*. He is by nature iconoclastic and questing and, at the end of the novel, he resumes his pursuit of Jadine by way of Gideon and Therese and Sydney and Ondine, on the Isle de Chevaliers. It is clear that Jadine's perception of Eloe has undermined his pastoral dream of welcoming women and ladies minding the pie table. Her photographs show him a different Eloe; "sad, poor and even poor-spirited" (254):

> Beatrice, pretty Beatrice, Soldier's daughter. She looked stupid. Ellen, sweet cookie-faced Ellen, the one he always thought so pretty. She looked stupid. They all looked stupid, backwoodsy, dumb, dead . . . (234–35)

His obsessive pursuit of the copper Venus on the cover of a fashion magazine suggests that she has succeeded in pressing some of "her dreams of gold and cloisonne and honey-colored silk into him" (103).

Reconnection with the copper Venus is not what Therese has in mind when, as water lady, she ferries Son in a heavy fog to the uninhabited side of Isle de Chevaliers to join the island's mythic race of black horsemen. At this point the ancestral figure as archetypal earth mother is a menacing, devouring figure: "Her voice was a calamitous whisper coming out of the darkness toward him like jaws. 'Forget her. There is nothing in her parts for you. She has forgotten her ancient properties'" (263). The closing image is not of blind horsemen racing thunderously across the hills, but of Brer Rabbit making his way across the briar patch. If Son is exactly where he wants to be, where he was born and raised as the Tar Baby tale tells us, then he is well poised to renew the phallic quest of the blind horsemen. The novel ends as it began. Son, repository of ancestral resonance, avatar of the trickster as hero, and would-be pastoral lover to Jadine's Chloe, may be running blind, but Brer Rabbit is a survivor and he is on home turf in the briar patch that is Isle de Chevaliers.

In *Their Eyes Were Watching God*, the national-historical boundaries of the African American experience are sharply defined within the segregated structure of black life in the southern United States. Zora Neale Hurston posits authoritatively that unity of being is a realizable goal within this historical framework. Ancestors may be unreliable, misguided, and even menacing, but folklore is celebrated as a stable source of cultural unity in the African American community irrespective of conflicts within that community.

Folklore does not belong to any special area, time, nor people. It is a world and an ageless thing, so let us look at it from that viewpoint. It is the boiled down juice of human living and when one phase of it passes another begins which shall in turn give way before a successor. ("Folklore," 41)

In the saga of Janie Crawford, reconnection with folk culture across class lines is both possible and necessary in a continuing cycle of regeneration and renewal within the African American community.

Morrison offers no such formula for cultural stability. In *Tar Baby* the national-historical boundaries that frame Janie's emergence as a heroine are redrawn to reflect a contemporary reality in which apartheid and integration coexist. The fundamental features of African American culture are inscribed in terms of diversity and conflict rather than the heroine's unity of being.[9] Morrison makes no attempt to resolve the ideological, social, and political conflicts that are embodied in Son's and Jadine's love affair. Problems of ancestry and cultural identity in the African American community are not resolvable by apportioning fixed value to folklore. The Tar Baby tale as a metaphor of entrapment has one meaning for Jadine and another for Son. It is this ambivalence that becomes the focus of Morrison's interest in the tale as a repository of cultural values. "The Tar Baby tale seemed to me to be about masks. Not masks as covering what is to be hidden, but how masks come to life, take life over, exercise the tensions between itself and what it covers" ("Unspeakable," 30). In *Tar Baby* a folk tale is reinvented as a polyphonic novel, exposing conflicts in the African American community between the inner self and the outer self, between the self and community.[10] The problem of cultural identity is redefined to reflect a changing historical situation, and an ancestral tale becomes a subtext for examining a community's need for stability and its coexistent need to adapt to historical change.

NOTES

1. Regarding the function of the novel Morrison states: "It should have something in it that enlightens; something in it that opens the door and points the way. Something in it that suggests what the conflicts are, what the problems are. But it need not solve those problems because it is not a case study, it is not a recipe" ("Rootedness," 341).

2. Michael Cooke has an interesting footnote on Janie's survival mechanism: "Janie, in fact, makes her first husband feel impotent, tells her second publicly that he is so, and kills the third. It is an arresting, anthropophobic pattern which the text does not allow us to search to its foundation" (77).

3. As Mary Helen Washington explains: "Janie's search for identity is an integral part of her search for blackness" (69), and Janie's "descent into the Everglades is the last in a series of steps by which Janie discovers and comes to terms with her own blackness" (74).

4. Janie is stereotyped as untrustworthy by both Logan Killicks and Joe Starks. Joe has her conceal her long hair in a scarf, while Logan reminds her that she was "born in a carriage 'thout no top to it, and yo' mama and you bein born and raised in de white folks back-yard" (51).

5. Houston Baker points out that Janie's property is not to be separated from her assumption of voice: "From an ideological perspective, Hurston's novel is a commentary on the continuing necessity for Afro-Americans to observe property relationships and to negotiate the restrictions sanctioned by the economics of slavery if they would achieve expressive wholeness" (59).

6. Eleanor W. Traylor (138) comments exhaustively on the meaning of Valerian's name.

7. It is worth considering, even casually, the historical role of Paris as home in exile to so many Afro-American intellectuals, artists, and performers, among them, Josephine Baker, Richard Wright, James Baldwin, and Chester Himes.

8. Hovet and Lounsberry explore Morrison's use of flight in a fine essay.

9. Susan Willis writes that "the problem at the center of Morrison's writing is how to maintain an African American cultural heritage once the relationship to the black rural south has been stretched thin over distance and generations" (274).

10. Craig H. Werner explores the multiplicity of meanings Morrison discovers in the tar baby myth.

WORKS CITED

Baker, Houston A., Jr. *Blues, Ideology, and Afro-American Literature*. Chicago: University of Chicago Press, 1984.

Cooke, Michael G. *Afro-American Literature in the Twentieth Century*. New Haven: Yale University Press, 1984.

Ellison, Ralph. *Shadow and Act*. New York: Signet, 1966.

Gates, Henry Louis, Jr. "The Blackness of Blackness: A Critique of the Sign and the Signifying Monkey." *Black Literature and Literary Theory*. Edited by Henry Louis Gates, Jr. New York: Methuen, 1984. 285–321.

Hovet, Grace Ann, and Barbara Lounsberry. "Flying as Symbol and Legend in

Toni Morrison's *The Bluest Eye, Sula,* and *Song of Solomon,*" *College Language Association Journal* 27 (1983): 119–40.

Hurston, Zora Neale. *Their Eyes Were Watching God.* Urbana: University of Illinois Press, 1978.

———. "Folklore Field Notes from Zora Neale Hurston." Intro. Robert Hemenway. *The Black Scholar* 7, 7 (1976): 41.

Morrison, Toni. "Rootedness: The Ancestor as Foundation." *Black Women Writers (1950–1980).* Edited by Mari Evans. New York: Anchor, 1984. 339–45.

———. *Song of Solomon.* New York: Knopf, 1977.

———.*Tar Baby.* New York: Signet, 1981.

———. "Unspeakable Things Unspoken: The Afro-American Presence in American Literature." *Michigan Quarterly Review* 28 (1989): 1–34.

———. with Gloria Naylor. "A Conversation." *Southern Review* 21 (1985): 567–93.

———. with Robert B. Stepto. "Intimate Things in Place." *Chant of Saints.* Edited by Michael S. Harper and Robert B. Stepto. Urbana: University of Illinois Press, 1979, 213–29.

Traylor, Eleanor W. "The Fabulous World of Toni Morrison: *Tar Baby.*" *Confirmation: An Anthology of African American Women.* Edited by Amiri and Amina Baraka. New York: Quill, 1983, 333–52.

Washington, Mary Helen. "The Black Woman's Search for Identity." *Black World* (August 1972): 68–75.

Werner, Craig H. "The Briar Patch as Modernist Myth: Morrison, Barthes, and Tar Baby As-Is." *Critical Essays on Toni Morrison.* Edited by Nellie Y. McKay. Boston: G.K. Hall, 1988. 150–67.

Willis, Susan. "Eruptions of Funk: Historicizing Toni Morrison." *Black Literature and Literary Theory.* Edited by Henry Louis Gates, Jr. New York: Methuen, 1984. 263–84.

PART 5
Beloved

Beloved and the New Apocalypse

Susan Bowers

Toni Morrison's *Beloved* joins a long tradition of African American apocalyptic writing. Early African American writers believed that "America, after periods of overwhelming darkness, would lift the veil and eternal sunshine would prevail" (Gayle, xiii). By the Harlem Renaissance, African American writers had begun to doubt a messianic age, but the middle and late 1960s saw a return to apocalypticism, emphasizing Armageddon. Many of these works by such writers as John Williams and John Oliver Killens conceived "the longed-for racial battle" as "the culmination of history and the revelatory moment of justice and retribution" (Bigsby, 149). Morrison's novel maps a new direction for the African American apocalyptic tradition which is both more instructive and potentially more powerful than the end-of-the-world versions of the sixties. She has relocated the arena of racial battle from the streets to the African American psyche from where the racial memories of black people have been taken hostage.

Morrison has remarked on the dearth of any "songs or dances or tales" about those who died in the Middle Passage and on what was left out of slave narratives.

> People who did dwell on it, it probably killed them, and the people who did not dwell on it probably went forward. They tried to make a life. I think that Afro-Americans in rushing away from slavery, which was important to do—it meant rushing out of bondage into

freedom—also rushed away from the slaves because it was painful to dwell there, and they may have abandoned some responsibility in so doing (Morrison, "In the Realm," 5).

She believes that her "job as a writer in the last quarter of the 20th century, not much more than a hundred years after Emancipation, becomes how to rip that veil drawn over 'proceedings too terrible to relate'" (Walters, 60).

The word "apocalypse" means unveiling, and this novel unveils the angry presence of the "disremembered and unaccounted for" (Morrison, *Beloved*, 274), those who died from slavery and on the Middle Passage (at least 50% of all Africans on slave ships died between Africa and the American plantations during the 320 years of the slave trade [Mannix and Cowley, 123]).

Apocalypticism is a form of eschatology. The root meaning of *eschaton* is "furthermost boundary" or "ultimate edge" in time or space. Apocalypses can be read

as investigations into the edge, the boundary, the interface between radically different realms. If the apocalypse is an unveiling (*apo* [from or away], *kalupsis* [covering] from *kalupto* [to cover], and *kalumma* [veil]), then clearly the veil is the *eschaton*, that which stands between the familiar and whatever lies beyond. In this sense the apocalypse becomes largely a matter of *seeing*. (Robinson, xii-xiii).

The veil or *eschaton* in *Beloved* is forgetting. The etymological sense of "forget" is to miss or lose one's hold. The characters of *Beloved*—and by implication, contemporary African Americans—have lost touch with those who have died from slavery and even with their own pasts. As a result they have lost part of themselves, their own interior lives. Their struggle is to lift the veil of Lethe to reveal the truth of their personal and collective histories. Morrison fuses Christian notions of apocalypse with West African beliefs to create a revised apocalyptic that principally looks backward, not forward in time, and concentrates on the psychological devastation which began with the horrors of slavery and continued when African Americans had to let the horrors of the Middle Passage and slavery disappear into the black hole of Lethe, that vortex of forgetting. Working from the foundation of West African philosophy, at the heart of which is communion with ancestors (Campbell, 145), Morrison presents an apocalyptic demolition of the boundaries between the earthly and spiritual realms, an invasion of the world of the living by the world beyond the veil. The narrative does not drive toward its apocalyptic moment but recounts the struggle of living through and beyond the reign of the Anti-Christ and of surviving the "mumbling of the black and angry dead" (*Beloved*, 198).

Beloved's focus on the past may seem contrary to the forward-looking spirit of apocalypse, especially in American literature, where the apocalyptic is considered fundamental (Robinson, xi). However, African American apocalypse must be clearly differentiated from White American apocalypse. The fact is that "American apocalypse" is founded on a premise that necessarily excludes African American writing: that America is the New World, land of rebirth and new life, as opposed to Europe, the Old World of decadence, decay and death. When Europeans discovered America in the sixteenth century, "America was conceived as mankind's last great hope, the Western site of the millennium," and "its future destiny was firmly and prophetically linked with God's plan for the world" (Robinson, xi). As a result, most White American apocalyptic literature has been based on the optimistic expectation of historical, material change. The reverse experience, of course, is true for African Americans. They did not leave an Old World of death and decadence for a New World of hope and rebirth but were torn from the world of their families, communities, their own spiritual traditions, and languages, to be taken to a world of suffering, death, and alienation. The good life lay not before them but behind them; yet, every attempt was made to crush their memories of the past. Slaves were isolated from other members of their tribes to keep them from communicating in their own languages and maintaining their own traditions. In *Beloved*, only when characters can recover the past do they begin to imagine a future.

One way Morrison avoids the end-of-the-world perspective of most apocalyptic fiction is by basing her novel, like Ralph Ellison's *Invisible Man* (Lewicki, 48), on West African philosophy, including the notion of cyclical time. The West African sense of time is part of an organic phi-losophy that views the world as living—"subject to the law of becoming, of old age and death" (Eliade, 45). For such a culture, apocalypse is re-peatable and survivable. On the other hand, there can be only one apoca-lypse if time is conceived of as linear and irreversible as it is in the Judeo-Christian tradition (Zamora, 3). The constant circling of the narrative in *Beloved* from present to past and back again enacts the West African per-spective and reinforces the importance of the past for both the individual and collective psyche.

Morrison shares with post-Holocaust Jewish artists the monumental difficulties attendant in depicting the victims of racial genocide. What Elie Weisel has stated about the Holocaust applies to the slaughter of ten times as many Africans and African Americans as the six million Jews killed by Hitler (Morrison has said that 60 million is the smallest figure she had gotten from anyone for the number of slaves who died as a result of slavery [Angelo, 120]).

> The Holocaust is not a subject like all the others. It imposes cer-tain limits. . . . in order not to betray the dead and humiliate the living, this particular subject demands a special sensibility, a dif-ferent approach, a rigor strengthened by respect and reverence and, above all, faithfulness to memory. (Wiesel, 38)

Betrayal would include sentimentalizing and thus trivializing the victims of slavery, rendering them merely pathetic and pitiable. Morrison does not do that. She dedicated *Beloved* to the "Sixty Million and More," and her novel conjures slaves back to life in many-dimensional characters with a full range of human emotions. They love and hate, sin and forgive, are heroic and mean, self-sacrificing and demanding. They endure in-credible hardships to sustain relationships, but the inconceivable brutal-ity and degradation which they experience fractures their communities and inflicts both physical and perhaps irreparable psychological damage on individuals.

One of the questions which *Beloved* asks is whether it is possible to transform unspeakably horrific experiences into knowledge. Is the mag-nitude of their horror too great to assimilate? Perhaps because the novel asks its readers, especially African Americans, to "dwell on the horror" which those rushing away from slavery could not, it addresses what happens when the magnitude of that horror is acknowledged, even suggesting how to survive the bringing into consciousness of what has lain hidden for so long. The struggle of *Beloved's* characters to confront the effects of the brutality and to recover their human dignity, their selves "dirtied" by white oppression—to transform their experiences into knowledge—is presented in the form of a slave narrative that can be read as a model for contemporary readers attempting to engage these brutal realities. Slave narratives emphasize personal quest as a means of "wrest[ing] the black subject out of anonymity, inferiority and brutal disdain" (Willis, 213). *Beloved* combines the personal quest theme with the collective memory of racial brutality, for although apocalyptic literature features the destiny of the individual and personal salvation, its "overall perspective is still that of the community" (Russell, 27).

It is important to note that *Beloved* is more explicit than most early slave narratives, which could not reveal fully the horror of slave experience, either because their authors dared not offend their white abolitionist audiences or because they too could not bear to dwell on the horror. *Beloved* does not subordinate the stories of slave life to abstract ideas, unlike the slave narratives which were usually "sandwiched between white abolitionist documents, suggesting that the slave has precious little control over his or her life—even to its writing" (Sekora, 109). Moreover, Morrison's modeling of her novel on the slave narrative is one way of giving African Americans back their voices. The slave narrative was an extremely popular form of literature until the Civil War. But after the war, the narratives were expelled from the center of our literary history.

While an editor at Random House, Morrison worked for 18 months in the early 1970s on a project to unveil the reality of African American life, *The Black Book*, which she called "a genuine black history book—one that simply recollected black life as lived" (Morrison, "Behind the Making. . . ," 89). *The Black Book* contains what became the germ of *Beloved*: the story of a slave woman in Cincinnati who killed one child and tried to kill the other three, to, in her words, "end their sufferings, [rather] than have them taken back to slavery, and murdered by piecemeal" ("A Visit to the Slave Mother," 10). But this "folk journey of Black

America" (Cosby, iii) had a far more profound impact upon Morrison than providing her with an initial spark, because it was a model of attempting to tell the truth about a part of African American life that has been either whitewashed or forgotten, a truth so horrible that it could make a mother see death as desirable for her child.

What *The Black Book* models is an uncensored exposure of brutality through newspaper clippings and photographs of lynchings and burnings of black people, for instance, juxtaposed with the celebration of African American strengths and achievements and folkways. Essentially, *The Black Book* models the remembering of African American experience.

"Rememorying" is what Morrison's characters call it, and it is the central activity in *Beloved*. Because of it the narrative moves constantly back and forth between past and present, mixing time inextricably, as memory escalates its battle against amnesia. The voice of the former slave "above all *remembering* his ordeal in bondage" can be "the single most impressive feature of a slave narrative" (Stepto, 1). The characters' rememorying in *Beloved* epitomizes the novel's purpose of conjuring up the spirits and experiences of the past and thus ultimately empowering both characters and readers. *Beloved* pairs the stories of a woman and a man, Sethe and Paul D. Sethe's name may be an allusion to Lethe, the spring of forgetfulness in Greek myth. The past that was too painful for either to remember alone can be recovered together: "Her story was bearable because it was his as well" (*Beloved*, 99). Their stories reveal that the worst brutality they have suffered "is less a single act than the systematic denial of the reality of black lives" (C. Davis, 323), the profound humiliation which both know can be worse than death:

> That anybody white could take your whole self for anything that came to mind. Not just work, kill, or maim you, but dirty you.
> (*Beloved*, 251)

Remembering is part of reversing the "dirtying" process that robbed slaves of self-esteem.

The concentration on the horrors of the past and present—the misuse of power, the cruelty and injustice—is characteristic of apocalyptic writing. However, the traditional apocalyptic anticipation of the messianic age—the time of freedom and redemption—is missing among these slaves and ex-slaves for whom hope has come to seem a cruel trick. The members of Paul D's chain gang try to destroy that part of themselves as they crush stone: "They killed the flirt whom folks called Life for leading them on" (*Beloved,* 109).

The typical format of the slave narrative is to trace the story of the individual's life in slavery, escape, and the journey to freedom (Willis, 220). What Morrison reveals is that the process must be repeated twice: first to leave physical enslavement by whites and the second time to escape the psychological trauma created by their brutality. The physical escapes of both Sethe and Paul D create the patterns for their psychological escapes: archetypal journeys of courage, descents into almost certain death, and rebirths into beauty and freedom. Sethe gives birth with the help of a young white girl when she reaches the Ohio River and thus freedom. Paul D is helped by Cherokees, who "describe the beginning of the world and its end and tell him to follow the tree flowers to the North and freedom" (112).

But the novel opens with characters still traumatized many years after their escapes from slavery. They are numb, almost incapable of emotion because they have suffered so deeply and seen such terror. Sethe and her daughter are literally haunted by the ghost of her murdered baby. Sethe is unable to feel; every morning she sees the dawn but never acknowledges its color. Paul D experiences his heart as a "tobacco tin lodged in his chest" (113), which holds the painful memories of his own past, the memories of one friend being burned to death, of others hanging from trees, his brothers being sold and taken away, of being tortured. "By the time he got to 124 nothing in this world could pry it open" (113). Paul D's arrival at 124, Sethe's home, 18 years after the two had last seen each other, begins their long and excruciating process of thawing frozen feeling.

Contemporary research on treatment for post-traumatic stress syndrome indicates that support and caring from others can help victims to heal, but that the most crucial part of healing is the unavoidable confrontation with the original trauma and feeling the pain again (Brown). *Beloved* enacts that theory. Sethe and Paul D are able to help each other to a point, but until they have intimate contact with the original pain and the feelings it created that had to be suppressed, they cannot be purged of its paralyzing effect.

What breaks open Paul D's tin heart and allows Sethe to see and love color again (color often appears in Morrison's fiction as a sign of the ability to feel) is Beloved's return from the dead, not as a ghost but a living being. She climbs fully dressed out of the water—perhaps representing the collective unconscious of African Americans—while, appropriately, Sethe, Paul D., and Sethe's daughter Denver are at a carnival (etymologically, "festival of flesh"). Beloved has "new skin, lineless and smooth" (*Beloved,* 50), no expression in her eyes, three thin scratches on her head where Sethe had held her head after severing her neck, and a small neck scar. Although Sethe does not consciously recognize her daughter for some time, her bladder fills the moment she sees her face and she voids "endless" water as if giving birth (*Beloved,* 51). For each of the three residents of 124—Sethe, Paul D and Denver—relating to Beloved addresses her or his most profound individual anguish, whatever lies at the core of each identity. For Sethe, it is mothering; for Paul D, his ability to feel, and for Denver, her loneliness. Their individual reactions to her reflect their respective voids and reveal their deepest selves.

Angela Davis has pointed out that slave women were not recognized as mothers having bonds with their children but considered only "breeders" and workers. Thus slave owners had no scruples about selling children away from their mothers: "Their infant children could be sold away from them like calves from cows" (A. Davis, 7). *Beloved* is characterized by mothers losing their children: Sethe's mother-in-law barely glanced at the last of her eight children "because it wasn't worth the trouble" (*Beloved*, 139). Sethe's own mother, hanged when Sethe was a small child, had not been allowed to nurse her. But Sethe defines herself as mother in defiance of the near-impossibility of that role. Even 18 years after her escape, Paul D recognizes that Sethe's mother-love is risky. "For a used-to-be slave woman to love anything that much was dangerous, especially if it was her children she had settled on to love" (*Beloved*, 45). It was to avoid a future in slavery for her children that led Sethe to plan escape and to get her milk to her baby—sent ahead with the other children—that made her attempt it alone. She experiences having her milk stolen from her by the nephews of her slave master as the ultimate brutality, even worse than the savage beating she received just before escaping. "They handled me like I was the cow, no, the goat, back behind the stable because it was too nasty to stay in with the horses" (*Beloved*, 200). Beloved's return enables Sethe to mother her abundantly with "lullabies, new stitches, the bottom of the cake bowl, the top of the milk" (*Beloved*, 240).

If mothering is at the core of Sethe's identity, feeling is at the core of Paul D's. "Not even trying, he had become the kind of man who could walk into a house and make the women cry. Because with him, in his presence, they could" (*Beloved*, 17). What had led to his own inability to feel was the systematic destruction of his manhood. Like many men, women, and children, he had had a bit in his mouth, but the worst part of the experience for Paul D was feeling the superiority of a rooster (called Mister):

> Mister was allowed to be and stay what he was . . . . But wasn't no way I'd ever be Paul D again, living or dead. Schoolteacher changed me. I was something else and that something was less than a chicken sitting in the sun on a tub. (*Beloved*, 72)

When Beloved seduces Paul D, making love with her breaks open the tobacco tin in his chest to release his red heart.

Sethe's anguish is about her mothering, and Paul D's, the ability to feel. Denver's is her loneliness. Its original cause is Beloved's murder, which alienated the community, made Denver afraid of her mother and of whatever was terrible enough to make her kill her own, and caused the haunting of 124 that made Denver's two brothers leave. She had gone deaf and withdrawn from others for a time after having been asked if she hadn't been in jail with her when her mother was charged with murder (*Beloved*, 104). Beloved's gift to Denver is attention. Under her gaze, "Denver's skin dissolved . . . and became soft and bright" (*Beloved*, 118).

But Beloved is much more than Sethe's resurrected daughter. She is the embodiment of the collective pain and rage of the millions of slaves who died on the Middle Passage and suffered the tortures of slavery. Therefore, her unconscious knows the desperately crowded conditions of a ship of the Middle Passage:

. . . there will never be a time when I am not crouching and watching others who are crouching too I am always crouching the man on my face is dead his face is not mine his mouth smells sweet but his eyes are locked (*Beloved*, 212)

West African religion believes that after physical death, the individual spirit lives, but because it is no longer contained by its "carnal envelope," it gains in power. Spirits "may cause havoc to people if they are spirits of people who were killed in battle or unjustly" (Mbiti, 8), and the spirits feel punished if their names are obliterated or forgotten (Mbiti, 9). (Beloved has no name but the epitaph on her gravestone, a word Sethe remembered from the funeral and which she could pay to have engraved only by enduring the sexual assault of the engraver.) The invasion of the world of the living by Beloved's physical presence is evidence of the terrible destruction of the natural order caused by slavery. No one had thought anything about a ghost haunting the house, because ancestral spirits were known to linger in the world. But her physical presence has the effect of Judgment Day on all those whom she encounters: Sethe, Paul D, Denver, and the community. However, because the West African sense of time is non-linear, judgment can be endured and redemption still achieved.

. . . if the apocalypse stands as one constant pole of the black imagination, as a present possibility, the other pole is an unfashionable conviction that change is possible—that the ghosts of the past can be laid if only they are freely engaged and honestly confessed. (Bigsby, 167)

Beloved proclaims that apocalypse and change are not necessarily at opposite poles: an apocalypse—that lifting of the veil on whatever lies beyond—can stimulate change. Its catharsis can be the beginning of transformation; apocalypse can thus become a bridge to the future, passage to freedom.

This novel makes very clear that physical escape into physical freedom was only the first step for the slaves. That fact is symbolized by

Beloved's equivalent of Charon, the figure in Greek mythology who ferries the souls across the Acheron to the underworld. This character is an ex-slave who, after handing over his wife to his master's son, changed his name from Joshua to Stamp Paid because "whatever his obligations were, that act paid them off." By ferrying escaped slaves across the Ohio into freedom, he "gave them their own bill of sale" (*Beloved*, 185), except that the freedom on the Ohio side of the river is illusory, and not only for political and economic reasons. The slaves who cross the river bring with them the memories of lynchings and torture, family members sold away, degradation, and cumulative loss, so that Stamp Paid, like Charon, actually carries them physically to an underworld, to "free" territory where, in *Beloved*, souls are dead even if bodies are alive. However, Stamp Paid also attempts to carry them out of this underworld into genuine freedom. He "extended the debtlessness [that he believed he had achieved by handing over his wife] to other people by helping them pay out and off whatever they owed in misery" (*Beloved*, 185).

Stamp Paid interprets the angry mumbling of the spirits around Sethe's home as "the jungle whitefolks planted" in black people, a jungle which grew and spread, "in, through and after life" (*Beloved*, 198). Among other things, Beloved is the embodiment of the white folks' jungle, the psychological effects of slavery. The three residents of 124—Sethe, Paul D, and Denver—find out that although Beloved, once no longer a ghost, did address their deepest needs, she is also malevolent. Sethe realizes that Beloved will never accept her explanation for the murder and Sethe can never make it up to her. Sethe becomes Beloved's slave, goes without food so that Beloved can eat, and begins to die. Paul D recognizes that making love with Beloved "was more like a brainless urge to stay alive" (*Beloved*, 265). Denver is finally deserted by Beloved when her mother recognizes her dead daughter. When Denver accuses her of strangling Sethe from a distance of several feet, Beloved denies it. "The circle of iron choked it" (*Beloved*, 101). Her reply reflects the complexity of her character, as both the ghost of Sethe's murdered baby who can't get enough love from her mother and as also the representative of all the angry spirits—the manifestation of the murderous rage created by whites in enslaved African Americans. Beloved as the spirit of slavery—the circle of iron around slave necks—did try to kill Sethe; murdered indirectly by

Sethe's slave master, Beloved is an unquiet spirit. The enormity of the wrongs wreaked upon the "60 million and more" has produced her, obsessed with revenge, desperately needy for love but incapable of giving it. Beloved is the tangible presence of the painful past. When Sethe finally recognizes her, Sethe is "excited to giddiness by all the things she no longer had to remember" (*Beloved*, 183). Even though sex with her filled Paul D with repulsion and shame, "he was thankful too for having been escorted to some ocean-deep place he once belonged to" (*Beloved*, 265).

Beloved's stream of consciousness reveals that she had waited "on the bridge" (*Beloved*, 212). She herself becomes a bridge between the "other side" and the living, the apocalyptic manifestation of the world beyond the veil. Like a bridge, Beloved enables passage to knowledge of the other side that otherwise would be impossible. We know that medieval chapels were constructed in the middle of bridges so that passengers could contemplate passage from one state of being to another. Beloved's very being forces such contemplation.

In terms of Christian apocalypse, Beloved is not the anti-Christ; that role belongs to Sethe's slave master, representative of the whites who oppressed African Americans through slavery. But as the product of slavery, she could be the Anti-Christ's beast. She is a constant sign that this novel is dealing with another level of reality but also a reminder of the paradoxes about which the novel circles: the killing of a child to protect her and the combined pathos and wrathfulness of the ancestral spirits. Yet, although Sethe's murder of Beloved is the center of the paradox, which occurred 18 years before the action that begins the novel, it is not depicted until nearly the mid-point of *Beloved*. Instead, the murder is anticipated so often that a dark foreboding is created, just as Sethe's mother-in-law sensed something "dark and coming" as the slave master and his accomplices were arriving (*Beloved*, 139).

The slave master, Schoolteacher, is definitely an Anti-Christ figure, the kind of character who usually functions in apocalyptic writing as a sign of the end. The Anti-Christ signals a return to chaos (Russell, 36), and Schoolteacher's arrival produces chaos which permeates Sethe's life and the lives of everyone in her family and in the entire community. Schoolteacher and the three other white men: his nephew, the slave catcher, and the sheriff, are Morrison's four horsemen of the apocalypse. Their appearance crystallizes the terror and horror of slavery, emphasized by the fact that this episode is the only one in the novel told from the point of view of a white person. When they discover Sethe's sons bleeding at her feet, her baby's head nearly severed, and her trying to kill the other infant, Schoolteacher concedes his economic loss. He believes that Sethe would be useless as a slave to him because she has "gone wild" (*Beloved*, 149) due to his nephew having "overbeaten" her; she resembles a hound beaten too hard and which, therefore, can never be trusted. He reflects slavery's treatment of African Americans as animals. Sethe's reaction to seeing the four horsemen is to protect her children in the only way she has left: to remove them from the reach of evil to try to carry them "through the veil, out, away, over there where no one could hurt them" (*Beloved*, 163).

This prefiguring of the novel's climactic, redemptive moment is the most violent episode in the novel. Although violence is characteristic of apocalyptic literature, this violence is especially notable because it consists of the victim inflicting the violence on her own children out of utter hopelessness. Stamp Paid calls this event "the Misery" and "Sethe's response to the Fugitive Act" (*Beloved*, 171). It demonstrates what the characters in *Beloved* recognize—that actual battle with whites is impossible because the odds are so stacked against blacks: "Lay down your sword. This ain't a battle; it's a rout" (*Beloved*, 244).

Biblical scholars read the four horsemen of the apocalypse as agents of divine wrath; Morrison's four horsemen are only emblems of evil. Her revision of the classic apocalyptic image suggests that she does not share with many apocalyptic writers a belief in a moral force at work in history, the invisible presence of a god who will come again to judge sinners and rescue and reward the oppressed. Instead, *Beloved* insists that if change is possible, it will happen only when individuals are integrated with the natural world and each other. The only moral agency is human, represented in *Beloved* by Denver. Born in a boat filling with the "river of freedom," she represents the generation born outside slavery: the future.

Denver is the redemptive figure in this novel. She was only a few days old when her mother murdered Beloved, and Sethe's nipple was covered with her sister's blood when she nursed. "So Denver took her mother's milk right along with the blood of her sister" (*Beloved*, 152). The image can be read as an allusion to Christ in Revelation "robed in the blood of martyrs" (Rev. 19:13). Like a Christ figure, Denver often functions as an intermediary between spirits and living. Even before Beloved materialized, she saw her in a white dress kneeling beside Sethe, and she was the first to recognize Beloved. Denver not only represents the future; she brings it into being. When neither Sethe nor Beloved seem to care what the next day might bring, "Denver knew it was on her. She would have to leave the yard; step off the edge of the world" and find help (*Beloved*, 243). Her efforts lead to everyone's salvation: the reunion of the community. It begins with gifts of food accompanied by the givers' names but culminates in the women coming to the yard of 124 to exorcise Beloved.

Ella, the former slave woman who had led Sethe and the just-born Denver from the Ohio River, leads Sethe's rescue. She had guided them to the community of former slaves, then led the community's ostracizing of Sethe for 18 years when Sethe had seemed not to need anyone after Beloved's death. Now, it is the idea of Beloved's physical presence which enrages Ella, for she understands that Beloved represents the invasion of one world by the other, and specifically, "the idea of past errors taking possession of the present" (*Beloved*, 256). As long as Beloved was only a ghost, even a violent ghost, Ella respected it.

> But if it took on flesh and came in her world, well, the shoe was on the other foot. She didn't mind a little communication between the two worlds, but this was an invasion. (*Beloved*, 257).

Ella and the others recognize that Beloved's being violates the boundary between the dead and the living. They know that she is the representative of "the people of the broken necks, of fire-cooked blood" (*Beloved*, 181) whose anger and suffering could not be contained in the other world as long as the living neither heard nor remembered them: the apocalyptic presence come to demand attention. When the community is forced to acknowledge what she represents in their own interior lives, Beloved can be exorcised. Like Beloved's murder, the exorcism takes place in the yard of 124. It shares several other characteristics with that appearance of the

Anti-Christ: the arrival of a white man with a horse, a violent reaction by Sethe, and the demise of Beloved. But it is the contrasts that are most important. This time, the white man's mission is innocent; Sethe does not succeed; Beloved's demise is necessary and beneficial, the community supports Sethe instead of deserting her, and, most important of all, the community achieves a shared revelation that ushers in a new age.

This second momentous gathering at 124 has a fated quality. For instance, at precisely the same moment that the black women are marching toward 124, Edward Bodwin, the white abolitionist who owns 124, is coming to take Denver to his house to work as a night maid. The women are coming to purge the house of the demon beating up on Sethe, armed with whatever they believe will work: amulets, their Christian faith, anything. It has been 30 years since Bodwin saw 124, the house where he was born, a place about which "he felt something sweeter and deeper" than its commercial value (*Beloved*, 259). The thought of it takes him back to his childhood, a time when he had buried his precious treasures in the yard. It has been 18 years since the women were in the yard of 124, at the picnic Sethe's mother-in-law had given the day before Schoolteacher's arrival to celebrate Sethe's escape. If the house is symbolic for Bodwin, it has symbolic value also for the women approaching it. Seeing Beloved on the porch makes them see themselves as young girls picnicking in the yard 18 years earlier, the day before Beloved was killed. What they see is also a reminder of how the community shares responsibility for Beloved's death. The community of former slaves had been so jealous of the huge party which Sethe's mother-in-law had thrown that no one warned 124 of the approaching horsemen. Then the community had not gathered around Sethe when she climbed into the cart for the ride to jail because they felt that she held her head too high. However, Beloved's presence does enable the women to go back in time to being "young and happy" (*Beloved*, 258). She also lets them recapture the paradisal time they had spent in the Clearing with Sethe's mother-in-law Baby Suggs as their spiritual leader. It is significant that by the end of the novel "rememorying" calls back positive moments instead of the painful, oppressive past. United in memories of joy and collective strength, the women can respond to the need to banish Beloved, the objectification of the angry and revengeful ancestral spirits, with the full power of their spiritual tradition. It is especially important that their leader Ella recognizes at last that she shares something very significant with Sethe. What Ella remembers is the "hairy white thing," fathered by her slave master, which she had let die. "The idea of that pup coming back to whip her too set her jaw working" (*Beloved*, 259). And she hollers, to be joined at once by the others.

> They stopped praying and took a step back to the beginning. In the beginning there were no words. In the beginning was the sound, and they all know what that sound sounded like. (*Beloved*, 259).

The primal sound exorcises Beloved and thus the evil of the "white folks' jungle" in their own lives as well as Sethe's family's. The moment takes them all outside of linear time into a type of apocalypse in which all is reduced to its most fundamental terms, to a purity of emotion and a brilliant clarity. In this moment the cycle has rolled around to begin again. When the women take a step back to the beginning, they touch the eschaton, the boundary, and momentarily escape from the flux of time to the place where clear vision is possible. They remind us that apocalypse is not a synonym for disaster or cataclysm; it is linked to revelation. Seeing clearly into the past, the women can take hold again of what they had lost in forgetting.

Apocalyptic literature is very like Greek tragedy in arousing emotion and creating the conditions for catharsis. Morrison's novel raises all kinds of emotion—pain, grief, remorse, anger, fear—and purges it once "intensified and given objective expression" (Robinson, xiii). Beloved focuses the objective expression of emotion. When the women create the powerful, timeless sound which exorcises Beloved, they purge themselves and Sethe and Denver of the emotion which had imprisoned them. It returns them all to a new beginning where, cleansed, they can create a new life.

> The apocalyptic imagination may finally be defined in terms of its philosophical preoccupation with that moment of juxtaposition and consequential transformation or transfiguration when an old world of mind discovers a believable new world of mind, which either

nullifies and destroys the old system entirely or, less likely, makes it part of a larger design. (Ketterer, 13)

The women's song or shout creates the moment of redemptive transfiguration in *Beloved*. Still caught in the mode of forgetting that had been their method of survival after physically escaping slavery, when the women focused on the image of Beloved standing on the front porch of 124, they were themselves dragged through the veil into a world rich with memory of their personal and collective lives and of the "unnamed, unmentioned people left behind" (*Beloved*, 92).

For Sethe it was as though the Clearing had come to her with all its heat and simmering leaves, where the voices of women searched for the right combination, the key, the code, the sound that broke the back of words. (*Beloved*, 261)

The Clearing was the open place in the woods where Sethe's mother-in-law, Baby Suggs, had led the community in spiritual ceremonies. Baby Suggs had begun those ceremonies by asking the children to laugh, the men to dance, but the women to cry, "For the living and the dead" (*Beloved*, 88). Then she would direct them all to love themselves deeply.

"Here," she said, "in this here place, we flesh; flesh that weeps, laughs, flesh that dances on bare feet in grass. Love it. Love it hard. Yonder they do not love your flesh." (*Beloved*, 88)

But Baby Suggs gave up after the "Misery" and went to bed to die. When Sethe is taken back to the Clearing by the women's song in her yard, it is a sign of both personal and community redemption; the community at this apocalyptic moment has returned finally to loving themselves but also to feeling compassion for those who have died. In the yard of 124 when the women found "the sound that broke the backs of words,"

it was a wave of sound wide enough to sound deep water and knock the pods off chestnut trees. It broke over Sethe and she trembled like the baptized in its wash. (*Beloved,* 261)

The women's song was powerful enough to break "the backs of words"— words used to define African Americans, such as "animal" and "breeding stock" and "slaves." It baptizes Sethe into a new life, into a radical spiritual transformation.

Ironically, Bodwin arrives at the peak of the women's song/shout. His appearance recalls Sethe to that moment when four white horsemen rode into her yard. So she acts again to protect her child, but this time she runs to kill the oppressor—whom she sees as Bodwin—instead of her own child. Denver stops her. We should not read Sethe's seeing Bodwin as her enemy as a crazed mistake but rather as evidence of a kind of clear-sightedness, Sethe having just been baptized in primal, sacred sound. Apocalyptic catharsis requires confrontation with hidden horror; it also provides a two-fold purgation by making the wronged one feel better and castigating the sinner. Although the Bodwins did help ex-slaves and worked for abolition of slavery, *Beloved* makes it clear that they are part of the problem, not the solution. They gave help to runaways "because they hated slavery worse than they hated slaves" (*Beloved,* 137). On a shelf by their back door is the figurine of a black child, his mouth full of money, kneeling on a pedestal with the words, "At Yo' Service" (*Beloved,* 255). When Bodwin returns to 124, his eyes are transfixed by the sight of Beloved. After she has disappeared Beloved is described as "a naked woman with fish for hair" (*Beloved,* 267) which may be an allusion to Medusa, the gorgon who turned men to stone. Perhaps Beloved has that effect on Bodwin. Perhaps he recognizes in her what Stamp Paid called "the white folks' jungle." Perhaps his encounter with Beloved— he doesn't even see Sethe approaching to stab him with the ice pick—is his experience of Judgment, occurring appropriately at the house where he was born, where his "treasure" lay hidden.

Apocalypse is a more diffuse experience in *Beloved* than traditionally conceived, and it is presented as something which can be survived, not as an event at the end of linear time. In *Beloved* it is an attempt to free African Americans from guilt and past suffering. What *Beloved* suggests is that while the suffering of the "black and angry dead" is the inescapable psychological legacy of all African Americans, they can rescue themselves from the trauma of that legacy by directly confronting it and uniting to loosen its fearsome hold. *Beloved*'s redemptive community of women epitomizes the object of salvation in biblical apocalyptic literature: "the creation of a new society" (Russell, 27).

Thus, like much African American writing, *Beloved* does not conclude with a climactic moment. "For the black writer, incompletion is a fact of private and public life and the basis for social and cultural hope" (Bigsby, 168). The experience of suffering and guilt can begin to be transformed into knowledge, once the trauma is purged, so that the novel leaves the powerful apocalyptic scene of the community's expurgation of Beloved to observe Sethe and Paul D rejoining their stories to each other's. Paul D, who had left upon learning of the murder, must return to Sethe's house to re-establish the intimate connection which will allow them each to find his or her own self and love it. Paul D, despite his inability to feel when he had first arrived at Sethe's, has a deep understanding of the meaning of slavery and freedom, that under slavery "you protected yourself and loved small," but finding freedom means "to get to a place where you could love anything you chose" (*Beloved*, 162). Linked with Sethe's mother in several ways, including the wearing of the bit, he mothers Sethe as her own mother never could, and when he does, the voice of his lynched best friend enters his mind, speaking about the woman he loved, "She is a friend of my mind. She gather me, man. The pieces I am, she gather them and give them back to me in all the right order" (*Beloved*, 272–73).

Beloved is a novel about collecting fragments and welding them into beautiful new wholes, about letting go of pain and guilt but also recovering what is lost and loving it into life. One of its most poignant images is the ribbon that Stamp Paid finds on the river bottom—"a red ribbon knotted around a curl of wet woolly hair, clinging still to its bit of scalp" (*Beloved*, 180). Although he knows all the horrors of 1874—the lynchings, whippings, burnings of colored schools, rapes, and lynch fires—it is this discovery which finally weakens Stamp Paid's bone marrow and makes him "dwell on Baby Suggs' wish to consider what in the world was harmless" (*Beloved*, 181).

What Morrison creates is far from harmless. She knows how painful it is to remember the horrors she presents. She has said in an interview that she expected *Beloved* to be the least read of all her books because "it is about something that the characters don't want to remember, I don't want to remember, black people don't want to remember, white people don't want to remember, I mean, it's national amnesia" (Angelo, 120). However, because *Beloved* insists on remembering, the novel is able to recover and honor the symbolic spirit of the black girl whose ribbon and piece of scalp Stamp Paid found. In so doing, it makes possible the contemplation and creation of a future in which African Americans can respect and honor themselves and their ancestors—be beloved. As Paul D says to Sethe, "Me and you, we got more yesterday than anybody. We need some kind of tomorrow" (*Beloved*, 273). What *Beloved* suggests is that tomorrow is made possible by the knowledge of yesterday, a knowledge that for contemporary African Americans can be gained from imagining what it was like to walk in the flesh of their slave ancestors.

> Auschwitz lies on the other side of life and on the other side of death. There, one lives differently, one walks differently, one dreams differently. . . . Only those who lived it in their flesh and their minds can possibly transform their experience into knowledge. (Wiesel, 1).

By giving its readers the inside view of slaves' lives—which bore uncanny resemblance to the Holocaust—the novel enables its African American readers to live the experience of slavery in their minds and to join in the healing primal sound of the women who come to Sethe's yard. By speaking the horror, Morrison assumes and helps to create the community that can hear it and transform it.

WORKS CITED

"A Visit to the Slave Mother Who Killed Her Child." *The Black Book*. Edited by Middleton A. Harris. New York: Random House, 1974.

Angelo, Bonnie. "The Pain of Being Black." *Time* May 22, 1989:120–22.

Bigsby, C.W.E. "Judgment Day is Coming! The Apocalyptic Dream in Recent Afro-American Fiction. *"Black Fiction; New Studies in the Afro-American Novel Since 1945*. Edited by A. Robert Lee. San Francisco: Harper & Row, 1980 .

Brown, Laura S. "From Alienation to Connection: Feminist Therapy with Post-traumatic Stress Disorder." *Women and Therapy* 5:1 (1986):13–26.

Campbell, Jane. *Mythic Black Fiction*. Knoxville: University of Tennessee Press, 1986.

Cosby, Bill. "Introduction." *The Black Book*. Edited by Middleton A. Harris. New York: Random House, 1974.

Davis, Angela. *Women, Race and Class*. New York: Random House, 1981.

Davis, Cynthia. "Self, Society and Myth in Toni Morrison's Fiction." *Contemporary Literature* 23: 3 (1982): 323–42.

Eliade, Mircea. *Myth and Reality*. Trans. Willard R. Trask. San Francisco: Harper & Row, 1963.

Gayle, Addison. *The Way of the World; The Black Novel in America*. Garden City: Anchor Press/Doubleday, 1975.

Ketterer, David. *New Worlds for Old; The Apocalyptic Imagination, Science Fiction, and American Literature*. Bloomington: Indiana University Press, 1974.

Lewicki, Zbigniew. *The Bang and the Whimper; Apocalypse and Entropy in American Literature*. Westport, Conn: Greenwood Press, 1984.

Mannix, Daniel P. and Malcolm Cowley. *Black Cargoes: A History of the Atlantic Slave Trade, 1518–1865*. New York: Viking Press, 1962.

Mbiti, John S. *The Prayers of African Religion*. Maryknoll, NY: Orbis Books, 1975.

Morrison, Toni. "Behind the Making of *The Black Book*. " *Black World*. February 1974: 86–90.

Morrison, Toni. *Beloved*. New York: New American Library, 1987.

Morrison, Toni. "In the Realm of Responsibility: A Conversation with Toni Morrison." With Marsha Darling. *The Women's Review of Books*. March 1988: 5–6.

Robinson, Douglas. *American Apocalypses; The Image of the End of the World in Literature*. Baltimore: The Johns Hopkins University Press, 1985.

Russell, D.S. *Apocalyptic: Ancient and Modern*. Philadelphia: Fortress Press, 1968.

Sekora, John. "Is the Slave Narrative a Species of Autobiography?" *Studies in Autobiography*. Ed. James Olney. New York: Oxford University Press, 1988. 99–111.

Stepto, Robert B. *From Behind the Veil: A Study of Afro-American Narrative*. Urbana: Urbana: University of Illinois Press, 1979.

Walters, Colin. "A Ghostly, Terrifying Tale of Lives in Slavery." *Insight* 12 October 1987: 60–61.

Wiesel, Elie. "Art and the Holocaust: Trivializing Memory." *New York Times*. June 11, 1989, eastern ed., sec. 2: 1+ 38.

Willis, Susan. "Black Women Writers: Taking a Critical Perspective." *Making A Difference; Feminist Literary Criticism*. Edited by Gayle Greene and Coppelia Kahn. New York: Methuen, 1985.

Zamora, Lois Parkinson. *Writing the Apocalypse; Historical Vision in Contemporary U.S. and Latin American Fiction.* New York: Cambridge University Press, 1989.

Fleshly Ghosts and Ghostly Flesh: The Word and the Body in *Beloved*

David Lawrence

In William Faulkner's *Light in August*, Byron Bunch reflects that no matter how much a person might "talk about how he'd like to escape from living folks . . . it's the dead folks that do him the damage."[1] The damage done by dead folks in Toni Morrison's *Beloved* points to the central position accorded to memory, the place where these dead folks are kept alive, in this novel of futile forgetting and persistent remembrance. Operating independently of the conscious will, memory is shown to be an active, constitutive force that has the power to construct and circumscribe identity, both individual and collective, in the image of its own contents. Sethe's "rememory," in giving substance to her murdered daughter and to the painful past, casts its spell over the entire community, drawing the members of that community into one person's struggle with the torments of a history that refuses to die.

In portraying the capacity of the past to haunt individual and community life in the present, *Beloved* brings into daylight the "ghosts" that are harbored by memory and that hold their "hosts" in thrall, tyrannically dictating thought, emotion, and action. The stories of the tightly woven network of characters culminate in a ritualistic sacrifice of Beloved, a ceremony that frees the community from this pervasive haunting. The supernatural existence of Beloved, who acts as a scapegoat for the evils of the past, threatens the naturalized set of inherited codes by which the community defines itself. The climactic scene shows how a culture may find it necessary in a moment of crisis to exorcise its own demons in order to reaffirm its identity.

Morrison first exposes, however, the workings of the internal mechanisms that have generated the need for exorcism in the first place. A deeply encoded rejection of the body drives the highly pressurized haunting in *Beloved*. The black community of Cincinnati is caught in a cycle of self-denial, a suffocating repression of fundamental bodily needs and wants. The inability to articulate such embodied experience, to find a text for the desiring body within communal codes, obstructs self-knowledge and does violence to the fabric of community. Woven into the dense texture of the novel, into what Morrison has called the "subliminal, the underground life of a novel,"[2] the interaction of language and body underlies the collective confrontation with the ghosts of memory. In her representation of this psychic battle, Morrison fashions word and flesh as intimate allies in the project of constructing a domain in which body and spirit may thrive. The exorcism of Beloved, an embodiment of resurgent desire, opens the way to a rewording of the codes that have enforced the silencing of the body's story, making possible a remembering of the cultural heritage that has haunted the characters so destructively. In the end, the communal body seems ready to articulate a reinvigorated language that, in returning to its roots in the body, empowers its speakers to forge a more open, inclusive community.

In a novel that examines the dehumanizing impact of slavery, one might expect that the white man, the monstrous enforcer of slavery's brutality, would haunt the black community. The haunting occurs, however, within a social structure relatively insulated from the white community and, in its most intense form, springs from the "rememory" of an ex-slave in the form of one victimized by slavery. There is nothing mysteriously threatening about whites; on the contrary, "whitefolks didn't bear speaking on. Everybody knew."[3] Of course, whites "spoke on" their slaves tirelessly, and, in the exploration of political power in the novel, ownership of body and authorship of language are shown to be insidiously linked. Under the regime of white authority, the "blackness" of the slave's body represents for "white folks" an animal savagery and moral depravity that, ironically, ends up remaking them in the image of their own fears:

Whitepeople believed that whatever the manners, under every dark skin was a jungle. Swift unnavigable waters, screaming baboons, sleeping snakes, red gums ready for sweet white blood. . . . But it wasn't the jungle blacks brought with them to this place from the other (livable) place. It was the jungle whitefolks planted in them. And it grew. It spread. In, through and after life, it spread, until it invaded the whites who had made it. . . . The screaming baboon lived under their own white skin; the red gums were their own (198–9).

This "belief," which underlies the chilling scientific rationality of School-teacher, abstracts the human corporeality of the slave into a sign for the other in the discourse of the dominant ideology. Further, such invasive signifying upon the black body generates a self-fulfilling prophecy, as blacks find themselves unable to assert an identity outside the expectations imposed upon them: "The more [colored people] used themselves up to persuade whites of something Negroes believed could not be questioned, the deeper and more tangled the jungle grew inside" (198).

In *Beloved,* the question of authority over one's own body is consistently related to that of authority over discourse; bodily and linguistic disempowerment frequently intersect. At Sweet Home, Sethe makes the ink with which Schoolteacher and his nephews define on paper her "animal characteristics"; the ink, a tool for communication produced by her own hands, is turned against her as ammunition for their "weapons" of torture, pen and paper.[4] Shocked, she asks Mrs. Garner for the definitions of "characteristics" and "features," vainly attempting to assert control over the words that have conscripted her body in a notebook (194–5). The terror she feels at seeing herself defined and divided (animal traits on the left, human on the right) concludes her list on ways whites can "dirty you so bad you forgot who you were" (251); the litany of brutality—decapitations, burnings, rapes—she provides Beloved as "reasons" for killing her ends with this bottom line: "And no one, nobody on this earth, would list her daughter's characteristics on the animal side of the paper. No. Oh no" (251).

As Stamp Paid, the community's literate newsbearer, reads about the post-Civil War violence against his people, he can "smell" the bloody brutality in the very words that attempt to communicate that violence in digestible form:

> The stench stank. Stank up off the pages of the *North Star,* out of the mouths of witnesses, etched in crooked handwriting in letters delivered by hand. Detailed in documents and petitions full of *whereas* and presented to any legal body who'd read it, it stank (180).

The primary means of entry into the realm of the written word for blacks is the atrocity that is inflicted upon them or that they inflict upon others. Looking at Sethe's picture in Stamp's newspaper clipping relating the story of Sethe's "crime," Paul D knows that "there was no way in hell a black face could appear in a newspaper if the story was about something anybody wanted to hear" (155).

Even on Sweet Home, where Garner believes he allows his slaves to be men, the power of naming remains with the white master.[5] Paul D wonders years later, "Is that where the manhood lay? In the naming done by a whiteman who was supposed to know?" (125). Of course, School-teacher, Garner's successor, destroys even this precarious sense of identity. Sethe recalls how Schoolteacher asserted his authority as "definer" after Sixo had dexterously challenged an accusation of theft. Sixo's rhetorical artistry—stealing and eating the shoat is "improving property" since such apparently transgressive behavior actually will increase his productive capacity—is futile: "Clever, but Schoolteacher beat him anyway to show that definitions belonged to the definers—not the defined" (190). Sethe tells Denver that what "tore Sixo up . . . for all time" was not the beatings but the questions that Schoolteacher asked them, presumably as part of his research into their animal nature. According to Sethe, it is the notebook Schoolteacher carries with him containing the answers that destroys Sixo, not the gunshots that eventually end his life (37).

Finally, in the first pages of the novel, Sethe remembers how she had to exchange "ten minutes" of sex with the engraver for the "one word that mattered"—Beloved (5). In order to acquire the inscribing power of the white man's chisel, she must transform her body into a commodity; he will grant the cherished script provided he first be granted the right of sexual inscription. Thus Sethe must temporarily "kill off" her own body (she lies on a headstone, "her knees wide open as the grave") to purchase the text that she thinks will buy her peace. The debt owed to her murdered daughter, however, will not be so "easily" paid.

As Sethe lies in the Clearing where her mother-in-law, Baby Suggs, used to preach the Word, she thinks about how her month of "unslaved life" made her realize that "freeing yourself was one thing; claiming ownership of that freed self was another" (95). This striving to claim ownership links Sethe's own horrifying story to the story of the entire community. Central to the pursuit of self-ownership is the articulation of a self-defining language that springs from the flesh and blood of physical experience and that gives shape to the desire so long suppressed under slavery. Baby Suggs discovers such self-definition immediately upon gaining her freedom. After she experiences the wonder of possessing her own body, of recognizing the pounding of "her own heartbeat" (141), she renames herself "Suggs" (her husband's name), forcefully rejecting Garner's uncomprehending defense of the "legal" name on her bill of sale, Jenny Whitlow. She thus begins to fill with "the roots of her tongue" (141) that "desolated center where the self that was no self made its home" (140).

Of course, it is precisely this kind of "self-generating" language that has been stifled by the mortifications of flesh endured under slavery. In defending itself against the bodily depredations of enslavement, the community has learned to choke off its capacity for pleasure and love, for the experience of jouissance. "Baby Suggs, holy," the "unchurched preacher" (87), tries to revise this legacy of self-denial in her self-loving exhortations, devoting "the roots of her tongue" to calling the Word. Eschewing such confining abstractions as sin and purity, Baby Suggs grounds her words in the earthly, sensual realm through which the body moves: "She told them that the only grace they could have was the grace they could imagine. That if they could not see it, they would not have it" (88). Rather than a divine state of being that descends from above, grace is a humanly conceived, embodied experience. In the oral text of her "sermon," which Baby Suggs draws from the powerfully felt fact of being alive within a body, "grace" is both noun and verb, a blessed touching of one's own body: "Here in this here place, we flesh; flesh that weeps, laughs; flesh that dances on bare feet in grass. Love it. Love it hard . . . grace it, stroke it, and hold it up" (88). In this open-ended, organic religion, Baby Suggs taps a bodily "organ music," imploring her listeners to love their "dark, dark liver" and "life-giving parts" (88–9). And when her words cease, Sethe recalls, she "danced with her twisted hip the rest of what her heart had to say while the others opened their mouths and gave her the music" (89). Using her own disfigured body as an instrument, Baby Suggs talks through dance to find the language adequate to the demands of their bodies: "Long notes held until the four-part harmony was perfect enough for their deeply loved flesh" (89). Her speech, both literally and metaphorically, comes from her "big old heart," providing a kind of scaffolding for the reconstitution of the damaged communal body. The members of the community must put themselves back together—re-member themselves—so that they can remember that the heart "is the prize" (89).

Sethe recalls how this "fixing ceremony" (86) had begun the work of asserting self-defined ownership: "Bit by bit . . . along with the others, she had claimed herself" (95). But the unwritten codes of the community cannot yet entirely accommodate such joyous self-celebration. After Baby Suggs hosts a spontaneous feast to mark the arrival of her daughter-in-law, the community finds itself resenting what they perceive as her prideful behavior. She has crossed the boundary of permissible pleasure: "Her friends and neighbors were angry at her because she had overstepped, given too much, offended them by excess" (138). Her former guests transfer their self-despising outrage at the poverty of their own lives onto the person who dares to dispense such a rare commodity as love with "reckless generosity": "Loaves and fishes were His powers—they didn't belong to an ex-slave" (137). Ironically, the communal voice that Baby Suggs "hears" the morning after the feast plays, in effect, the role of the white master by reprimanding the "slave" who has violated the code of acceptable behavior. The oppression enforced by slaveowners is now perpetuated by the oppressed themselves. As a unit, the community itself remains an "ex-slave," unable to define itself outside the parameters of the slave experience.

To be sure, Morrison makes it clear that under slavery the self-imposed prohibition on "reckless generosity" worked as a necessary survival strategy, an indispensable means of self-defense. Paul D learned "to love just a little bit; everything just a little bit, so when they broke its back, or shoved it in a croker sack, well, maybe you'd have a little left over for the next one" (45). Loving "big," according to Paul D, "would split you wide open," so "you protected yourself and loved small" (162). On the chain gang in Alfred, Georgia, Paul D and the men vent their rage in songs, fictions that permit them to act out through their labor their desire to "kill the boss" as well as "the flirt whom folks called Life for leading them on" (109). But this life-killing strategy of self-defense has become, after slavery, a deadly form of self-destruction. Listening to Sethe's own story of desperate self-defense (her "explanation" of why she had to kill her children in order to protect them), Paul D reflects upon the need to find a space for uninhibited love: "To get to a place where you could love anything you chose—not to need permission for desire—well now, that was freedom" (162). Freed from slavery, the community must now learn to permit itself the freedom to desire. The denial of this permission to Baby Suggs, apparently an act of collective self-assertion only implicates the community in Sethe's self-destructive defense of her own flesh and blood. Because her neighbors are furious at Baby Suggs' presumption, they do not send someone to warn her of Schoolteacher's approach, a warning which might have prevented the slaughter of one of their own by one of their own.

Having moved from "the center of things" (137) to the margins of the community, 124 is haunted, its residents three phantoms (after Sethe's sons run away) and a ghost. Baby Suggs, her heart "collapsed" and her voice silenced, spends the last eight years of her life contemplating the colors on her quilt. Sethe devotes herself to beating back the past that is "still waiting" (44) for Denver, who goes deaf rather than remember the dark time she spent with her mother in prison (104). They lead sterile, isolated lives, the ghost the only member of the family who seeks the intimacy of physical contact.

But Paul D's arrival eighteen years after "the Misery" (171) disturbs the unhealthy equilibrium at 124. In evicting the ghost and touching Sethe, he initiates the process of articulating "word-shapes" (99) for the past that still imprisons them. The marks of violence and humiliation must be "read," translated into a shared understanding, before that body language called by Baby Suggs in the Clearing can be rediscovered and respoken. With instinctive compassion, Paul D goes straight to the source to learn of Sethe's suffering, the network of scars inscribed by Schoolteacher's nephews that has numbed her entire back: "He rubbed his cheek on her back, and learned that way her sorrow, the roots of it, its wide trunk and intricate branches" (17). The sexual union that allows Sethe to "feel the hurt her back ought to" (18) also brings about a psychic union; they silently recall, in tandem, the safe memory of love at Sweet Home. Morrison's narrator creates seamless transitions between their separate but simultaneous memories of Sethe and Halle's first lovemaking in the cornfield. The recollection culminates in the shared trope for sexual arousal and fulfillment expressed in the husked corn: "How loose the silk. How quick the jailed-up flavor ran free" (27). This convergence of sexuality, memory, and poetic figure beautifully illustrates the intimate communion of linguistic and bodily experience enacted in the text of the novel.

As Sethe and Paul D "make talk" (20), what had previously been "unspeakable" begins to be speakable: "Her story was bearable because it was his as well—to tell, to refine and tell again. The things neither knew about the other—the things neither had word-shapes for" (99). In his presence, Sethe rediscovers her own capacity for bodily sensation and reestablishes contact with the outside world that induces such sensation: "Emotions sped to the surface in his company. Things became what they were. . . . Windows suddenly had view" (39). After a day spent at the carnival enjoying Paul D's gregarious companionship, Sethe allows herself to imagine that the three hand-holding shadows she observes on their return will shortly be a fully fleshed unit. The desire that Paul D stirs up, however, taps a reservoir of repressed feeling that seems to trigger Beloved's emergence from Sethe's rememory. The spoken text of their love cannot accommodate Beloved, and their storytelling intimacy is soon broken by the ghost's return in full-grown, fleshly form.

Beloved acts as an embodiment of uninhibited desire, projecting a "bottomless longing" (58) for love that places impossible demands upon the human body. Her appearance at 124 fresh from the waters of the Ohio causes Sethe to run desperately for the privy to relieve the incredible pressure of her own waters, an emergency evacuation reenacting Beloved's natural birth. Her touch, "no heavier than a feather but loaded with de-sire" (58), dissolves the "tobacco tin" into which Paul D has crammed his painful, humiliating memories, moving him involuntarily from the house he thought he had claimed. She absorbs Denver's devotion only to give her more strength for consuming Sethe's love: "Sethe was licked, tasted, eaten by Beloved's eyes" (57). Her appetite is an insatiable "life hunger" (264), a "downright craving to know" (77) the life and love that was de-nied her. Like a vampire, she sucks out Sethe's vitality, fattening on her mother's futile attempts to "make her understand," to explain and justify the necessity of murdering her own child to save her from the murder of slavery.[6]

When Stamp Paid approaches the newly haunted 124, he hears "a conflagration of hasty voices" speaking a language incomprehensible save for the word *mine* (172). He senses that this is the "roaring" of "the people of the broken necks, of fire-cooked blood and black girls who had lost their ribbons" (181). Beloved magnetizes 124, attracting all that lost life now returning to lay claim to its own. The impossibility of articulating such possessive claims in an "earthly" language suggests the life-threat-ening potency of Beloved's desire. As an infant in a nineteen-year-old body, Beloved has not yet learned the codes that give shape to and control desire. Her unadulterated narcissism permits her to "seduce" her mother in the Clearing, an impulsive sensuality that probably derives from her memory of breast feeding. Here, though, the libidinal element in normal breast feeding becomes dominant, as Beloved's tender kisses entrance Sethe until she finds herself forced against the wall of the incest taboo: "You too old for that" (97–8). Beloved recognizes no social bounds, show-ing a resistance to conventional form that is registered in the disturbing "cadence" (60) of her own words. While she craves adult language, par-ticularly those stories that "construct out of the strings" of Denver and Sethe's experience "a net" to hold her (76), she is incapable of such con-struction herself.

The sections of the novel dominated by Beloved's voice reflect her lack of a socially circumscribed identity; her "word-shapes" embody her tenuous physical and psychical shape. Before she finds "the join" with Sethe that enables her to escape the "dark place" (210-13), her "units" of self-representation are fragmented memories, word-pictures, and sensations, articulated without clearly established frames of reference- inside and outside, past and present, cause and effect. Even the gaps on the printed page suggest the danger of the disintegration of her being.[7] After she assumes physical form (214–17), her self-projection in language integrates itself syntactically but continues to obfuscate the boundary between self and other; Beloved's image of her mother's face—"She smiles at me and it is my own face smiling" (214)—suggests her inability to distinguish her own body from that of her mother.

At the end of the sections expressing the "unspeakable thoughts, unspoken" of "the women of 124" (199), the voices of Sethe, Denver, and Beloved merge into a single chorus that effaces individual identity in a possessive love sounded by the refrain

> You are mine
> You are mine
> You are mine. (217)

The fusion of identity expressed in this refrain can only be destructive, as Sethe and Denver lose themselves in the overpowering "mine" asserted by Beloved. In the end, their "conversation" is a monologic discourse dictated by a fleshly ghost, a univocal tyranny silencing any attempt at dialogic communication. In her insistence on absolute possession of her mother, Beloved resurrects the slavemaster's monopoly over both word and body, enforcing the internalized enslavement that has become a legacy of institutionalized slavery.[8]

In order to free itself of the haunting past embodied in 124, the community must tap a deeper level of language, a more primitive source of cultural experience that creates communal bonds rather than destroying them. When Paul D's chain gang rescues itself from the muck flooding their below-ground cages, it discovers this kind of instinctive communication in the chain that binds them together: "They talked through that chain like Sam Morse and, Great God, they all came up" (110). This "talking" is born out of the ooze, a pre-Genesis chaos—"All Georgia seemed to be sliding, melting away'" (111)—from which the human community is delivered. Ironically, the "best hand-forged chain in Georgia" (107) acts as a linguistic tool for forging the communal identity that enables each one of them to survive the flood. Conversely, as Paul D reflects, had just one not "heard" the message, they all would have perished. Individual and community survival are thus inseparable; the trials of one body are, in some form, the trials of everybody.

This unity of the one with the whole is reaffirmed when the townswomen, alerted by Denver, come to rescue Sethe. The community resuscitates itself by again giving voice to the power of the life-affirming language that Baby Suggs had called out in the Clearing and that now demands the complete devotion of their bodily efforts. Eighteen years ago, the community, outraged at Sethe's prideful self-possession, had turned its back to her as she rode off to prison. The narrator observes that, had Sethe not been so seemingly convinced of her rectitude, "a cape of sound would have quickly been wrapped around her, like arms to hold and steady her way. . . . As it was, they waited till the cart turned about, headed west to town. And then no words. Humming. No words at all" (152). The people withhold the support that their songs would have bodied forth, their words disdaining to touch the offending flesh. Now, however, the community, led by Ella, tries to sing Sethe back into its embrace. Like the singing of Paul D's chain gang and that of Sixo just before he is shot to death, the human voice in song is a potent material force. Sixo's song, triumphant because the Thirty-Mile Woman has escaped with his "blossoming seed," culminates in a laugh "so rippling and full of glee it put out the fire" (229).

But when the women's singing prayer does not have the power to make contact with the "roaring" around 124, they must go all the way back to the first page of the text in their collective memory: "In the beginning was the sound, and they all knew what the sound sounded like" (259). This familiar, original sound precedes and overwhelms words,[9] revitalizing Sethe's body and allowing her to break the lock Beloved has had upon her:

> For Sethe it was as though the Clearing had come to her with all its heat and simmering leaves, where the voices of women searched for the right combination, the key, the code, the sound that broke the back of words. Building voice upon voice until they found it, and when they did it was a wave of sound wide enough to sound

deep water and knock the pods off chestnut trees. It broke over
Sethe and she trembled like the baptized in its wash. (261)

This preverbal language seems to flex its muscles as it bursts forth from
the deepest roots of human knowing, tapped by the "building" of a chorus of individual voices. Unleashed, Sethe rushes toward Bodwin (mis-
taking him for Schoolteacher) with ice pick raised, her body partially
transformed into the shape of the weapon she must use to protect her
daughter: "The ice pick is not in her hand; it is her hand" (262). But the
reconstituted community intervenes, absorbing her in what Beloved sees
as a "hill of black people falling (262). Now that Sethe and Denver have
both reentered the communal fold, Beloved senses she has been left behind "Alone. Again" (262), and the "devil-child" (261) vanishes.

In the aftermath of her baptism, though, Sethe is devastated, her "best
thing" taken from her a second time. She has taken a crucial step towards
self-ownership in directing her protective violence against the oppressor
(Schoolteacher in the form of Bodwin) instead of against her own flesh
and blood, but, alone, she cannot recuperate from the tragic repetition of
her loss. To open the way to such recuperation, Paul D's own story of
self-recovery is reunited with Sethe's. After he first leaves 124, ostensibly in horror at the news of Sethe's murderous past, he retreats into isolation, drinking alone in the cold church.[10] When Stamp Paid visits him,
Paul D resists his attempts to humanize Sethe's actions. But when Stamp
asks whether he might have been "run off" 124 by Beloved, not Sethe, he
is shocked into recognizing that his condemnation of Sethe's shameful
act actually covered his own shame at his emasculation in Beloved's company (234–5). Now, returning to 124 to check on Sethe, he recalls his
peculiar lovemaking with Beloved:

> Coupling with her wasn't even fun. It was more like the brainless
> urge to stay alive. Each time she came, pulled up her skirts, a life
> hunger overwhelmed him and he had no more control over it than
> over his lungs. And afterward, beached, gobbling for air, in the
> midst of repulsion and personal shame, he was thankful too for
> having been escorted to some ocean-deep place he once belonged
> to. (264)

His gratitude suggests a recognition that his rival for Sethe's affections had actually started the work of prying open his rusty tobacco tin and restoring to him the pulse of his "red heart" (117).

Paul D must discover this "life hunger" within himself by sounding that "ocean-deep place" that the community tapped into in exorcising Beloved. To find that place "he once belonged to," he must begin drawing a "map to discover" himself (140), one charting those regions of memory that block the way to the ocean-deep self. Standing over the half-conscious Sethe, not knowing what to make of this powerful woman, he suddenly recalls how Sixo described his love for the Thirty-Mile Woman: "'She is a friend of my mind. She gather me, man. The pieces I am, she gather them and give them back to me in all the right order. It's good you know, when you got a woman who is a friend of your mind'" (273). Then, "thinking about her wrought-iron back," that map of Sethe's sorrow and suffering, he remembers a moment that previously had been "packed away" in his tobacco tin:

> The mean black eyes. The wet dress steaming before the fire. Her tenderness about his neck jewelry—its three wands, like attentive baby rattlers, curving two feet in the air. How she never mentioned or looked at it so he did not have to feel the shame of being collared like a beast. Only this woman Sethe could have left him his manhood like that. He wants to put his story next to hers. (273)

This remembering of his haunting past is constructive rather than destructive, giving him the freedom, finally, to choose his own desire. In effect, he regains the authorship of his own text; he wants to put the story of his body, as well as the body of his story, alongside Sethe's. The next words inscribed into that text, communicated through the "holding fingers" (273) of Paul D's "educated hands" (99), begin the restoration of Sethe's own self-authorship: "You your best thing, Sethe. You are." Her wondering response, "Me? Me?," implies its own affirmation (273). Reviving her with the knowing touch of his words, Paul D rescues Sethe from mute oblivion, reconnecting her with the talking spirit of companionship and community.

In the end, Beloved again becomes one of the "disremembered and unaccounted for" (274),[11] lurking in the liminal space of communal memory perhaps, but not a part of that community's consciousness. As Morrison's narrator puts it, "remembering seemed unwise," for Beloved's story "was not a story to pass on" (274–5). Her demonic "life hunger" simply cannot be encompassed within the "word-shapes" of the community's storytelling language. Provoked by Beloved's intrusion, the neighborhood has widened the circle of community to reincorporate Sethe and 124, but that circle must exclude the unassimilable otherness of Beloved.

Having accomplished its spontaneous "fixing ceremony" (86), the kind Baby Suggs had led in the Clearing, the community is free to lay down "the heavy knives of defense against misery, regret, gall, and hurt" (86), those weapons of self-defense that had turned against them as weapons of self-denial and self-destruction. Morrison has commented on the need for the novel as a way of dispensing "new information": "It should have something in it that enlightens; something in it that opens the doors and points the way. Something in it that suggests what the conflicts are, what the problems are. But it need not solve those problems because it is not a case study, it is not a recipe."[12] In *Beloved,* Morrison suggests a way through the door of memory, even if that way entails a precarious balancing act between the danger of forgetting a past that should not be forgotten and of remembering a past that threatens to engulf the present. While the painful heritage of slavery cannot simply "pass on," cannot die away (to use another meaning suggested by that ambiguous phrase), enslavement to that heritage, Morrison implies, must "pass on," must die away, in order to undertake the task of re-membering and re-articulating the individual and the communal body.

NOTES

1. William Faulkner, *Light in August* (New York: Vintage Books, 1987), p.81.

2. Toni Morrison, "Unspeakable Things Unspoken: The Afro-American Presence in American Literature,"*MQR,* 28 (1989), 32.

3. Toni Morrison, *Beloved*. (New York: Alfred A. Knopf, 1987), p. 53. Subsequent page references are cited parenthetically in the text.

4. In her analysis of the slave mother's role as reproducer in and of the slave system, Anne E. Goldman points out the "conflation between reproduction and literary production" in schoolteacher's use of Sethe's ink to record the taking of her milk by his nephews: his "gaze collapses Sethe's milky maternal product into the inky literary one. . . ." See Anne E. Goldman. "'I Made the Ink': (Literary) Production and Reproduction in *Dessa Rose* and *Beloved*," *FSt*, 16 (1990), 324.

5. Cynthia Davis asserts that "power for Morrison is largely the power to name to define reality and perception." See "Self, Society, and Myth in Toni Morrison's Fiction," *ConL*, 23 (1982), 323.

6. Likening Sethe to a "Greek protagonist faced with a tragic dilemma," Terry Otten argues that the "moral authority" of the novel "resides less in a revelation of the obvious horrors of slavery than in a revelation of slavery's nefarious ability to invert moral categories and behavior and to impose tragic choice." See *The Crime of Innocence in the Fiction of Toni Morrison* (Columbia: Univ. of Missouri Press, 1989), pp. 82–3.

7. Deborah Horvitz identifies the way in which Beloved's voice in these sections works as a kind of collective voice for all those women who suffered on slave ships, asserting that Beloved's "sickening fear of her body exploding, dissolving, or being chewed up and spit out links each enslaved Beloved with her sister in captivity." See "Nameless Ghosts: Possession and Dispossession in *Beloved*," *SAF*, 17 (1989), 164.

8. Similarly, Deborah Horvitz suggests that the possessiveness inherent in this tortured mother-daughter relationship is "reminiscent of the slave-master relationship." See "Nameless Ghosts," 161.

9. Missy Dehn Kubitschek argues that "the beginning" the women go back to "revoices not only God's creation of the world in Genesis but women's creation of other life, the sounds accompanying birth." See *Claiming the Heritage: African-American Women Novelists and History* (Jackson: University Press of Mississippi, 1991), p. 171. While it is true that the bodily experience of women seems more closely tied to the articulation of this powerful "feminine" voice, it should also be remembered that the men of the community are equal participants in Baby Suggs' calling in the Clearing. Such communion between the sexes is consistent with the sense of community expressed in the novel: that "to belong to a community of other free Negroes" means to love and be loved by them, "to counsel and be counseled, protect and be protected, feed and be fed" (177).

10. The church and its minister are otherwise absent in the novel, supplanted by the more organic religious rites inspired by Baby Suggs in the natural setting of the Clearing. The freedom from the physical restrictions of being "indoors" permits the "deeply loved flesh" of the "congregation" to respond more intensely

and uninhabitedly to the emotions elicited by Baby Suggs' calling. Further, in stripping this ceremony of Western convention, Morrison emphasizes the importance of remembering the religion that had been practiced in Africa and carried to America. Thus the fleeing Sethe instinctively draws on her memory of the "antelope dance," in which the men and the women "shifted shapes and became something other," to get her body and the "little antelope" stomping inside of it to the point where Amy rescues her (30–1).

11. Deborah Horvitz connects Beloved's fate to that of "those African women who did not survive the Middle Passage," glossing "disremembered" as "meaning not only that they are forgotten, but also that they are dismembered, cut up and off, and not remembered." See "Nameless Ghosts," 165.

12. See Toni Morrison, "Rootedness: The Ancestor as Foundation," in *Black Women Writers (1950–1980)*, edited by Mari Evans (New York: Doubleday, 1983), p. 341.

Margaret Atwood and Toni Morrison: Reflections on Postmodernism and the Study of Religion and Literature

Ann-Janine Morey

Born in the 1940s and flourishing by the sixties, the specialty study first called "literature and theology," or "Christianity and literature," and later "religion and literature," flourished as a small but vigorous academic endeavor through the mid-seventies, but has since suffered a decline.[1] I am not attempting an historical review of the field, nor am I trying to offer a comprehensive assessment of causes and probabilities.[2] Rather, I am in this essay illustrating and discussing *one* significant reason why the field of religion and literature is in difficulty: the marginalization of women's fiction from the study of religion and literature.[3] Both the content and the fact of women's writing is threatening to the study of religion and literature as it has been traditionally articulated. Using Margaret Atwood's *Surfacing* and Toni Morrison's *Beloved* to model the terms for discussion, I explore the inadmissible *content* of women's writing as it is situated relative to postmodernism and the practice of religion and literature. I conclude from this discussion that even the *fact* of women's writing is threatening to traditional religion and literature study. Women's narratives propose a determined disruption of conventional intellectual and religious norms. Finally, I close with a brief reflection on the challenge for religion and literature as we continue to reconceptualize our task.

I

Although much is often made of the shift from modernism to postmodernism, both descriptors engage a fairly traditional theological view of the universe, as I argue in the second half of this essay. Not surprisingly, women's narratives have been ignored in the formulation of such cultural-analytic categories, are not easily classified as "modern" or "postmodern," and so are often dismissed as irrelevant to the literary mainstream. Rita Felski and Molly Hite both argue that women's writing stands outside the consideration of most postmodern theory because women do not value stylistic experimentation as the best expression of women's concerns, and what is hailed by the androcentric establishment as "innovative" or "radical" may be largely irrelevant to women writing. Nonetheless, no matter what genre and critical label we give it (metafiction, realism, magical realism, postmodernism), we find that the content of women's writing (which may or may not employ stylistic experimentation) offers a radical challenge to conventional canonical universes. Contemporary women's writing makes knowing use of the metaphoric duplicity of language in order to dissolve (without entirely destroying) the authoritative boundaries of traditional, western knowledge about meaning and the ultimate nature of things.[4] Although this is certainly a threatening move, the boundary dissolutions that are so common in women's writing represent a fictional and cultural moment of opportunity for conversation that issues a challenge with no sure or predictable conclusion.[5]

A number of contemporary women writers such as Margaret Atwood, Mary Gordon, Louise Erdrich, Toni Morrison, and Marilynne Robinson facilitate our encounter with boundary and authority by making extensive use of a common metaphor for bodily life, sexual love, time and memory, that of water. Women write about entering water willingly in order to dissolve, escape, and rethink the imprisoning boundaries governing conventional wisdom about male/female, natural/supernatural, self and other. In these fictions, the world is flooded with the awesome, indifferent finality of life promise and all that we call solid and real is seen to be of illusory solidity. Crossing the margin of normality sends the characters into a condition I call *watertime,* a confluence of time and space in which all normal boundaries are suspended, in which the gods are dislocated, or redefined by an underwater perspective without necessarily being abolished or denied.[6] In so doing, the writer affirms the ambiguous structures of representation, preserving a rare moment of cultural flexibility, a textually created space inhabited by both hope and warning about the powers of language.

Margaret Atwood's *Surfacing* [7] and Toni Morrison's *Beloved* are examples of how women's fiction is shaped around a watertime knowledge that threatens the boundaries of traditionally represented (religious) reality. While the unnamed narrator of *Surfacing* enters water, Sethe in *Beloved* is visited by water. But there is no Lethe in either novel, for although water may sometimes offer cleansing, it also represents the irrepressible fluidity of the inbreaking past, what Sethe calls "rememory." In both novels, the female characters are haunted by their children, and each mother is implicated in that loss. *Surfacing*'s narrator has had an abortion she pretends to forget, while Sethe slashes the throat of her youngest daughter to spare her child a life of slavery. In both *Surfacing* and *Beloved,* the skeletal structure of a Christian universe is exposed and partially refleshed through alternate cosmologies. Both novels draw upon an inverted Demeter and Persephone cycle in which a daughter goes looking for her mother. In *Surfacing,* once the traditional religious realities have been abandoned, the narrator's exploration of water is guided by various Native American mythologies, while *Beloved* incorporates the accents of Hindu mythology and the defiance of slave religion. Finally, both female characters find themselves in a world where language, as irresistible as the waters of rememory, is considered as an ambiguous instrument of fullness and autonomy, or damage and alienation.

In *Surfacing*, the lake is a simultaneous site of redemption and nausea, for the water that symbolizes life is also the solution of death and holds for the narrator the memory and knowledge of two important deaths, her father and her fetus. One of the familiar pivotal scenes in *Surfacing* occurs when the narrator dives into the lake near her parent's wilderness cabin and discovers the drifting corpse of her missing father, an event which also plunges her into her repressed memory about her abortion. Most commentary focuses upon this spectacular entrance into water, because that dive into the lake initiates her separation from the "normal" world and opens to her a mysterious world of alternative power. But this action is not completed until her literal dive into lake water in search of her father is connected with a metaphorical plunge in search of her mother. After discovering the body of her father, and after her friends have departed, the narrator returns to the cabin and lies down next to her mother's jacket whose leather smell is that of "loss irrecoverable," and as she tries not to think about this loss, the rain begins, "sound of an avalanche surrounding. I feel the lake rising, up over the shore and the hill, the trees toppling into it like sand collapsing, roots overturned, the house unmoored and floating like a boat, rocking and rocking" (207–8). This long-delayed plunge into her grieving love for her mother is the entrance that concludes her passage from the visible world of firm earth to the felt world of natural transience. From here on she belongs to watertime.

In *Beloved,* as in *Surfacing,* water or fluidity, representing the simultaneity of life and death, danger and redemption, overwhelms conventional realistic notions of the proper boundaries between physical/metaphysical and natural/supernatural. Thus, *Beloved* is filled with sacred fluids—milk, blood, and water—which finally are indistinguishable as they course through the beating heart that is the center of the novel. "The dragon swam the Ohio at will," and on these perilous banks Sethe's second daughter, Denver, is born and then nearly drowns in her mother's blood commingled with the Klan-infested river water (66). Later, Denver is suckled at Sethe's bloody breast—taking in with her mother's milk the blood of the infant Sethe has just murdered. Like Kali, Sethe has devoured her child, and then her lost child returns to devour her. Sethe tries to live as though she has put grieving behind her, but she is engulfed by her suppressed water world when one day "a fully dressed woman walked out of the water" (50). Sethe's first sign of ontological slippage is most prosaic. Just as the enigmatic young woman approaches, Sethe has an unmanageable urge to urinate, for "there was no stopping water breaking from a breaking womb and there was no stopping now" (51). Once a baby poltergeist in Sethe's lonely house, an annoying but acceptable manifestation of other world, Beloved violates conventional wisdom about how ghosts are supposed to act by appearing in the flesh. As an outraged neighbor says, "a little communication between the two worlds" is to be respected, but "this was an invasion" (257). From the moment Beloved appears as an embodied memory, Sethe is steadily and willingly sucked into the voracious demands of the personal and historical memory pool brought from the suppressed other side. Sethe, too, now belongs to watertime.

In both novels, then, entering water or being invaded by fluidity exposes the illusory objectivity of "reality" as the backwash of the past arrives to claim all present and future in the name of spiritual honesty. Moreover, the relentless water pressure submerges the conventions of western Christianity without necessarily establishing any alternative utopic promises. In *Surfacing* and *Beloved*, as with many other women's narratives, Christ and Christianity are not denied or erased but rather displaced and relocated by being washed clean of transcendent pretense. Jesus can be seen as just one of the gods in a world of transience and uncertainty.

Her father has tried to protect her from the "distortions" of Christianity, teaching her that Jesus was an historical figure and God a superstition, so the narrator in *Surfacing* knows Jesus only as an "alien god" (11) whom she associates with the severed extremities of church history (26), or the "desperate beggar's whine" of sexual incantation—"Jesus jesus Oh yes please jesus" (95). In Sunday School, she gets a picture of Jesus, "alive and draped in a bedsheet, tired-looking, surely incapable of miracles" (60). As her logical father has so reasonably pointed out to her, people may sing about resurrection, but they "are not onions. . . . they stay under" (122). She finds nothing in her experience to refute his ideas about Christian efficacy, and in her time of spiritual crisis she knows instinctively that there is no power in the "bland oleo-tinted Jesus" (170), and she must turn somewhere else for sacred assistance.

But she does not leave Christianity behind. Rather, she weaves her version of the Jesus story back into the natural fiber of physically defined existence. She associates a slaughtered heron "hanging wrecked from the tree" with Christ, for both are desecrated by a gratuitous death at the hands of profane humanity. And she decides that "whether it died willingly, consented, whether Christ died willingly, anything that suffers and dies instead of us is Christ . . ." (164). Thus the dead heron functions as a Christ symbol, weaving together two old stories, one about the successive rhythms of natural life, the other about sacrificial death in the name of eternal life. But, given the dissolved boundaries of the novel, there is reciprocity in the image, for in deciding that "anything that suffers and dies instead of us is Christ, if they didn't kill birds and fish they would have killed us," she puts Christ in line with any number of natural, sacrificial victims. The heron is a Christ symbol, but Christ is also a heron symbol. He's just one of the gods, taking definition from the world which has given him birth rather than the transcendent way around, just one more destructible and receding deity. In the exchange, the Christian word does not stand apart from the world of history, pronouncing, guiding, or judging but rather speaks only in dislocated and re-shaped fragments from within the newly flooded "real."

Similarly, in *Beloved,* Sethe's mother-in-law, Baby Suggs, is a Christ symbol. She makes a feast with blackberries that taste so good that "to eat them was like being in church," and her feast expands like loaves and fishes to feed the entire neighborhood. She operates a safe house for escaped slaves, gives advice, heals the sick, preaches from the center of the ring shout; she is holy. But despite the scriptural parallels between Baby Suggs and Jesus, the same reciprocity operates between Jesus and Baby Suggs as between Christ and the heron. Jesus is a Baby Suggs symbol, for her claim to authentic word and her judgment on scriptural efficacy are the authoritative perspective by which sacrality is measured. Where conventional Christian teaching—and especially that promulgated by white slaver owners—violates human dignity, Baby Suggs replaces it with her own life-giving word, advising the freed slaves in ecstatic outdoor preaching, singing and dancing to obey the sacred call to self and bodily love:

> She did not tell them to clean up their lives or to go and sin no more. She did not tell them they were the blessed of the earth, its inheriting meek or its glorybound pure.
>
> She told them the only grace they could have was the grace they could imagine. That if they could not see it, they would not have it. (88)

She calls them to love their bodies and names each part, for Baby Suggs, like all enslaved peoples, knows about the lethality of the disembodied W/word, and she rightfully reclaims holiness from within history and physical, loving life. No Christian Jesus and no Christian God can presume to judge her or her people; rather, she supersedes the first Jesus-word as a latter day judgment upon Christianity, for lurking behind her deliberately embodied preaching is the most devastating ghost of all: white Christian rationalization about slavery.

But like any prophet who can gain no respect in her own hometown, Baby Suggs suffers the wrath of her neighbors, who grow jealous of her spiritual generosity, and they betray her by allowing Schoolteacher, Sethe's slave master, to approach Baby Sugg's sheltering house without warning. When Sethe sees the approaching party, she hustles her children into the woodshed to kill them and succeeds in dispatching her infant daughter before Baby Suggs and Stamp Paid can intercede. Devastated by that tragedy and its years of haunting, and embarrassed by the failure of Christian promise, Baby Suggs relinquishes all claim to holy word and takes to her bed to think about color.

All language is on trial in watertime, not just traditional religious language. The narrator of *Surfacing* knows language to be meaningless, except as the enabling surgical instrumentality that divides and amputates human from natural, mind from body, and man from woman. This use of amputating language she associates specifically with males or those she also labels as "humans," or "Americans." As she listens to a companion, David, chortling about "split beaver" and "cunt," she swiftly associates the linguistic violence of scatological language with its acting out in literal violence against nature and against women. "A part of the body, a dead animal. I wondered what part of them the heron was, that they needed too much to kill it," she says, correctly identifying the body loathing and self-hatred implicit in gratuitous male predation. Later, having gleefully taken pictures of the mutilated heron, David bullies his wife, Anna, into taking off her clothes so he can take pictures of her. "You'll go in beside the dead bird" (157) he says, confirming her as one more male-devastated animal. Repulsed by David, but also by Anna's submission and complicity with his visual and linguistic violence, the narrator flees this "human" condition and tries to recover some sort of pre-linguistic body language. Hoping she is newly impregnated by her lover, she imagines her unborn child as a god with shining fur, saying "I will never teach it any words" (193).

In women's fiction, the brutality of language is a physical event, giving new meaning to any literary critical notion of "symbolic" action. "My throat constricts, as it learned to do when I discovered people could say words that would go into my ears meaning nothing," reports *Surfacing*'s narrator at the beginning of her journey. Later, she trusts only her physical communication with her lover and finally tries to abandon language altogether. Similarly, Sethe's daughter, Denver, goes deaf for several years, having encountered words "that would close your ears shut" (243). Sethe is driven to infanticide by Schoolteacher's lists of words dividing human from animal qualities, a list which also separates white from black. This, she wants to tell Beloved, was far worse than dying, "that anybody white could take your whole self for anything that came to mind. Not just work, kill or maim you, but dirty you. Dirty you so bad you couldn't like yourself any more. Dirty you so bad you forgot who you were and couldn't think it up. . . . And no one, nobody on this earth would list her daughter's characteristics on the animal side of the paper" as Schoolteacher had listed hers (251). Sethe sends her child to the other side, where she fully intended to join her, in protection against this dehumanizing devastation by enemy language.

The writing of *Beloved*, of course, affirms the integrity of black story telling against the presence of linguistic terrorism, but the novel itself actually submerges the ambiguously regarded "master" tongue by suggesting how much meaning may reside in non-verbal communication. Sethe has rememories of her mother in a language she can no longer remember, in "words which would never come back. But the message— that was and had been there all along," and she "picks meaning out of a code she no longer understood" (62). When the women gather in Sethe's yard to exorcise Beloved, first they pray, and then they leave words altogether and take "a step back to the beginning. In the beginning there were no words. In the beginning was the sound, and they all knew what that sound looked like" (259). They are making a tidal wave of sacred sound, finding

> the right combination, the key, the code, the sound that broke the back of words. Building voice upon voice until they found it, and when they did it was a wave of sound wide enough to sound deep water and knock the pods off chestnut trees. It broke over Sethe and she trembled like the baptized in its wash. (261)

In *Beloved,* the characters may *feel* a different tongue, and meaning, both holy and ordinary, can outwit the depredations of the master tongue through authentic physical life. Sethe's lover, Paul D, accepts and learns her story first by putting his cheek against her scarred-up back. Then the ear of his mouth touches every ridge and branch of wounded flesh, and in this way he hears her sorrow, "the roots of it; its wide trunk and intricate branches" (17). When he returns to her, he does so because "he wants to put his story next to hers" (273).

Although the act of writing each novel claims the power of word, clearly, both novelists keep before us the reasons why disenfranchised voices must dislocate the "master" tongue. Indeed, both novels fill in the failure of language with the efficacy of touch or wordless sound, a form of representation which evades verbal signification while affirming the subtle speech of the loving, physical body. The charge to white people is the same as the charge to all men—that language has literally devastating capacities, and language that can be used as an instrument of domination and degradation can never be used uncritically or thoughtlessly again, lest the user forfeit his or her own claim to human consideration.

II

Religion and literature study foregrounds the soul of all literary study; indeed, as Terry Eagleton and Gerald Graff both point out, the academic study of literature was founded upon and later supplanted a religious vision of creation and meaning (Eagleton 22–30; Graff 24–5). Clearly, then, the issue of goodness, meta/physical danger and linguistic integrity pronounced by women's fiction and feminist criticism should be central to religion and literature study and ongoing conversations about postmodernism. As we have seen, however, the content of women's fiction threatens the verities of traditionalist world views. A brief examination of modernist and postmodernist thought will further clarify why the fact of women's writing is as offensive to the conventionally postured academic as is the content.

Religion and literature study flourished during the literary and academic period now identified as postmodern, but the foundational scholars in the field were shaped by modernist sensibilities and concerns.[8] Until recently, religion and literature study largely ignored postmodern discourse, although in many ways, postmodernism completes and depends upon modernist concerns. Where modernism is ironic, postmodernism is parodic. Where modernism relies upon a subtextual sense of coherence despite experimental narrative structure, postmodernism challenges an assurance of representational coherence at every possible level. Thus, where modernism expresses teleological anxiety through the use of open endings and self-referential narrative experiment, postmodernism pushes that anxiety to its limits, using multiple endings, false endings, narrative labyrinths, and "kitty-litter" (McHale, 151) litanies in a final effort to abolish any false sense of order. What in modernism is "intractable epistemological uncertainty" becomes in postmodernism "ontological plurality or instability: push epistemological questions far enough and they 'tip over' into ontological questions" (McHale, 11). Finally, despite the modernist suspicion that order is an artistic, human construct, modernism does not relinquish a basic theocentrism, for although the modernist mind fears that God has dropped out of view, there remains a sense, however faint, that some sort of objectively coherent world view still exists. Here is where postmodernism pushes religion and literature study beyond acceptable modernist limits, for most religion and literature scholarship has long staked its identity on a traditional Christian cosmos and assumes a meaningful connection between God and language about God. In contrast, the postmodern attack on mimesis jeopardizes all such representational assurance, suggesting that the "realistic" novel has never been concerned with "real" experience but rather with our human constructions of raw experience, constructions built of language which inevitably will betray us. With its free-wheeling skepticism about representation and language, postmodern literature about literature posts a serious challenge to old order and cultural authority. At stake is the representational transparency of language, the possibility of an objectively obtained truth, and the meaningful presence of self, author, and even God.[9]

Naturally, such an agenda would not be immediately appealing to a traditionally inspired study of religion and literature. Yet the irony of postmodern literary radicalism and the subsequent efforts by some religion and literature scholars to repel these innovations is that if we continue to bracket feminist postmodernism (as I've been doing by and large in my general survey of postmodernism), we see that postmodern discourse is not as hostile to traditional literary and religious outlooks as might appear. If God ever disappeared in the postmodern carnival, "he" was replaced by postmodern authors, who have been obsessed enough with resuming the guise of God to "sacrifice novelistic illusion for the sake of asserting their 'authority' in the most basic sense, their mastery over the fictional world, their ontological superiority as authors. . . . The postmodern author arrogates to himself the powers that gods have always claimed: omnipotence, omniscience" (McHale, 210).

Furthermore, some postmodern literary practice suggests, at least by example if not directly, that secular literary texts might be an alternative, or at least partner, to biblical inspiration. Commenting on the quasiscriptual protections built up around postmodern literature, Rita Felski notes that the profound critical and literary fascination with theory that has so much defined postmodernism has also served to mystify the text "as an esoteric site of subversion" such that "'in a way analogous to religion, the work of art alludes mysteriously to a superior but now essentially opaque and unknowable order'" (Felski, 158).[10] What we must not lose sight of is the intrinsic connection between the human and divine author, modeled, of course, on male deity. This is still a universe in which male persons claim the exclusive privilege of creation and definition, and the usual gender constructions of traditional western literature and criticism have found a relatively undisturbed home in postmodern discourse. As Molly Hite announces, the postmodern canon is "rigidly masculinist" (12).[11]

The source of continuing inspiration for this covert embrace of the androcentric status quo in Western literary traditions is Jewish-Christian monotheism. "Let us note," Julia Kristeva says, "that by establishing itself as the principle of a symbolic, paternal community in the grip of the superego, beyond all ethnic considerations, beliefs or social loyalties, monotheism represses, along with paganism, the greater part of agrarian civilizations and their ideologies, women and mothers" (1986a: 141). Just as traditional representation *and* postmodern representational defiance are dependent upon the absence and difference of which the m/other is the sign, this principle of sexual difference wherein one sex is necessarily silenced in order to guarantee (l)awful speech for the other, is intrinsic to

Christianity. Thus, the reappearance of divine authority as the white male postmodern author is not a very daring transfiguration and not a very far step from traditional literary and religious universes.

At this point, however, we must release postmodernism from an artificial captivity to monolithic definition. Although what I am about to suggest also simplifies the reality of postmodern thought, it might be helpful to think of postmodernism in at least two forms, an oxymoronic "traditional postmodernism" and an ambiguously situated "feminist postmodernism." The former postmodernism is "traditional" despite its experimentation with form-meaning structures, because the masculinist postmodernism I've been surveying retains its lock upon traditional Western gender constructions. When Leland Ryken complains about canonical degradation as a product of postmodernism, for example, he is complaining about feminist postmodernism, for it is feminist critical theory which has inaugurated the break-up of phallocratic literary canons, and it is feminism which has foregrounded difference as the key to discussion over representation and authority. Thus, as Kristeva argues, religion is the necessity of speaking animals to provide themselves with representation, and the women's movement is situated in "the very framework of the religious crisis of our civilization" (1986b: 208). Indeed, Alice Jardine suggests in her reading of Kristeva that predictions about the End of History or the Death of the Author may be "nothing but paranoid reactions on the part of male thinkers to the concrete changes brought about by women's massive reawakening" (9). That is, lamentations for the decentered subject, like lamentations for the displaced Word, fixate on the decentered male subject, for with Irigaray, "we can assume that any theory of the subject has always been appropriated by the 'masculine'" (1985b:133). Within this androcentric structure, postmodern discourse appropriates "woman" as the unrepresentable, the necessarily unspoken and unspeaking matrix of pre-symbolic language. As Carolyn Allen points out, "woman has so often been the object of someone else's articulation, so constructed by her culture as an object, especially an object of desire, that she has yet to speak clearly as subject. . . . It is ironic that just when postmodernism argues for a decentered subject woman is struggling socially and economically to become a subject as all" (281–2).

Not only is "woman" denied the authority of her own representation, while serving as the object of someone else's representation, she may not even have been included as a significant audience for representation. For example, in her study of white middle class women's reading groups, Elizabeth Long found her educated and articulate female respondents reading for realism, self-knowledge and morally significant characters—reading in short, within the parameters of traditional mimesis, while dismissing the products of postmodernism with its decentered and fragmented self as "incoherent" and uninteresting. Either educated reading women are too ignorant to realize that realism and referentiality are suspect, or they simply aren't interested. Does this audience count? Clearly, I am suggesting here that the female reader and writer occupy a different location relative to representation and postmodernist issues than the male reader and writer, hence the necessity of distinguishing feminist postmodernism from its traditional, masculinist variation.

Perhaps it is not surprising that it is possible to read feminist literary theory and never meet the word "postmodern," for having found themselves silenced in most postmodern discourse by phallogocentric structures, some feminist theorists have chosen to bypass postmodern discussion for more fruitful engagement elsewhere. Others argue that the usual postmodern constructs simply don't address what women do. Molly Hite talks about contemporary women's writing as a "category almost completely outside the dominant experimental movement of postmodernism" (14), although if we could consider more than certain kinds of stylistic innovation as the only definition of "experimental," we might very well see how much women writers have established an "other" side to the story. Similarly, Rita Felski defends the efficacy of feminist realism and confessional modes of fictional autobiography as the most appropriate expression of and response to women's frustrating cultural location. Although much postmodern discourse makes it sound as if language is an inescapable loop of androcentric satisfaction, other theorists have pointed out that while we may not be able to entirely undercut the essential linguistic sexism of Western speech, simply to identify how the system works is to disrupt it. Margaret Homans suggests we can follow the lead of contemporary women's fiction, which accepts the necessity for representation while undercutting the premises of representation. Thus, by "simultaneously appropriating and rejecting the dominant discourse," women's writing duplicates "the female experience that they thematize the experience of both participating in and standing outside the dominant culture" (205).

Where Felski and Hite tend to argue that women do not, by and large, write postmodern fiction *as it is usually defined*, Canadian critic Linda Hutcheon sees feminism (if not women's writing) as a shaping force of postmodernism. In fact, by prioritizing content over style, critics like Felski and Hite validate Linda Hutcheon's description of feminism *as* postmodernism by taking cognizance of difference as a cultural and biological construct without being trapped by essentialist inevitabilities. As Hutcheon describes it, both postmodernism and feminism "share a concern for power—its manifestations, its appropriations, its positioning, its consequences, its languages," and both feminism and postmodernism work to "challenge our traditional essentialized anchors in God, father, state and Man through acknowledgment of the particular and different" (1988a: 70). Postmodern fiction problematizes all notions of absolute authority by using the language of the authoritative master narrative as its own elegiac or self-mocking referent. Women's writing, along with African American and Native American writing, has been especially effective in this task, for "these are the voices whose questions of discourse and of authority and power. . . are at the heart of the postmodern enterprise in general" (1988a:16).

Hutcheon's response to postmodern anxiety about referentiality is that the metafiction of the postmodern imagination recognizes that the gap between word and experience cannot be avoided, that "we can know the real, especially the past real, only through signs, and that is not the same as wholesale substitution" (1988a: 230). Knowing this, the postmodern imagination also confronts the fact that while our agreement to representation cannot be avoided, it is an agreement which automatically legitimates certain kinds of power and knowledge over others. As Craig Owens says, "it is precisely at the legislative frontier between what can be represented and what cannot that the postmodernist operation is being staged not in order to transcend representation, but in order to expose that system of power that authorizes certain representations while blocking, prohibiting or invalidating others" (59). Postmodern fiction, in other words, does not deny representation but rather dislocates referentiality by making us self-conscious about the assumptions governing representation.[12] Those assumptions about representation—who writes it, who reads it, and who says what it means—are precisely the assumptions traditional postmodernism and religion and literature study have avoided examining.

In short, while traditional postmodernism postures about challenging conventional language and ontological structures, feminist postmodernism and women's writing actually does so. *This,* not ten thousand and one issues of literary merit or the threatened integrity of Western cultural history, is why women's fiction has been marginalized. Women's speech truly, and literally, decenters the male subject and speaker, for if a woman is speaking and writing, a man cannot be doing so in the same space. "He" is no longer the center of attention. As Joanne Frye says, "the literary dangers to patriarchal wholeness. . . originate in the woman's voice. Once the female 'I' has spoken, the subversion is begun. . ." (50).

This challenge of women's criticism and fiction to the cosmic and cultural egocentrality of man is an important reason why women's writing has been avoided by traditional postmodernist scholarship and religion and literature study. Scholars have engaged in a politics of silence, for there is little even in the way of explicit negative response with which to assess the reaction of religion and literature scholarship to feminist criticism and/or women's fiction.[13] Commenting on this form of cultural condescension, Stephen Heath says, "any discourse which fails to take account of the problem of sexual difference in its own enunciation and address will be, within a patriarchal order, precisely indifferent, a reflection of male domination" (quoted by Hutcheon, 1988a: 53). That is, androcentric academics have no intention of admitting women's speech, because to do so would require rewriting the entire religious and literary story of western civilization. God as we know "him" might truly disappear.

III

At the close of *Beloved,* Paul D. returns to help Sethe recover from the drowning waters of her past because she has done the same for him before. "The pieces I am, she gather them and give them back to me in all right order. It's good, you know, when you got a woman who is a friend of your mind" (272–3). I wish I could use this as a closing inscription, but this vision of a gendered reciprocity of representation is still unclaimable for most of us. It is more like this: At the close of *Surfacing*, the narrator watches her lover as he returns for her, and poised on the dissolved margins between what she once knew and what she does not yet know, she says—and there is my more realistic inscription—"We can no longer live in spurious peace by avoiding each other, the way it was before, we will have to begin. For us it's necessary, the intercession of words" (224).

Surely religion and literature study cannot continue to refuse this intercession of words and expect to sustain a reputable scholarly identity. The claim of different people and cultures to representation and inclusion in the empowering definitions of "culture," "Western," "human," or "religion," is undeniably difficult, and undeniably just. Any time a generalization is to be ventured, any time an expansive sense of coherence is sought after, a leveling process occurs, and difference disappears. In this essay, I am critical of the continued use of white male experience and products as universals that efface and deny other human realities, but in order to do so, I rely upon an equally challengeable universal, that of "woman." For example, the narrator of *Surfacing* tries to exorcise her past by denying "humanity," which she sees an intrinsically destructive. She tries to become an instinctively worshipful animal-person. Sethe, on the other hand, tries to exorcise the past by repudiating the imposed animality of slavery, even into death for herself and her children. She yearns for the chance to live in human dignity. The meaning of "human" and "animal," much like the meaning of "universal," depends very much upon whose perspective is invoked. Somehow we must assume some common ground of good will even as we are suspicious of unexamined claims to universalism. But how to manage this?

Susan Bordo suggests that "while it is imperative to struggle continually against racism and ethnocentrism in all its forms, it is impossible to be "politically correct," for "all ideas (no matter how "liberatory" in some contexts or for some purposes) are condemned to be haunted by a voice from the margins. . . awakening us to what has been excluded, effaced, damaged" (138). It is this kind of insight that is modeled in women's fiction. In the novels I've discussed, as well as many others, women characters encounter watertime in desperate grief and anger at the limitations of human power, at the power of human limitations. As the narrator of *Surfacing* discovers, primeval naturalism driven by the arbitrary and brutal rituals of the old gods is not a sufficiently honest response to human pain any more than blaming "Americans," men, her parents or Christianity for all the perplexities of human life. There is no easy choice, which is why the novel closes with her poised upon a critical, wavering margin, the wilderness at her back, the city of "man" before her. Waiting, watching, unsure, she knows only this:

> No gods to help me now, they're questionable once more, theoretical as Jesus. They've receded, back to the past, inside the skull, is it the same place? They'll never appear to me again, I can't afford it; from now on I'll have to live in the usual way, defining them by their absence. . . I regret them; but they give only one kind of truth, one hand. . . . No total salvation, resurrection. . . their totalitarian innocence was my own. (221)

This is a scary ontological position for anyone who is comfortable with traditional reassurances, but it should be just as admonitory for the enthusiastic feminist as the defensive Christian. In Atwood's fiction, as in most contemporary women's writing, domination of Christian interest is portrayed as archaic and tragically self-important. But Atwood does not dismantle one set of absolutisms and dualisms in order to construct another. Rather, her writing challenges us to outwit these antimonies in the name of human decency. She—and the numerous other women writing with her—urges us to consider how we are required to take responsibility for our limitations, all of us.

There is no easy solution, no miraculous rescue, and finally, no room for self-righteousness. Here is what our best contemporary fictional resources have to tell us: the mutual conversation between religious experience and literary expression cannot belong only to Christians any more than it could flourish were it colonized exclusively by feminists, Marxists or womanists. Commenting critically on separatism among lesbian critics, Carolyn Heilbrun (quoting Elizabeth Abel) argues that the "'shifting boundaries of sexual difference' must not, at any arbitrary point, be prevented from shifting" (297).[14] That, I argue, is the possibility offered to religion and literature study by women's fiction—in refusing absolutism, women's writing preserves our cultural flexibility for the hope and danger of a yet unrealized inclusiveness.

NOTES

1. In 1990 the AAR section of Arts, Literature and Religion was suspended and charged with reconstructing and revalidating its enterprise.

2. For some representative historical and definitional reviews of the field, see Comstock; Detweiler, 1978; Gunn; Hesla; Kauffman; and Magee. For a recent essay on the relationship of religion and literature to postmodernism, see Kort.

3. Although there are some scattered exceptions to this generalization (e.g., Ficken; Detweiler 1989), virtually the only pluralistic entry to the field was offered by Carol Christ a decade ago (1976, 1980, 1986), and her groundbreaking work was ignored by the religion and literature establishment. I invite my readers to verify the accuracy of this claim by perusing the national AAR program catalogues for the last fifteen years to see just how often women's fiction and feminist criticism entered the mainstream of religion and literature dialogue.

4. Brian McHale identifies the "transgressions of ontological levels or boundaries" and "vacillation between different kinds and degrees of 'reality'" as a central characteristic and purpose of postmodern fiction (232), and a number of feminist commentators have noted the fluidity and function of boundary in women's writing. for example, Chodorow; Hutcheon (1988b: esp. Ch. 5); Irigaray (1985a, 1985b); and Rubenstein. For a discussion of the use of water in some androcentric writers, see Morey (-Gaines).

5. This challenge is as pertinent to feminist ideology as to androcentrist. Women's writing does not simply discover goddesses hidden in the picture, just waiting to pop out with the "correct" reading. After all, if we mean an authentic challenge to traditional authority and its representations, feminists must be willing to challenge the tempting absolutisms of our own authority as well, and not even goddesses can be exempt from such scrutiny.

6. The dislocation of the gods is not an invention of contemporary women's fiction but rather a fulfillment of the promise of the sixties. See, for example, Miller.

7. My discussion of *Surfacing* and boundary dissolution in women's fiction is adapted from Chapter Eight of Morey.

8. For example, Cleanth Brooks, Stanley Romaine Hopper, William F. Lynch, Amos Wilder, Nathan Scott, and (of later vintage) Robert Detweiler and Wesley Kort. For historical accuracy I might also mention Sallie (TeSelle) McFague, although her work moves so decisively away from traditional religion

and literature study that she, like Carol Christ, becomes absent as a standard field reference. An informal tabulation of the modernist-inspired religion and literature canon finds these authors: Hemingway, Faulkner, Yeats, Eliot, Updike, Stevens, Bellow, Auden, Kafka, Camus, Greene, Penn Warren, Mailer, Malamud, Lawrence, Percy, and Flannery O'Connor (the only twentieth-century woman routinely admitted to the standard canon). Nathan Scott includes black authors Richard Wright and Ralph Ellison.

9. My own reading and summary of modernism and postmodernism is enhanced here by Bertens and Fokkema; Barth; Hassan (1982, 1987), Hite (1983, esp. 3–10); Lodge; and McHale.

10. Felski is quoting McBurney (100–101).

11. Among others Hite is referring explicitly to John Barth, whose discussion of postmodernism in "The Literature of Replenishment" (1984) mentions one woman, Nathalie Sarraute, among the usual fellows: Gass, Hawkes, Barthelme, Coover, Elkin, Pynchon, Vonnegut, Nabokov, Beckett, Borges, and maybe Bellow and Mailer. Ihab Hassan (1982; 1987) uses the following authors to typify postmodernism: Sade, Hemingway, Kafka, Genet, Beckett, Barth, Burroughs, Pynchon, Barthelme, Abish, Ashbery, Antin, Shepard, and R. Wilson. Brian McHale does a better job of inclusivity by mentioning Angela Carter, Brigid Brophy, Monique Wittig and Muriel Spark. His list of representative postmodernists, however, contains no women: Beckett, Robbe-Grillet, Fuentes, Nabokov, Coover, and Pynchon (11).

12. Bertens (1986) describes a similar process when he discusses "midfiction" (43).

13. Leland Ryken is the recent exception. He says the problem with the field of religion and literature is the Marxist-feminist-deconstructive-nihilist effort to dismantle the great works of our Western civilization and "give prominence to writers and works that are admittedly deficient in literary value" (27).

14. Heilbrun is quoting Elizabeth Abel.

WORKS CITED

Abel, Elizabeth, ed. *Writing and Sexual Difference*. Chicago: University of Chicago Press, 1982.

Allen, Carolyn. "Feminist Criticism and Postmodernism." In *Tracing Literary Theory*. Ed. Joseph Natoli. Urbana and Chicago: University of Illinois Press, 1987, pp. 278–305.

Atwood, Margaret. *Surfacing*. New York: Fawcett Crest, 1973.

Barth, John. *The Friday Book: Essays and Other Nonfiction*. New York: G.P. Putnam's Sons, 1984.

Bertens, Hans, and Douwe Fokkema, eds. *Approaching Postmodernism*. Amsterdam and Philadelphia: John Benjamins, 1986.

Bordo, Susan. "Feminism, Postmodernism, and Gender-Skepticism." In *Femi-

nism/Postmodernism. Edited by Linda J. Nicholson. New York and London: Routledge, 1990, pp. 133–56.

Chodorow, Nancy. *The Reproduction of Mothering: Psychoanalysis and the Sociology of Gender*. Berkeley: University of California Press, 1978.

Christ, Carol. "Feminist Studies in Religion and Literature: A Methodological Reflection." *JAAR* . 44 (1976): 317–25.

———. *Diving Deep and Surfacing: Women's Writers on Spiritual Quest*. Rev. ed. Boston: Beacon Press, 1986.

Comstock, W. Richard. "Religion, Literature and Religious Studies: A Sketch of Their Modal Connections." *Notre Dame English Journal*. 14 (Winter, 1981): 1–25.

Detweiler, Robert. "Recent Religion and Literature Scholarship." *Religious Studies Review*. 4 (April, 1978): 107–17.

———. *Breaking the Fall: Religious Readings of Contemporary Fiction*. San Francisco: Harper & Row, 1989.

Eagleton, Terry. *Literary Theory: An Introduction*. Minneapolis: University of Minnesota Press, 1983.

Felski, Rita. *Beyond Feminist Aesthetics: Feminist Literature and Social Change*. Cambridge, MA: Harvard University Press, 1989.

Ficken, Carl. *God's Story and Modern Literature: Reading Fiction in Community*. Philadelphia: Fortress Press, 1985.

Frye, Joanne S. *Living Stories, Telling Lives: Women and the Novel in Contemporary Experience*. Ann Arbor: University of Michigan Press, 1986.

Graff, Gerald. *Professing Literature: An Institutional History*. Chicago and London: University of Chicago Press, 1987.

Gunn, Giles B. *The Interpretation of Otherness: Literature, Religion and the American Imagination*. New York: Oxford University Press, 1979.

Hassan, Ihab. *The Dismemberment of Orpheus: Toward a Post-Modern Literature*. Madison: University of Wisconsin Press, 1982.

———.*The Postmodern Turn: Essays in Postmodern Theory and Culture*. Columbus: Ohio State University Press, 1987.

Heilbrun, Carolyn. "Critical Response II: A Response to *Writing and Sexual Difference*." In *Writing and Sexual Difference*. Ed. Elizabeth Abel. 1982.

Helsa, David H. "Religion and Literature: The Second Stage." *Journal of the American Academy of Religion*. 46 (1978): 181–92.

Hite, Molly. *Ideas of Order in the Novels of Thomas Pynchon*. Columbus: Ohio State University Press, 1983.

——— *The Other Side of the Story: Structures and Strategies of Contemporary Feminist Narratives*. Ithaca and London: Cornell University Press, 1989.

Homans, Margaret. "'Her Very Own Howl': The Ambiguities of Representation in Recent Women's Fiction." *Signs*. 9 (Winter, 1983): 186–205.

Hutcheon, Linda. *A Poetics of Postmodernism: History, Theory, Fiction*. New York and London: Routledge, 1988a.

———. *The Canadian Postmodern: A Study of Contemporary English-Canadian Fiction*. New York: Oxford University Press, 1988b.

Irigaray, Luce. *This Sex Which Is Not One*. Trans. Catherine Porter with Carolyn Burke. Ithaca: Cornell University Press, 1985a.

———. *Speculum of the Other Women*. Trans. Gillian Gill. Ithaca: Cornell University Press, 1985b.

Jardine, Alice. "Introduction to Julia Kristeva's 'Woman's Time.'" *Signs*. 7 (Autumn 1981): 5–12.

Kauffman, S. Bruce. "Charting a Sea Change: On the Relationships of Religion and Literature to Theology." *Journal of Religion*. 58 (October 1978): 405–27.

Kort, Wesley A. "'Religion and Literature' in Postmodernist Contexts." *JAAR*. 58 (1990): 575–88.

Kristeva, Julia. "About Chinese Women." In *The Kristeva Reader*. Ed. Toril Moi. New York: Columbia University Press, 1986a., pp. 138–59.

———. "Women's Time." In *The Kristeva Reader*. 1986b. pp. 187–213.

Lodge, David. *The Modes of Modern Writing: Metaphor, Metonymy, and the Typology of Modern Literature*. London: Edward Arnold, 1977.

Long, Elizabeth. "Women, Reading and Cultural Authority: Some Implications of the Audience Perspective in Cultural Studies." *American Quarterly*. 38 (Fall 1986): 591–612.

Magee, Rosemary. "Art, Literature and Religion: A Decade of Scholarship." *JAAR Thematic Studies*. 49 (1983): 191–7. Chico Scholars Press.

McBurney, Blaine. "The PostModernist Transvaluation of Modernist Values." *Thesis Eleven*. 12 (1985): 94–109.

McHale, Brian. *Postmodernist Fiction*. New York and London: Methuen, 1987.

Miller, David L. *The New Polytheism: Rebirth of the Gods and Goddesses*. New York and London: Harper & Row, 1974.

Morey (-Gaines), Ann-Janine. "Religion and Sexuality in Walker Percy, William Gass and John Updike: Metaphors of Embodiment in the Androcentric Imagination." *Journal of the American Academy of Religion*. 51 (1983): 595–609.

Morey, Ann-Janine. *Religion and Sexuality in American Literature*. Cambridge: Cambridge University Press, 1992.

Morrison, Toni. *Beloved*. New York: Alfred A. Knopf, 1987.

Owens, Craig. "The Discourse of Others: Feminists and Post-Modernism." In *The Anti-Aesthetic: Essays on Postmodern Culture*. Ed. Hal Foster. Port Townsend, WA: Bay Press, 1983, pp. 57–82.

Rubenstein, Roberta. *Boundaries of the Self: Gender, Culture, Fiction*. Urbana: University of Illinois Press, 1987.

Ryken, Leland. "The Contours of Christian Criticism in 1987." *Christianity and Literature*. 37 (Fall, 1987): 23–37.

PART 6
Jazz

The Function of Jazz in Toni Morrison's *Jazz*

Barbara Williams Lewis

It don't mean a thing
If it ain't got that swing.
Doo wop, doo wop, doo wop, doo wah...
       —Duke Ellington, 1932

If we look at the beginning and end of Toni Morrison's *Jazz*, the novel appears to be structurally backwards. The opening paragraph tells the whole story: Joe Trace

> . . . fell for an eighteen-year old girl with one of those deepdown, spooky loves that made him so sad and happy he shot her just to keep the feeling going. When the woman, her name is Violet, went to the funeral to see the girl and cut her dead face they threw her to the floor and out of the church (3).

So, we know what happens and to whom. But these few lines "ain't got that swing," and are essentially meaningless until we read the rest of the book. Once we get to the end, however, we are left with the impression that the story is unfinished, will continue, and will repeat itself.

I thought of this as a flaw in Morrison's writings. In an interview conducted by Claudia Tate in *Black Women Writers at Work*, Morrison says that when she finishes a book she misses "the characters, their company, the sense of possibility in them" (Tate, 131). This statement validated, for me, the suspicion that Toni Morrison, with all her great talent, simply does not know how to bring closure to her narratives.

During my research for an earlier version of this paper, I discovered the term "jazz literature." Then I realized that Morrison's stylistic approach in *Jazz* is no accident; it is a very carefully structured technique that she executes supremely well as I will show in this essay. Nor is it the first time she has used it; much of her work, especially *Beloved* and *Sula* are jazz novels. Moreover, the jazz text is not even Morrison's invention; I am thinking particularly of Ann Petry's *The Street.* As Gayl Jones points out:

> The writer's attempt to imply or reproduce musical rhythms can take the form of jazz-like flexibility and fluidity in prose rhythms (words, lines, paragraphs, the whole text), such as non-chronological syncopated order, pacing or tempo. A sense of jazz—the jam session—can also emerge from an interplay of voices improvising on the basic themes or motif of the text, in key words or phrases. (Jones, 200)

Thus, while the unnamed narrator assumes omniscient authority over the text, each of the main characters of *Jazz* takes a turn telling the story from her/his point of view.

Before I move into my analysis of the text, I think it is important to examine some of the elements of jazz and its presumed origin (s), usage and meanings.

No one is exactly certain how the word *jazz* originated. Emerging sometime around 1910, the term is usually associated with the folk mores of black men, and therefore its roots have been linked to Africa. Eileen Southern, author of *The Music of Black Americans*, suggests that *jazz* may have derived from an itinerant black musician named Jazbo Brown whose appreciative audience chanted, "More, Jazbo! More, Jaz, more!" (Southern, 362).

The development of jazz and the creation of Morrison's *Jazz* complement each other in terms of historical accuracy. The novel is set in the

1920s, and it was in the 1920s that jazz began to flourish. As blacks migrated from the south to the north prior to and during the '20s they demanded "their kind of music" (Southern, 363)—the kind that reflected their plight. Performers used their songs to express their inner-most feelings as is exemplified in pieces such as "John Henry," "Down by the Riverside," and "This Thing Called Love."

Jazz is a music with a vocabulary of its own: a *break* is a brief flurry of notes played by the soloist during a pause in the ensemble playing. You will recall that the narrator of *Jazz* calls them "'cracks'. . . Not openings or breaks, but dark fissures in the globe light of the day" (22). A *riff* is a short phrase repeated over and over again by the ensemble—the way the story is told about the death of Dorcas. A *sideman* is any member of the orchestra other than the leader—in this case side *woman*, the narrator of *Jazz*.

As Southern points out:

> The most salient features of jazz derive directly from the blues. Jazz is a vocally oriented music; its players replace the voice with their instruments, but try to recreate its singing style and blue notes by using sliding, whining, growling, and falsetto effects. Like the blues, jazz emphasizes individualism. The performer is at the same time the composer, shaping the music in style and form. A traditional melody or harmonic framework may serve as the takeoff point for improvisation, but it is the personality of the player and the way he [sic][1] improvises that produces the music. . . the pre-existent core of musical material . . . is generally short. The length of the jazz piece derives from repetition of the basic material. (Southern, 363)

This sounds like a summary of Morrison's *Jazz*. The "core" of the material is short; as I mentioned earlier, it is all on the first page. The length of the novel is derived from "repetition of the basic material."

Like jazz, *Jazz* moves back and forth in time. At one moment we are in 1906, then 1926, then back again:

Arriving at the train station in 1906, the smiles they both smiled at the women with little children, strung like beads over suitcases, were touched with pity. They liked children. Loved them even. Especially Joe, who had a way with them. But neither wanted the trouble. Years later, however, when Violet was forty, she was already staring at infants, hesitating in front of toys displaced at Christmas (107).

This passage is extremely important. It gives us insight into Violet's character. She has, indeed, a bad case of the blues. Though we know that she is physically as strong as John Henry's Polly Ann—she "could handle mules, bale hay and chop wood as good as any man" (105)—she suffers from "mother hunger" as she remembers her last *miscarried* child. Violet owns a parrot that says "I love you," sleeps with a doll, tries to steal a baby, and is haunted by the memory of that last child, "a girl probably" (108). But her loss is as deliberate as the melody of a jazz piece. Yet, she is unwilling to accept the blame for her abortion. Instead, she blames the child for not being strong enough to survive the "mammymade poison" of "soap, salt and castor oil" (109). She makes the connection that her daughter and Dorcas would have been the same age, and at this point, Violet replaces "the daughter who fled her womb" with her husband's lover: "bitch or dumpling, the two of them, mother and daughter, could have walked Broadway together" (108).

The language in *Jazz* represents "the name of the sound, and the sound of the name," as Morrison quotes on the fly sheet. That is to say, Morrison chooses words that keep the concept of jazz on the forefront. The word *slide*, for example, is associated with a trombone, indeed, "The Trombone Blues" (21). Joe Trace says, "The quiet money whispers twice: once when I *slide* it in my pocket; once when I *slide* it out" (123, my emphasis). And the narrator tells us: "He forgets a sun that used to slide up like the yolk of a good country egg. . ." (34).[2] One can almost hear the slide of a trombone, or the lonesome wail of a saxophone.

The notion of sliding symbolizes the slipperiness of Joe Trace. He slips out of prosecution for the murder of Dorcas because "nobody actually saw him do it" (4). The reader, too, forgives him because he "cried all day. . . and that was as bad as jail" (4). Also, Dorcas' death is not entirely

Joe's fault; he shoots her in the shoulder, but Dorcas *chooses* to bleed to death, as shall be discussed in detail later.

Joe has no ties, except for Violet whom he treats "like a piece of furniture" (123). He admits to changing "into new seven times" before he meets Dorcas. He does not leave us wondering what those changes are, and we experience a *break* in *Jazz* as I defined it earlier: Joe names himself after his parents abandon him. The second change occurs when Joe is taught how to hunt and "trained to be a man" (125). He marries Violet in 1893, the third change. In 1906 he and Violet travel to Rome, where they board a train to the City and find menial labor. The move from West Fifty-third to uptown constitutes the fifth change, the one Joe thinks is his "permanent self" (127). But Joe changes again when, during the riots of 1917, he is rescued by a white man. Then, two years later, he changes for the seventh time when he "danced in the street" as the colored troops of the 369th Regiment marched proudly through the streets of New York.[3]

I mention these changes—these variations in the character of Joe Trace, because they illustrate the concept of jazz in *Jazz*. Joe continues to change, especially in the epiphany we witness here:

> I dismissed the evil in my thoughts because I wasn't sure that the sooty music the blind twins were playing wasn't the cause. It can do that to you, a certain kind of guitar playing. Not like the clarinets, but close. If that song had been coming through a clarinet, I'd have known right away. But the guitars—they confused me, made me doubt myself, and I lost the trail. Went home and didn't pick it up again until the next day when Malvonne looked at me and covered her mouth with her hand. Couldn't cover her eyes, though; the laugh came flying out of there (132).

The clarinet has a single reed; its notes are easier to follow. But the guitar, with its variable ranges, has six strings that can be played simultaneously. The melody (Dorcas) is difficult to trace.

The guitar has a special value in the text of *Jazz*. In the 1920s the guitar emerged as leader of the jazz ensemble. Southern writes:

... they worked out special devices—drawing the blade of a knife across the strings of the guitar as they played ... —to produce whining tones reminiscent of the human voice, so that their instrument could "talk". . . . (Southern, 371)

Joe Trace is the leader of the ensemble; all action is centered around his relationship with Dorcas. Joe realizes that, like the guitar, he has been played. Here, too, the music takes on a character of its own. Joe calls it "the sooty music" that "confused" him. Earlier, the narrator alludes to the diabolic nature of jazz from Alice Manfred's point of view: ". . . she was no match for a City seeping music that begged and challenged each and every day. 'Come,' it said. 'Come and do wrong'" (67).

The idea of drawing a blade across the strings of a guitar symbolizes not only dislocation and severed ties, but also the overall image of violence in the City: "Daylight slants like a razor cutting the buildings in half" (7); "Black women were armed; black women were dangerous and the less money they had the deadlier the weapon they chose" (77); and, of course, Violet wields a blade as she approaches Dorcas' coffin.

So, *Jazz* thematically represents a contrast of good and evil. Everything everybody does in this book can be *excused*, in effect, because it is the *music* that makes them do it. The music—that "lowdown music," that manifests itself in " (s)ongs that used to start in the head" and then dropped on down, "down to places below the sash and the buckled belts" (56); that "nasty" music that somehow connects itself to the "silent black women and men" (57), anger, riots, and violence; the "something evil" that "ran the streets and nothing was safe—not even the dead" (9).

Like Sula Peace in Morrison's *Sula*, the community needs a scapegoat, someone or something upon which to unload their burden of guilt. Music serves this purpose.

Even in making that comparison we can see another element of jazz: *repetition*. As I mentioned earlier, there are intratextual repetitions in *Jazz*. There are also intertextual repetitions, as well. In *Sula*, Shadrack proclaims a "National Suicide Day" (*Sula,* 41), January 3, 1941. In *Jazz*, Violet's mother commits suicide by throwing herself down a well. Violet, herself, tries to cut the face of the dead Dorcas on January 3, 1926 (9).

When Dorcas chooses to die from a gunshot wound in her shoulder, she repeats the suicide of Violet's mother.

Sula Peace watches her mother, Hannah, burn to death because she is "interested." Dorcas, whose mother dies in a house fire, "must have seen the flames, must have, because the whole street was screaming" (57). Each girl remains silent as her mother dies. And the end of each novel is open, without a final chord.

I can remember a time in my childhood when my mother and I listened to "Sepia Serenade," a radio show intended for black audiences. Songs like "Work with Me Annie" and its sequel, "Annie Had a Baby, Can't Work No Mo'" permeated the walls of our little house. Then my mother "got religion," as we say, and the "devil's music" was no longer allowed in our home.

But music is not the only role that jazz plays in *Jazz*. The *Dictionary of Word Origins* explains that *jazz*:

> ... originated in a West African language, was for a long time a Black slang term in America for 'strenuous activity,' particularly 'sexual intercourse'. . . . (307)

In fact, the word *jazz*— (nouns, verbs and adjectives)—can mean a number of things: business, affairs, nonsense, bureaucratic red tape, sex, etc., and especially gossip or signifying, which is precisely what our narrator does. She tells the story, with a difference, because surely she was not present at the actual crime. And it is she who admits near the end that she doesn't know exactly what happened. In other words, she presents herself as an authority on the lives of Violet, Joe, Dorcas and Felice when she says, "Sth, I know that woman. . . Know her husband, too" (3), and then "changes her tune," so to speak, when she realizes that she has been watched as much as she did the watching:

> I thought I knew them and wasn't worried that they didn't really know me . . . they knew me all along . . . they watched me . . . and when I was feeling most invisible, being tight-lipped, silent and unobservable, they were whispering about me to each other . . .
>
> So I missed it altogether. I was sure one would kill the other. I

waited for it so I could describe it. . . . the past was an abused record with no choice but to repeat itself at the crack and no power on earth could lift the arm that held the needle . . . . they danced and walked all over me. Busy they were, busy being original, complicated, changeable—human . . . . (220)

What does this mean? Well, if we go back to page six of the text, the narrator introduces (but does not name) Felice: "another girl with four marcelled waves. . . that's how that scandalizing threesome on Lennox Avenue began. *What turned out different was who shot whom"* (emphasis mine). She predicts another murder, another climax to the story. The reader anticipates this action as the story unfolds, but it *never* happens. No one else gets shot. Or, rather, I should say, no one except the narrator who gets "shot down" in her prophesy. She, too, experiences an epiphany. Her own imagination has betrayed her: "It never occurred to me that they were thinking other thoughts, feeling other feelings, putting their lives together in ways I never dreamed of" (221). With that thought she realizes that she has not even known herself.

I am aware that critics have tried to "de-genderize" the narrator, and that my reference to her as female is unpopular. Interestingly, John Leonard, in his article, "Her Soul's High Song," suggests that the narrative voice is "the book itself" (718). This argument has some merit when we consider the last lines of the book: "Say make me, remake me. You are free to do it. . . because look, look. Look where your hands are now" (229). But it brings up the question, can a book write itself? I think it is safer to say that the narrator tries to write her own story and discovers that *she* is the open book we are reading. I see her as a character similar to Mrs. Hedges in *The Street.* Or, perhaps she solicits the reader's participation in the "remake" of this *Jazz.* Whatever the explanation, *everybody* knows somebody who knows everybody's business except her own.[4] The fact that she has no name is another example of Morrison's brilliance; anonymity is a key element of gossip. (You did not hear it from me.)

In an article entitled "Riffs on Violence," Paul Gray discusses what he terms "the unsolved mystery" of *Jazz.* Gray argues that the novel "never answers the question of 'why'?" I disagree. I think that Joe, Dorcas and the narrator form an ensemble that tells us exactly why Joe shoots Dorcas and why she chooses to die, although the psyche behind the *why* is far beyond the realms of my psychoanalytic expertise.

Joe brings gifts to his lover. At each meeting he gives her money, or candy, or cologne. He is devoted to her just as she is: "He didn't care what I looked like. I could be anything, do anything—and it pleased him" (190). But Dorcas is not happy with that. She needs a challenge, like Acton. She wants someone who wants to change her; she wants a man everybody else wants. She tells Joe that he makes her sick, and threatens, "You bring me another bottle of cologne I'll drink it and die you don't leave me alone" (189). Dorcas would rather be dead than stay with Joe. She knows he is coming for her; he's been searching for five days. She begins to "see him everywhere" (190). He will never let her go.

Thanks to Malvonne's laughter, Joe knows about Acton, one of the "wise, young roosters" who don't have to do anything except "wait for chicks to pass by and find them" (132). He equates Dorcas with Eve: "you were the reason Adam ate the apple and its core" (133). She is the forbidden fruit he wants to "bite. . . chew up. . . and. . . carry around for the rest of my life" (134). He experiences a kind of love he has never known before: "I didn't fall in love, I rose in it" (135). She has given him life, meaning. Like the phoenix, he is renewed.

When Malvonne laughs, she laughs at Joe, a laugh which says, in essence, *there's no fool like an old fool.* Joe is humiliated, stripped of his manly pride. He can take anything from Dorcas as long as he is allowed to sustain the illusion that he possesses her, and as long as her abuse is private. When she takes that away from him, he tracks her down and shoots—"Frankie and Johnny" in reverse.

When Violet tries to cut the dead girl's face, she wants to strip Dorcas of identity, to sever her ties with Joe, to "de-face" her, in other words. With Dorcas , Violet does not have to face the possibility that something is "wrong" with her. Her failure in that attempt forces her to come to terms with the desire Joe has for the girl. She then chooses to fuse herself with Dorcas, to "re-make" herself in an effort to recapture Joe's love. She learns how to dance like the girl, wear make-up like Dorcas, listen to the same kind of music. She conducts quite an extensive investigation into the life of Dorcas and even places on her mantle a picture of the girl "alive at least and very bold" (6), so that she and Joe could look at it "in bewilderment" (6).

Joe jazzes Dorcas. In so doing, he jazzes over Violet. Joe sells cosmetics; Violet fixes hair. They are both in the business of making women look jazzy.

So, Morrison's choice of title is not based solely on the theme of music in the lives of her characters. It is a manifestation of the conditions of life among migratory Negroes, their family love, romantic love and desire. It is an ongoing development of her writing style that bears the absence of a final chord and leaves the reader wanting something more. And it is, indeed, a mastery of technique used to give voices to women, and ears to all who would hear.

NOTES

1. If this is done by six influential people usage will begin to change quickly. Most of the great jazz vocalists have been women, and many fine instrumentalists, too.

2. The egg is also connected with the fertility that has been separated from the child-bearing by abortion.

3. For more information see Franklin and Moss, Jr., *From Slavery to Freedom*, (New York: Knopf, 1988), pp. 297–318.

4. Consider what Job tells Jason in *The Sound and the Fury:* "You fools a man whut so smart he cant even keep up wid hisself" (pp. 311–12).

WORKS CITED

Ayto, John. *The Dictionary of Word Origins*. New York: Arcade Publishing, 1990.

Ellison, Ralph. *Invisible Man*. New York: Vintage, 1947, 1981.

Franklin, John Hope, and Alfred A. Moss, Jr. *From Slavery to Freedom*. New York: Knopf, 1988.

Faulkner, William. [1929 and 1956] *The Sound and The Fury*. New York: The Modern Library. 1992.

Gray, Paul. "Riffs on Violence." *Time*, April 27, 1992, 69.

Jones, Gayl. *Liberating Voices, Oral Tradition in African-American Literature*. New York: Penguin Books, 1991.

Leonard, John. "Her Soul's High Song." *The Nation*, May 25, 1992, 706–18.

Morrison, Toni. *Sula*. New York: Plume, 1973.

———. *Jazz*. New York: Knopf, 1992.

Petry, Ann. *The Street*. Boston: Beacon Press, 1946.

Southern, Eileen. *The Music of Black Americans.* New York: W. W. Norton and Company, 1983.

Tate, Claudia. *Black Women Writers at Work.* New York: Continuum Publishing Corporation, 1983.

Movin' on up: The Madness of Migration in Toni Morrison's *Jazz*

Deborah H. Barnes

Well, we're moving' on up
To the East Side
To a deluxe apartment in the sky
Yeah, we're movin' on up
To the East Side
We've finally got a piece of the pie
    Fish don't fry in the kitchen
    Beans don't burn on the grill
    Took a whole lotta tryin'
    Just to get up that hill
    Now we're up in the big leagues
    Gettin' our turn at bat
    From now on it's you an' me baby
    Ain't nothin' wrong with that
Well, we're movin' on up. . . [1]

From 1975 to 1985 television viewers witnessed the weekly antics of *The Jeffersons,* a hard-working, aspiring African American family, as they fumbled and bumbled their way into the mainstream of upper-middle-class society.[2] George Jefferson, the family's patriarch, became the comic icon of the promise and the problem inherent in black social and economic upward mobility. Having overcome the impediments of being born black, poor, and therefore, disadvantaged, George pulled himself up by his gnome-sized bootstraps to build a prosperous dry cleaning empire with the help of his loving (though often contentious) family. Claiming to have been born in a sharecropper's shack in Alabama, George often fictionalized his genesis, apparently to make his entrepreneurial accomplishments seem more dramatic and his personal history more authentically "black." While George may not have made the same historical trek his African American ancestors made to New York from various points in the South, his physical and spiritual migration from Houser Street in Queens (where he had once neighbored bottom-dweller Archie Bunker) was exceptional and representative in its own right. Nevertheless, as George struggled to adjust to a new life in the "big time" of New York's exclusive East Side, America laughed.

The show's comedy resided in George's bungled attempts to imitate the ways of his wealthy, educated, mainly white neighbors and colleagues. Because he lacked the social skills necessary to mediate his new society, George's mimetic impulses were generally ludicrous. George was funny because—episode after episode—he believed that all he needed to play (and win) in the "big leagues" was a fat bank account and the right address. In the world of television, stubborn maladaptation makes good comedy; so, George never did find the nexus between his old life and the new. Like so many other aspiring cultural sojourners of fact and fiction, George believed that the opportunity to abandon the poverty and the limitations of his past—the opportunity to "move on up"—was all he needed to be happy and to make his family secure.

In her most recent novel, *Jazz,*[3] Toni Morrison shows that "success" won at the expense of cultural isolation, abandonment, or alienation— like the success George Jefferson "enjoys" in his "deluxe apartment in the sky"—is success won too dear. Morrison's fiction demonstrates historical fact: that cultural estrangement and loss too often accompany the African American's social, economic, and political "progress." *Jazz's* urban newcomers are shattered by significant geographic, social, and economic change. They yearn to recover a vital essence that they lose in the quest for a better life. This theme is not unique to *Jazz.* Significantly, Toni Morrison's *oeuvre* resonates with "movin' on up" stories—the costs and consequences of hoped-for and sought-after upward mobility for American blacks. Morrison does not satisfy herself with simple tales of personal agency. Instead, she proffers a unique depiction of migration that interrogates the destructive and distorting effects of physical and emotional dislocation on culturally mobile blacks.

Morrison's novels show in serious ways that ameliorative change—opportunity, mobility, and "success"—have a counterweight: culture shock.[4] Anthropological studies demonstrate that culture shock—the massive psychic reaction to cultural displacement—ensues when travel or migration require an individual to function in a culture that is vastly different from his or her own.[5] All of Morrison's novels inscribe (some might say, bemoan) the varied maladjustments of blacks who lose contact with or have been denied access to native, enculturating, and authenticating communities. Like George Jefferson, these maladapted blacks become ludicrous, pathetic, and dysfunctional when they abandon traditional cultural values and practices for alien ones. Without a native culture to inform or to mediate their existence, life often becomes alienating, meaningless, and indecipherably "foreign" for cultural itinerants.

The phenomenon of culture shock is well documented throughout Morrison's *oeuvre*. For example, in *The Bluest Eye,* newlyweds Cholly and Pauline Breedlove leave the backwoods of rural Kentucky to pursue the promises of economic mobility in "urban" Lorain, Ohio—a hostile environment that ultimately destroys their love and their lives. Ultimately, neither is able to make the necessary transitions demanded by a migratory experience. When Sula Peace ends her ten-year sojourn through the world beyond Medallion, her cultural disorientation is heralded by a prophetic plague of dead robins in *Sula.* She divulges the degree of her estrangement from Bottom culture when she puts her grandmother in an (interracial) old folks home, ruins her best friend's marriage, and reputedly sleeps with white men. Consequently, she dies alone and unloved. Governed by his greed and a lust for power, Macon Dead rejects his holistic cultural roots to adopt disabling mainstream ideologies of success in *Song of Solomon.* Psychologically maimed after witnessing the brutal murder of his father by white men, Macon seeks revenge by vowing to master the white man's game. The only white man's game Macon knows or understands, however, is the oppression of black people. Jadine Childs, *Tar Baby*'s cultural orphan, is perhaps Morrison's most fully developed and, therefore, most pathetic victim of cultural contamination and rootlessness. Notwithstanding her media success and her reputation as a brilliant international beauty, Jadine is condemned to Sisyphean wandering because she is unable to affiliate authentically or meaningfully with any cultural group. In *Beloved*, Sethe, a slave, matures to Selfhood without benefit of an enculturating community. After fleeing Kentucky's slavery for life on the "free side of the Ohio," she enjoys freedom and "kin" for only twenty-eight days before she attempts to kill all of her children rather than see them reclaimed by slave catchers. Sethe's newly adopted community rejects her because she clearly does not share their cultural vision.

Jazz recounts various migration experiences and their consequences. We are told, for example, that the once-happy Joe and Violet Trace begin their descent into marital discord after a succession of ameliorative moves that take them further and further from their cultural roots. Like so many other real-life (and fictional) African Americans, the Traces reify the ambitions of rural blacks who believed that the urban North was the promised land: the land of opportunity, equality, and plenty. Their plans and dreams there are thwarted, however, when the Traces undergo a series of disabling culture shocks. Without an orienting cultural community to sustain them in the North, Joe and Violet fail to cope with the challenges of city life. Accordingly, in this and other novels, Morrison portrays culture shock as a traumatic, yet inevitable, consequence for upwardly mobile, migrating, or rootless blacks.

Jazz is a redemptive novel that ends "happily." Morrison does not conclude the story (as she does her other novels) with a relocated family's destruction, desiccation, or despair. She moves beyond the nadir of Joe and Violet Trace's sensational post-migratory crisis—when they each attempt to murder Joe's young mistress, Dorcas—to chronicle their eventual healing, that is, their adjustment to and commensalism with their new environment and each other.[6] Thus, it is important to note that Joe and Violet are not ruined by culture shock. After many years of attempting to meet the demands of city living, they discover they cannot solve their adaptive dilemma by abandoning their southern roots and traditions for northern ones. In order to recover their personal and social equilibrium, they find, instead, they must reinterpret and tailor mutable native culturalisms to fit their new environment and evolving needs. Upon doing so, they reestablish community and with it a concomitant sense of identity. In the Morrisonian tradition, the Traces retreat to and find rootedness in (re)memories of their individual and communal pasts. Their (re)memories—historically enacted cultural perceptions and interpretations of reality—help them to deconstruct and to negotiate the present. As Joe's and Violet's stories show, one's native culture is ever and always present, even when it is repressed, displaced, or obscured. Thus, in *Jazz* Morrison not only maps the psychic path of culture shock but also chronicles the diasporizing of African American culturalisms from the South to the North (and to the Midwest) during the Great Migration.

The cultural critic's U-shaped curve is an effective tool for mapping the migrant's cultural adjustment experience—an experience described repeatedly by Morrison. This paradigm, widely known to social psychologists, offers an interpretive grid that plots the sojourner's reactions to the altering effects of migration in four configurative stages: honeymoon, crisis, recovery, and adjustment.[7] While *Jazz* recounts many migration stories, I will use this model to illuminate the textual record of Joe and Violet Trace's migratory experiences. I will show that the Traces' "movin' on up" story is more than a detailed depiction of aspiration, struggle, and loss. Rather, it plots the course of evolving cultural and personal identities as they undergo the voluntary or forced transformation that accompanies migration. Finally, my critique will reveal also the novel's prescriptive powers for contemporary cultural sojourners.

*　　*　　*

Social psychologists agree when people significantly change their geographical venue—as do Joe and Violet when they leave the rural, agrarian South for the urban, industrial North—they encounter major discrepancies in social reality. They soon discover that their relationships with people and things change radically from one place to another. Thus, the sudden shift in contingencies that reinforce social conduct, shape human relationships, and control outcome leave cultural sojourners at a behavioral disadvantage. Their anxiety, disorientation, and social difficulty are directly proportional to the degree of control the migrant exercised in initiating the cultural change and the "cultural distance" between the new and the old culture. In other words, if a person is forced to relocate (like Joe does when Vienna burns to the ground) or if a person moves to a "culturally far" environment that is profoundly alien and/or perceived to be hostile (like Golden Gray does when he searches for and finds his father), that person may experience significant difficulty in adjusting to the new environment. On the other hand, if a person migrates *willingly* to a "culturally near" or culturally similar environment (like Joe and Violet do when they move from Little Africa to 140th Street), then he or she is prone to adapt more easily. Cultural adjustment is influenced further by an index of other variables (which include but are not limited to) the individual's age, extent of previous travel, personal resourcefulness, independence, appearance, language skills, tolerance of ambiguities, and the nature and extent of his or her support group. While all migrants will experience some measure of culture or transition shock, the ease with which they overcome it is determined largely by their disposition to the move and their expectations toward its outcome. In short, the sojourner's desire for change plays a significant role in the adjustment process.

When the move is considered to be ameliorative—as it is for Joe and Violet—attendant physical, behavioral, and cognitive change is usually welcomed. The promise of newness and the privilege of starting over is part of the migrational boon. So, to the newcomer, the "foreignness" they encounter is exotic and alluring. They gladly ignore transitional complications because the city, in this case, beguiles them to forget what is for them the useless past.

> Part of why they loved [the city] was the specter they left behind. The slumped spines of the veterans of the 27th Battalion betrayed by the commander for whom they had fought like lunatics. The eyes of thousands, stupefied with disgust at having been imported by Mr. Armour, Mr. Swift, Mr. Montgomery Ward to break strikes then dismissed for having done so. The broken shoes of two thousand Galveston longshoremen that Mr. Mallory would never pay fifty cents an hour like the white ones. The praying palms, the raspy breathing, the quiet children of the ones who had escaped from Springfield Ohio, Springfield Indiana, Greensburg Indiana, Wilmington Delaware, New Orleans Louisiana, after raving whites had foamed all over the lanes and yards of home. (33)

Thus, cultural metamorphosis begins with forgetting, letting go of the old and embracing the new. In other words, newcomers must not only act, think, and perceive differently, they must also *be* different. The question is, What happens when cultural sojourners abandon what they know and what they are for the opportunity to begin again? The answer: culture shock. But that comes later.

In the beginning, newcomers are euphoric and optimistic about the move. Their delight helps to diminish the disorientation of outsider status and stimulates their desire to make the necessary adjustments to the new home. In the honeymoon stage—the first point at the top of the U-curve that maps the migration process—cultural sojourners are enchanted and enthusiastic about resettling despite conflicts over new and differing values, behaviors, and relationships. According to the novel's narrator

> That kind of fascination, permanent and out of control, seizes children, young girls, men of every description, mothers, brides, and barfly women, and if they have their way and get to the City, they feel more like themselves, more like the people they always believed they were. Nothing can pry them away from that; the City is what they want it to be: thriftless, warm, scary and full of amiable strangers. (35)

As a result, instead, their excitement conceals evidence of incipient culture shock.

To cope in the new environment, migrants often adjust their conduct to match local standards without attempting to understand the underlying cultural ideology. They find that the easiest way to negotiate an unfamiliar environment is to learn the indigenous culture's appropriate behaviors, attitudes, and responses to various social situations. In this way, newcomers quickly learn how "to get along," that is, metaphorically, how to play the game and win. Thus, Joe and Violet are able to "move on up" from a sharecropper's cabin in Tyrell County to a stately, elegant building on Lenox Avenue because they learn how to play the game. With Joe doing hotel work and selling Cleopatra cosmetics on the side and with

Violet doing hair, they surpass by far the quality of their lives sharecropping down home. For the first time they are winning: they have earned the right to direct their lives and to improve the material quality of their existence. But they find, as all newcomers do, that "playing the game" is not enough, in the long run. In order to play the game strategically, that is, to reason or to plan their next move, they must be able to decode the alien culture's underlying epistemological framework as well. The narrator portends, "If you don't know how, you can end up out of control or controlled by some outside thing. . ." (9). If newcomers fail to engage the cognitive processes founding their adopted culture they will misinterpret cultural cues. Thus, it is clear that Violet does not really know how to play the "City game" when she finds herself confronted by an angry crowd that accuses her of attempting to steal a baby she claims only to have been watching for its errant sister. Violet is deceived like other newcomers the narrator describes, when she believes she "can do what she wants and get away with it" (8). Such errors in judgment will lead, eventually, to the newcomer's social rejection and self-estrangement.

The adjustment process segues into the second phase, crisis—the bottom of the U-curve—as the migrant's adaptation stalls and begins to deteriorate. As the old folks might say, the honeymoon is over. Cultural differences once considered delightful at this point become unfathomable and unbearable. As a result, newcomers begin to feel frustrated, anxious, isolated, inadequate, lonely, and angry. Their native culture fails them in the new environment. Because they have not yet become acculturated to the host culture whose behaviors they have adopted, they find themselves culturally unmoored and adrift. Consequently, they become disoriented, their identities begin to erode, and they experience themselves as fragmented, foreign, without function. Without an operative cultural base to inform them, they no longer know who they are, what they are, or what they should do. Likewise, the Traces' self-identity begins to deteriorate when they can no longer experience unity and coherence between their being and doing. Violet, for example, is disoriented and confused to the point of "public craziness." She feels fragmented, disassociated from her life. She sees her day, we are told, as "a string of small, well-lit scenes."

In each one something specific is being done: food things, work things; customers and acquaintances are encountered, places entered. But she does not see herself doing these things. She sees them being done. (22)

On the other hand, Joe's shock is made plain when he forgets his native enculturation, a rudimentary premise of the Hunter's Hunter: females and the tender "ain't prey." He loses himself totally, tracking and killing the seventeen-year-old girl who has become for him the mother-sister-daughter-lover he never had. As Joe's and Violet's various social dilemmas show, the shock phase represents a kind of existential confrontation with the abyss that separates the two cultures the individual has internalized.

The unraveling of identity is a slow, degenerative process. Thus, Violet's narrative describes twenty years of attempted adjustment to urbanity. Her "private cracks" evolve over time into "public craziness" as her increasing inability to make sense of herself worsens. Depressed, Violet becomes increasingly sociopathic and, then (as her nickname indicates) violent. She flounders in a world devoid of meaning, watching "that other Violet" do what she would never do: steal a baby or slash a dead girl's face. Who she once knew herself to be—"a snappy, determined girl. . . .who liked, and had, to get her way"—ceases to be in the City. She cannot see herself as whole or recognizable. She loses all control: she sleeps with a doll, breaks up a funeral, throws out her birds, and takes a lover to her husband's home. Baffled by the discrepancies between her old self and her new self, Violet sits down in the middle of the street to think things through.

At the point of crisis, all newcomers must rethink themselves and their situations. They must decide either to return to their native cultural context where they can, once again, make sense of themselves (and things), or they must find a way to adapt fully to the new culture by bridging the ontological gap that separates the host culture from their native culture. Adaptation—the ability to "think" in the idiom of the host culture—ends the experience of being "foreign." However, if newcomers fail to chose either of the adjustment alternatives, then they will be considered (and rendered) insane by the host culture's standards and will be ostracized by or eliminated from the community, depending on the nature and degree of their insanity.

The third phase, recovery, moving across the bottom of the U-curve— begins *after* migrants realize that their personal and cultural identities have disintegrated and require immediate rescue if they are to survive. The reconfiguring process requires migrants to cull from their native cultural legacies those values, behaviors, and traditions worth keeping and to translate them into the idiom of the local culture. Interrogating the self to determine what is essential and what is dross is the primary work of this phase. The culture-shocked must come to *new* terms with the nature of social reality and their place in it. They may turn to cultural natives and/or enculturated members of their support group for help in the sorting process. Thus, communication and group (re)orientation is essential to survival.

At the nadir of her crisis, Violet knows intuitively that she must find a cultural mediator to teach her how to proceed. Ironically, she turns to Alice Manfred, Dorcas's aunt, and a former migrant herself, for help because they are "sisters" in age, experience, and loss. Confused, Violet begs Alice to tell her "something real," something that will help her figure things out and put them to rights. Alice, too, is unsure of herself, unsure that she is an appropriate cultural mentor for Violet because she has failed to properly enculturate (and, thus, protect) Dorcas. All of her advice to the girl about navigating the streets, disguising her good looks, and avoiding white people had been useless to Dorcas in the long run. Dorcas is destroyed by a horror that exists beyond the cultural framework Alice knows or can imagine. Thus, she cannot protect her. While Alice cannot intellectualize the existential dilemma that Violet faces any better than Violet can, she can and does offer her pragmatic advice: "You want a real thing?. . . I'll tell you a real one. You got anything left to you to love, anything at all, do it. . . . Mind what is left to you. . . . I'm saying make it, make it" (112–13). In order to "do it" or "to make it," Violet must reclaim the powerful and controlling identity (or as she thinks of it, the muscles and the hips) she lost upon leaving the South. In regaining her self, Violet also recovers a stable orientation that rekindles her love for and dedication to Joe. Violet realizes if she had not messed up her life by forgetting it was hers, if she had not run "up and down the streets wishing [she] was somebody else" (208), perhaps Joe would not have forgotten her or wished that she were somebody else. too.

By their example, Violet and Alice, sitting in that kitchen, plot the transient's rocky path back to wholeness and recovery. The culture shocked must search what Morrison calls "the useful past" to recover and to reconcile the identity that was forgotten in the honeymoon stage of migration. As in all Morrison novels, memory is the saving grace. Without memories of a historical, cultural, and personal foundation, the sojourner will have no identity, no point of orientation, no way to proceed and nowhere from which to begin anew. Even an evolving identity must be rooted in a past. It is critical, then, for newcomers to recognize that they cannot throw away the past—no matter how inconvenient or horrid it may be. They must reclaim it to reclaim the self's foundation and power.

The final stage, adjustment—climbing back up to the top of the U-curve—requires newcomers to build a bridge between the past and the present that will forge a new orientation towards their adopted environment. They learn to live commensally with the natural order and each other, forging into an functional whole the surviving elements of their native culture and the newly learned interpretations of reality. This new posture allows them to enjoy authentic interpersonal relationships with family and friends. Joe and Violet save themselves and their marriage when they reinvent the substance and pattern of their lives. Thus, newcomers become as adept as natives (and sometime even sharper than natives) when they gain the cognitive control that makes life predictable, certain, and, therefore, pleasant. Once the victims of culture shock determine where and how they fit into their adopted environment, they recover and exit the culminating phase of the migration process—Adjustment.

Clearly, Toni Morrison is fascinated by the effects of "progress" and cultural change. Her six novels describe the full range of consequences that result from integration and geographic dislocation. For example, the Breedloves are ruined when they adopt (what is for them) inauthentic white, urban definitions of reality. Sula destroys the natural order of her native community with culturally inappropriate behaviors when she returns to the Bottom from an extended sojourn after college. Macon Dead experiences culture shock when he is orphaned and dispossessed of his paternal legacy, Lincoln's Heaven. Jadine Childs lacks the authentic cultural base or community to give her life meaning and substance despite her beauty, brains, talent, and wealth. Sethe is so confused after her emancipating trek from Kentucky's slavery to Ohio's freedom, she falls into the abyss of meaningless that separates the two cultures—slaughtering her "best thing," a beloved daughter.

Jazz, however, is not only descriptive but also prescriptive, as this study demonstrates. In it, Morrison serves as the reader's cultural mentor, by inscribing a solution to the culture shock that ravages the spirits and minds of many aspiring, upwardly mobile African Americans. Thus, her sixth novel, *Jazz*, is a parable of resilience and recovery that shows contemporary blacks not only how to "move on up," to but also how to survive the good life at the top.

NOTES

1. The opening theme from *The Jeffersons,* a popular television situation comedy on CBS from 1975 to 1985.

2. *The Jeffersons,* a successful spin-off from Norman Lear's popular sitcom *All in the Family,* first aired January 17, 1975. The show's popularity and longevity marked an important change in the American social, economic, and cultural tableau. A comedic chronicle of an aspiring middle-class African American family's interpretation of the American dream's privilege and plenty, *The Jeffersons* aired on Saturday night after the domestic antics of narrow-minded, working-class Archie Bunker and before the professional striving of a happily unmarried, upwardly mobile *Mary Tyler Moore.* The show's unparalleled success firmly enshrined the reality of an African American middle class into the American tableau.

3. All page references to *Jazz* are to the Knopf edition (New York, 1992) and will be indicated in the text.

4. The term "culture shock" was introduced into the English language in 1954 by Kalervo Oberg. See *Culture Shock: Psychological Reactions to Unfamiliar Environments* by Adrian Furnham and Stephen Bochner. Methuen: London, 1986.

5. See Barbara C. Anderson, "Adaptive Aspects of Culture Shock." *American Anthropologist.* 73 (Oct, 71): 1121–1125; and Furnham and Bochner, 1986.

6. Commensalism, a holistic perspective, dictates that constituent elements of an environment exist in harmony with or at least without detriment to each other.

7. Furnham and Bochner (1986) describe numerous analytical hypoth-

eses that measure and interpret culture shock on extended sojourns, 112–140. They credit Lysgaard for the "idea" of the U-curve that plots the migrant's adjustment experience in three stages—initial adjustment, crisis, and regained adjustment—although he does not describe the shape of a "U" in his treatise. Oberg's paradigm characterizes culture shock as a "disease" of four phases—honeymoon, crisis, recovery, adjustment. My theoretical model is a conflation of these two ideas. To make my thesis visually memorable, I have plotted Oberg's four phases on Lysgaard's U-shaped grid. Lysgaard's model omits the recovery stage.

The Problem of Narrative in Toni Morrison's *Jazz*

Katherine J. Mayberry

Toni Morrison's novels reveal an intricate ambivalence about the function and implications of the narrative act. As a writer who repeatedly chronicles the stories of those too often deprived of the opportunity and means to record them themselves, Morrison is on good terms with narrative (or a certain kind of narrative). For her African American characters who are story-tellers, the act of narrating is personally and politically restorative. At the personal level, story telling is often coincident with the discovery of identity and self-knowledge. At the political level, as Valerie Smith puts it, the gift of narration grants African American narrators "significance and figurative power over their super ordinates" (2).

Morrison's narrative method does more than restore voice and grant authority; it aspires as well to be the literary representation of distinctly African American art forms—women's blues (most notably in *The Bluest Eye*), jazz, and oral story telling (Dittmar; Rushdy). In doing so, it abandons what Ursula LeGuin calls the "father tongue," which makes "a gap, a space between the subject . . . and the object," in favor of language that is relationship, whose power is "not in dividing but in binding" (3–4). Morrison's ambitions for narrative are similar to her ambitions for language in general, which ideally should (in her words) arc "toward the place where meaning may lie . . . . Its force, its felicity . . . in its reach toward the ineffable" (Nobel Lecture, 20).

Yet for all this, Morrison's novels do not seem entirely easy with the narrative medium—more particularly, with the implications inherent in the relationship between narrating subject and narrated objects. Traditional narrative can be regarded as a literary inscription of the dominant values of a hierarchical system: like the culture in which it evolved, traditional narrative is based upon a series of discriminatory logics that empower a dominant voice to promote, demote, include, exclude, and finally, at the end, to emerge victorious over the other voices or characters of the narrative. Non-traditional narratives, like those practiced by Morrison, Virginia Woolf, and Alice Munro, for example, partially resist this analogy through their manipulation and modification of narrative conventions. But even those narratives like Morrison's that emerge from a tradition very different from that of patriarchal narrative and which serve to restore voice to historically silenced characters, to deliver knowledge and experience, are not entirely free of these ideological implications. Finally, all narrators must tell the stories of other people, even when their primary focus is their own experience. And in doing so, they move characters around, speak for them, and to some degree, in recording their fates, determine them. If the granting of narrative authority bestows upon African American narrators "significance and figurative power over their super ordinates" (as Valerie Smith would have it), it inevitably grants them power over *all* the characters within the narrative.

Morrison's *The Bluest Eye*, *Beloved*, and *Jazz* are deeply concerned with the function and implications of narrative. While the two earlier novels take as their premise the value and necessity of narrative, both also seem to concede that the ideological traces of traditional narrative cannot be completely erased, that narrative is thus a potentially dangerous medium for the characters whose stories it tells. In *Jazz* , this ambivalence toward the function of narrative is explicitly addressed and at least partially resolved.

The Bluest Eye is a powerful indictment of a particular formula of oppression from which few of the novel's characters are exempt: In hierarchical societies, the less powerful inflict their masters' oppressive tactics upon the least powerful. This formula is inscribed not only within the plot but also within the narrative. The novel consists of at least four distinguishable narrative voices: the voice of Claudia McTeer, a young black girl in the Ohio community where most of the novel occurs; Pauline Breedlove, who directly narrates a series of personal reminiscences set between narrative bridges supplied by an anonymous third-person voice; that anonymous third-person voice, which supplies the narrative that no other character has the knowledge or experience to provide; and the double voice of Pecola Breedlove, who, gone mad at the end of the novel, presents directly—unmediated by any narration—a conversation between the two parts of her now bisected personality.

Through her use of multiple narrators, Morrison seems to be testing different relationships between narrator and narrated, determining both from which vantage point Pecola's story can be most successfully recorded *and* whether the economy of serial oppression is recalculable within narrative.

Of all the narrative voices in the novel, the anonymous, conventional third-person narrator plays the greatest part in the chain of serial oppression: Empowered by its very anonymity, this voice sanitizes, manipulates, and silences. Morrison reveals these oppressive practices in the second section of "Spring," where the literate, organizing voice of the narrator alternates with Pauline's own reflections. The narrator writes:

All the meaningfulness of her life was in her work. For her virtues were intact. She was an active church woman, did not drink, smoke, or carouse, defended herself mightily against Cholly, rose above him in every way, and felt she was fulfilling a mother's role conscientiously when she pointed out their father's faults to keep them from having them, or punished them when they showed any slovenliness, no matter how slight, when she worked twelve to sixteen hours a day to support them. And the world itself agreed with her. (102)

This passage is followed by Pauline's words:

He [Cholly] shivers and tosses his head. Now I be strong enough, pretty enough, and young enough to let him make me come. . . . I begin to feel those little bits of color floating up into me—deep in me. That streak of green from the june-bug light, the purple from the berries trickling along my thighs, Mama's lemonade yellow runs sweet in me. Then I feel like I'm laughing between my legs,

and the laughing gets all mixed up with the colors, and I'm afraid
I'll come and afraid I won't. But I know I will. And I do. And it be
rainbow all inside. And it lasts and lasts and lasts. (103–4)

Those two voices are strikingly different: the narrator summarizes,
contains, limits Pauline; Pauline, in the brief spaces allotted to her, au-
thenticates and liberates herself. The contiguity of voices here forces us
to recognize the damage that narrative representation can do—to admit
its tendency toward the complete falsification and alienation of its object.
Like the white uniform and pompadour hairdo Pauline wears at the home
of her white employers, this narrative constrains and falsifies, obscuring
deep truths about its object.

The oppressive operations of a distanced, anonymous narrator are
evident again in the section abut Geraldine and Junior. Geraldine is one
of many characters in the novel whose stereotyping of Pecola is a complete misinterpretation, fueling reactions of considerable cruelty against
Pecola. To Geraldine, Pecola is merely a type: "She had seen this little
girl all of her life. . . . They were everywhere" (75). But Geraldine's position within the narrative makes clear that she too is victimized by just this
habit of generalization and reduction. The narrator's attitude towards
Geraldine is very close to Geraldine's attitude toward Pecola. At the beginning of this section, Geraldine is herself introduced as a type, as one
of a group that "come from Mobile. . . . [that] soak up the juice of their
home towns, and it never leaves them" (67). Contained, classified, stereotyped, Geraldine is as much a victim as Pecola, although in Geraldine's
case, the abuser is a literary operation that constrains and dismisses its
objects. This section, then, re-enacts the novel's main point about social
oppression—that hierarchical societies are characterized by an economy
of serial oppression in which the less powerful visit their masters' oppressive tactics upon the least powerful; Geraldine, oppressed by the third-
person narrator, aims the same oppressive tactics at someone beneath her
on the social ladder.

While Claudia's first-person narrative is more capable of telling
Pecola's story without falsifying or controlling it, the novel concludes
that even this fresh, unconventional voice is ultimately powerless to rescue Pecola's story. At the end of the novel, Claudia concludes that Pecola's

community, including Claudia herself, "had failed her" (158). By this she presumably means that they were finally powerless to wrest her from the series of ugly crimes that victimized her, ending ultimately in her madness. But Pecola is failed in another way as well. She is failed by the narrative that must concede its inability to substantiate, subjectify her. Try as Claudia might to avoid the objectifying dangers of narrative, her story is incapable of moving Pecola from the position of victim at the margin of life to subject at its center. Claudia's narrative finally realizes no one but Claudia. While it may provide us with the story of Pecola's tragedy that would otherwise have gone unrecorded, it remains the story *of* Pecola, not Pecola's story.

In *Beloved*, the stories that must be told are clamorous and the risks posed by their telling huge. Like *The Bluest Eye*, *Beloved* also uses multiple points of view. The dominant voice is that of a third-person anonymous narrator that provides literate, eloquent translations of the otherwise unspoken reflections and memories of the novel's characters. The impression is of a presence at the same time separate from the characters and virtually elided with them. This narrative voice is significantly different from the anonymous, controlling, sanitizing narrator in *The Bluest Eye*. Unlike its predecessor, this voice comes out of the African American tradition of orality, placing *Beloved* in that class of novels that Henry Louis Gates characterizes as "speakerly texts"—those texts which, in creating a narrative suggestive of oral narration "privilege the representation of the speaking black voice" (Gates, 296). This narrator suggests a kind of privileged, trans-historical story teller—deeply sympathetic to its black characters, at times almost indistinguishable from them, capable of composing their memories into stories when they themselves are failed by denial or ignorance or loss of memory.

While this narrator is enabling, not silencing, the risks of oppressive narration are abundantly evident in the novel, particularly when narrative is practiced by whites. We see the dangers of narrative discourse in Schoolteacher's "book about us" (37), in the de-humanizing, repetitive naming of slaves (a form of narrative), in the newspaper report of Sethe's murder of Beloved. Even narrative practiced by blacks can be treacherous: Sethe's true report to Mrs. Garner of the atrocities of Schoolteacher's nephews results in her brutal whipping; Nelson Lord's report to Denver of her mother's attempt to kill all her children strikes Denver deaf for two years; and Sethe's own partial account to Paul D of the same event drives him temporarily out of her life.

It is no wonder, then, that many of the novel's black characters give up on narrative discourse—because it is treacherous, but also because it is inadequate, incapable of sounding certain deep realities and meanings. Sethe can talk *around* "the Misery" to Paul D (just as the term "the Misery" talks around the actual event), but she is well aware of the powerlessness of any narrative to capture the truth:

> Sethe knew that the circle she was making around the room, him [Paul D], the subject, would remain one. That she could never close in, pin it down for anybody who had to ask. If they didn't get it right off—she could never explain. Because the truth was simple, not a long-drawn-out record. (163)

It is difficult to know to what extent the novel's persistent and relatively direct indictment of narrative—at least as it is used by and against some of its characters—also interrogates its own dominant narrator. But there do appear to be suggestions that for all its beauty, lyricism, and distinctly non-hierarchical elements, the narrator's language does jeopardize the characters whose stories it tells, just as Beloved herself ultimately jeopardizes the lives of the people she revisits. Like Beloved, the narrative immobilizes its characters within a past that has been created for them and a language which, for the most part, is not their own. It is, as all narrative must be, highly selective and exclusionary in its rendering of experience, making powerful choices about what will and will not be told. Like the masters of an inequitable political system, like a ghost from the past that won't let go, this narrative deprives its characters of self-command and of will. An uncanny analogue of Beloved herself, it also deprives its characters of the promise of living in the present, condemning Sethe and Denver and Paul D to live within its manipulations until the final pages, when it makes the ceasing of narration a condition of the characters' accession to their present and future—"This is not a story to pass on" (275).

In *Jazz*, Morrison confronts the question of narrative power head-on, probing in particular the problematic relationship between the narrator and its (her? his?) characters. The use of an anonymous first-person omniscient narrator allows Morrison to stretch our credulous acceptance of the convention of the narrator so far that the mask finally slips, and we recognize that a narrator's authority is only a pretense, his or her omniscience a logical impossibility that we pretend to believe in for the sake of the story.

In the beginning pages of the novel, the narrator summarizes her characters' drama from a seemly distance, observing the proprieties of what a first-person narrator can and cannot know. But these proprieties don't last much beyond the twentieth page, as the narrator begins to claim increasingly impossible intimacies with her characters. She explains Violet's silence, reveals the pillow talk of Joe and Dorcas, relates all manner of events and reflections to which a first-person narrator could not be privy. If the narrator agreed to remain invisible, we would accept her omniscience. But as the following passage illustrates, the frequent juxtaposition of omniscient narrative and insistent self-reference draws attention to the impossibility of the narrator's knowledge.

So they [Joe Trace's female customers] looked right at him [Joe] and told him any way they could how ridiculous he was, and how delicious and how terrible. As if he didn't know.

Joe Trace counted on flirty laughing women to buy his wares, and he knew better than to take up with any of them. Not if he wanted to be able to lean over a pool table for a shot exposing his back to his customers' husbands. But that day in Alice Manfred's house, as he listened to and returned their banter, something in the wordplay took on weight.

I've wondered about it. What he thought then and later, and about what he said to her. He whispered something to Dorcas when she let him out the door, and nobody looked more pleased and surprised than he did. (71)

As the novel progresses, the strain of omniscience—or its pretense—begins to tell, and the narrator gradually concedes the impossibility of her apparent knowledge and control of the characters. She begins to let slip that her story is not a record of their histories but a record of her own imagination. She prefaces the long section recounting True Belle's return from Baltimore to Vesper County with the admission that this is imagination, not fact. She is "trying to figure out. . . [someone's] state of mind," but like Joe, she doesn't really know what happened, "although it's not hard to imagine what it must have been like" (137). By the end of the novel, she has dropped the pretense of control completely, admitting how limited and powerless her perspective on these characters has been. What power the narrative contains, she admits, resides not with the teller but with the characters whose lives she tries to shape: "when I invented stories about them. . . I was completely in their hands, managed without mercy. . . . I thought I'd hidden myself so well. . . and all the while they were watching me" (220).

The narrator (and the reader as well) has learned that the power of narrating is in fact a spurious power, that the narrator's authority is granted only in play by the reader. In the final pages of the novel, she is exposed— an Oz-like figure operating a cantankerous and unreliable machine dedicated to the production of artifice. Morrison seems to suggest that while narrators do reveal and disclose a considerable amount in their stories, it is they themselves who are revealed, their own agendas inevitably bleeding through their seeming manipulation of the characters. If there is a powerful force in narrative, it is the *story* itself, which gathers its own momentum and inevitability independent of the teller. Perhaps it is for this reason that the novel is so forgiving of the narrative impulse. Though the impulse to narrate may be universal (Violet asks "What's the world for if you can't make it up the way you want it"? [208]), in this novel, at least, it is not a harmful impulse.

The conclusions that Morrison seems to reach in *Jazz*, then, are quite different from those implied in *The Bluest Eye* and *Beloved*. In the earlier novels, the narrative act was suspect, with even the friendliest narrators (like Claudia in *The Bluest Eye* and the almost transparent narrator in *Beloved*) posing risks to the characters in their stories. But in *Jazz*, the risks of being narrated seem to have evaporated; if anyone is at risk here, it is the narrator herself, who ends up (unintentionally) revealing as much if not more about herself than about the characters whose stories she tries to tell. What can account for this detoxification of narrative that is effected in *Jazz* ? What is different in this novel that allows Morrison so completely to disarm this convention that has been represented as suspect in earlier novels? Are we seeing merely authorial sleight-of-hand at work here, or is Morrison representing in *Jazz* certain conditions under which the narrative act need not be harmful?

Certainly one important difference between *Jazz* and the two earlier novels is that the *Jazz* narrator is not allowed the luxury of self-effacement nor the virtual invisibility with which the other third-person narrators cloak themselves. From her opening "Ssth, I know that woman" (3), she draws attention to herself, voluntarily abrogating the privilege of self-concealment. Within traditional narrative taxonomy, she would qualify as a first-person narrator, despite the facts that she goes unnamed and that the particulars of her life and the exact nature of her relationship with Violet, Joe, and others is never specified. If we accept the designation of first-person narrator, we are left with a not particularly original demonstration of the pressures that subjectivity place on first-person narratives, of the inevitability of self-revelation through narrative. Understood in this way, the *Jazz* narrator is closely related to Claudia in *The Bluest Eye*, who, while intending to render, even liberate, Pecola through her narrative, ends up realizing herself far more successfully.

But the *Jazz* narrator does not exactly conform to the first-person narrator tradition: She is too shady, too vague, too openly illogical in her pretense to knowledge. Further, her exclusively narrating function completely precludes an interaction with other characters at the level of plot—an interaction which typifies traditional first-person narrators. Reading the narrative method of *Jazz* within the context of *The Bluest Eye* and *Beloved* suggests that in the later novel Morrison *is* demonstrating those conditions that must be satisfied in order for the narrative function to be harmless: narrators must admit the impossibility of their claims to know other characters; they must reveal that behind all narrative there is a narrating figure who is human and fallible and enormously pretentious. To disclose the nature of that powerful voice that works so (seemingly) powerfully behind the screen of anonymity and invisibility is to translate narrative from a language of mastery to one of exploration, from a force so concealed that it is answerable to no one to a medium held accountable through its presence and self-awareness. Narrators honest about their own complexities, granted "access to. . . their human instincts" are far more likely (to paraphrase Morrison's Nobel Lecture) to exercise deference to the uncapturability of the life they represent (15, 21). Such narratives, like the one in *Jazz*, are not merely harmless; they are, in their willingness to engage with their material, to institute a conversation with it, productive of new levels of awareness, just as, through her narrative, the *Jazz* narrator reaches new insights about herself and her relationship to others.

Just as the hierarchical narrative in *The Bluest Eye* can be read as a metonymy for oppression, narrative as it is conceived in *Jazz* offers a deconstructed, destabilized version of hierarchical systems (political, racist, sexist) that objectify and control the other. Thus, Morrison's method in *Jazz* is more than literary experiment; metonymically, it represents a utopian vision of human interaction in which "heads of state and power merchants" no longer "speak only to those who obey, or in order to force obedience." Instead, they use language, always "an act with consequences," to generate possibility, surge toward knowledge, "arc toward the place where meaning may lie" (15, 20).

*　　*　　*

Morrison's detoxification of the relationship between a narrator and her characters leads me to wonder whether, by analogy, we can reach the same conclusion about the relationship between the critic and the text that is his/her object? Critics, like conventional narrators, control, arrange, objectify their texts; the old and still-dominating critical idiom is one of mastery and reduction. While the analogy may not be a perfect one, it provides an opening for some very incomplete remarks on a problem that this essay cannot afford to ignore—that of white feminist critics working with texts by African American women writers.

This is a very hot and very complex issue that touches all literary critics at professional, political, and personal pressure points. It is a problem about which conversation is exceedingly difficult, but without conversation, impasse and resentment seem guaranteed. One helpful voice has been that of Ann duCille, who, in a recent issue of *Signs*, clarifies the complex response of an African American feminist critic to the appropriation by white feminists and African American men of texts by African American women. DuCille pulls no punches in this article, but she does not rule out a future in which black and white feminist women can work cooperatively and productively with these texts.

One particularly difficult facet of the problem is the political implications of whites writing about texts by African Americans. This issue is implicit throughout duCille's article, but with the help of *Jazz*, I'd like to take it on more directly. The idiom of literary criticism is one of certainty, control, and mastery. Traditionally, graduate schools have taught apprentice critics to eschew subjectivity and uncertainty; even today, under the influence of contemporary literary theories that approve of textual ambiguity and perversity, literary scholars are still in the business of controlling, organizing, and interpreting texts. There remains a powerful amount of certainty in our acknowledgment of uncertainty.

Our training carries risks: it instills in us a false sense of our own power and of the docility of the texts we claim to master. Our critical codes can come uncomfortably close to Morrison's own characterization of "dead language," language that in its arrogance seeks to pin down, conclude, capture. Can we infer from Morrison's earlier novels and from her remarks in her Nobel Lecture that *any* writing that claims objectivity, certainty, and invisibility for its practitioners is dangerous for the same reasons that anonymous, pretentious, conventional narrating can be dangerous? That criticism so practiced objectifies and immobilizes literary texts when it would be far more valuable to animate them? The traditional critical method may risk only the venial offense of reductiveness when applied to the canonical writers, but when we impose it on writers from marginalized, oppressed cultures, I fear the wrong becomes more profound, that the imposition of this traditional critical idiom upon texts by African American writers brings white critics uncomfortably close to a reinscription of oppression.

The particularly uneasy relationship that can exist between white criticism and African American texts might represent an opportunity for a fundamental re-consideration of the function of criticism. Indeed, works like *Beloved* and *Jazz* insist upon such a re-consideration. These works draw powerful responses from readers of all races that should not necessarily be factored out of our criticism. They require us to stretch our critical practice beyond the conventional function of illuminating and explicaticating texts, of, as Henry Louis Gates puts it, elucidating "the complexities of figuration peculiar to our literary traditions" ("Criticism," 6), they ask us to use the critical act as well to record and ponder the intersection of text and reader. Such a practice would give the critic permission to be self-conscious about the ways her historical, cultural, and personal identities are involved in, implicated through, that intersection. In other words, perhaps we should recognize that a significant part of the knowledge gained through criticism, like that gained through narrating in *Jazz*, is understanding of ourselves, of the ways our personal and collective identities are mapped through our engagement with texts. If we pursue the analogy between the critical and the narrative acts, one conclusion inevitably reached is that criticism that acknowledges its relationship to the text it studies and its inevitable 'otherness' from that text (just as the *Jazz* narrator acknowledges the nature of her relationship to the lives of those she narrates) promises to be far more productive than criticism that hides behind what Morrison calls "the calcified language of the academy" (Nobel Lecture, 16).

One corner of this intersection of critic and text is the original impulse of white feminist critics to work with texts by black women writers. DuCille's explanation for our gravitation to these texts is comparatively— perhaps justifiably—cynical. We are "restless" with an "already well-mined white female literary tradition," or we write about these texts to wring dry middle-class consciences sodden with racist guilt. She argues that these motives tempt us to ignore that African American literary studies is a rigorous, rich, complicated field, that it is not just an "anybody-can-play pick-up game" (601, 603). On this last point it would be impossible to disagree, but surely there is something else motivating the gravitation of white critics to black women writers, something to be recorded and pondered and learned from. I am hopeful that the attraction issues from positive, potentially constructive motives (as well as, if not instead of the motives duCille cites), that the powerful feelings ignited by novels like *Beloved* do not necessarily demean or commodify the text but can serve as a starting point for building a bridge between cultures that doesn't have to be made from *anyone's* back, that is constructed instead of reading and writing and honesty and good intentions. All this, while acknowledging that the text is primary and powerful, that it will most enrich and be enriched by those who are equipped with the proper knowledge and tools, and equipped as well with the objective of animating rather than immobilizing.

These possibilities, it seems to me, should not be discounted until we can be more certain about them—one way or the other—and this certainty can only be reached by permitting this critical engagement to continue, by encouraging conversations between critics of all identities and texts issuing from all cultures, and by encouraging conversations between African American critics and white critics. *"Talking to you and hearing you answer—that's the kick"* (*Jazz*, 229).

WORKS CITED

Dittmar, Linda. "'Will the Circle Be Unbroken?' The Politics of Form in *The Bluest Eye*." *Novel* 23 (1990): 137–55.

duCille, Ann. "The Occult of True Black Womanhood: Critical Demeanor and Black Feminist Studies." *Signs: Journal of Women in Culture and Society* 19 (1994): 591–629.

Gates, Henry Louis, Jr. "Criticism in the Jungle." *Black Literature and Literary Theory*. Edited by Henry Louis Gates, Jr. New York: Methuen, 1984, 1–24.

LeGuin, Ursula. "The Mother Tongue." *Bryn Mawr Alumnae Bulletin* (Summer 1986): 3–4.

Morrison, Toni. *Beloved*. New York: Knopf, 1987.

———. *The Bluest Eye*. New York: Washington Square Press, 1970.

———. *Jazz*. New York: Knopf, 1993.

———. *The Nobel Lecture in Literature*. New York: Knopf, 1994.

Rushdy, Ashraf H.A. "Daughters Signifyin(g) History: The Example of Toni Morrison's *Beloved*." *American Literature* 64 (1992): 567–97.

Smith, Valerie. *Self-Discovery and Authority in African-American Narrative*. Cambridge, Mass: Harvard University Press, 1987.

Contributors

Deborah H. Barnes is an Assistant Professor of English at Gettysburg College, where she teaches American, African American, and women's literatures. Currently she is working on two books, one a scholarly edition of Arthur P. Davis' collected editorial columns "With a Grain of Salt," the other a socio-historical examination of African American journalistic writings from the 1930s to the 1950s.

Susan R. Bowers is an Associate Professor of English and Director of Women's Studies at Susquehanna University, where she has taught for 11 years. She has taught also at the College of St. Catherine and Gustavus Adolphus College. Dr. Bowers holds a Ph.D. from the University of Oregon. She has published articles on Morrison, Theodore Roethke, and the grotesque in women's art and literature and co-edited three books on women, the arts, and society. She presently is working on a book on contemporary American women's love poetry.

David Cowart directs Graduate Studies in English at the University of South Carolina. He is the author of *Literary Symbiosis: The Reconfigured Text in Twentieth-Century Writing* (1993) and *History and the Contemporary Novel* (1989) as well as other books and articles. He is working on a book on Don DeLillo.

Diane Gillespie is a Professor in the Goodrich Scholarship Program at the University of Nebraska, Omaha. Professor Gillespie teaches in the social science sequence there as well as a qualitative research class in the graduate program at the Teachers College at the University of Nebraska, Lincoln. She was named Nebraska CASE Professor of the Year in 1992, the same year she published a book on cognition and contextualism focusing on narrative, the title of which is *The Mind's We: Contextualism in Cognitive Psychology* (Southern Illinois Press, 1992).

Ed Guerrero is the author of *Framing Blackness: The African American Image in Film*. He teaches film and literature at the University of Delaware.

Missy Dehn Kubitschek is a Professor of English, Afro-American Studies and Women's Studies at IUPUI (Indiana University Purdue University at Indianapolis). She has written *Claiming the Heritage* about the relationship of history and female identity in twentieth-century African American women's novels. Her other work has explored constructions of history in the fiction of August Wilson, David Bradley, and Gloria Naylor.

David W. Lawrence earned his Ph.D. in English from the University of Pennsylvania (1993). His dissertation, *Figuring the Flesh: The Intimate Horrors of Authority*, examined volatile confrontations of authority and the corporeal body in the fiction of Toni Morrison, Thomas Pynchon, Djuna Barnes, and William Faulkner. Currently he is Visiting Assistant Professor in Education at Brown University teaching courses in and researching curricular and pedagogical responses to multicultural classrooms, with particular attention to the teaching of English.

Lauren Lepow received her Ph.D. from the University of Connecticut in 1980. She has taught at the University of Missouri-St. Louis and is now a Senior Manuscript Editor at Princeton University Press.

Barbara Williams Lewis, Assistant Professor of English at the University of Texas, Austin, completed her Ph.D. at the University of Southern California with specialties in English, Women's Studies, African American Studies or African American Literature and Cultures. Her dissertation, *Prodigal Daughters: Female Heroes, Fugitivity and "Wild" Women*, focused on Morrison, Ann Petry, and Zora Neale Hurston. She is at work on a collection of critical essays on Morrison's *Jazz* and has an autobiographical novel in progress.

David L. Middleton, is Professor of English at Trinity University, San Antonio, Texas. He teaches principally Renaissance drama but has published on Flannery O'Connor, Joseph Heller, and Carlos Fuentes, as well as on Shakespeare. He has an earlier book on Toni Morrison, *An Annotated Bibliography* (1987) and an oral history, *The Newton Boys, Portrait of an Outlaw Gang* (1994).

Ann-Janine Morey taught Religious Studies for ten years before transferring her tenure to the Department of English at Southern Illinois University at Carbondale (SIUC), where she is a Professor teaching Religion and Literature and Women's Fiction, and the Director of the University Core Curriculum. The author of two books, *Apples and Ashes: Culture, Metaphor and Morality in the American Dream* (Scholars Press, 1982) and *Religion and Sexuality in American Literature* (Cambridge UP, 1992), she is currently preparing a book about her experience as a juror for a child murder trial.

Sandra Pouchet Paquet is Associate Professor of English at the University of Miami. The author of *The Novels of George Lamming* as well as numerous articles on African American literature and Caribbean literature, Professor Paquet teaches in those areas and is the Director of the Caribbean Writers Summer Institute. Her book on Caribbean autobiography is forthcoming.

Timothy B. Powell is Assistant Professor of English at the University of Georgia. He is currently editing a collection of essays dealing with the multicultural understanding of "American" identity for Rutgers University Press. In addition, he is working on a book-length manuscript which affords a multicultural interpretation of the American Renaissance.

Ashraf H.A. Rushdy is an Associate Professor of English and African American Studies at Wesleyan University. He has published articles on African American literature and culture, literary theory, and Renaissance literature, as well as studies of the works of John Milton, Jonathan Swift, Miguel Cervantes, E.B. White, Toni Morrison, John Edgar Wideman, Barbara Chase-Riboud, Charles Johnson, Octavia Butler, Sherley-Anne Williams, Ishmael Reed, and William Styron. He is the author of *The Empty Garden: The Subject of Late Milton* (1992) and is currently working on a book-length study of African American modes of representation in contemporary narratives of slavery.

Lynne Tirrell, Associate Professor of Philosophy at the University of Massachusetts, Boston, earned her doctorate in Philosophy from the University of Pittsburgh in 1986 and was formerly Associate Professor of Philosophy at the University of North Carolina at Chapel Hill. Her articles include essays on the theory of metaphor, the power politics of language, Nietzsche, Simone de Beauvior, and feminist theory. She is currently writing a book on the discursive practices and power associated with derogatory terms.

Gay Wilentz, Associate Professor of English at East Carolina University, a constituent institution of the University of North Carolina, teaches and publishes on African, African American, and Caribbean literatures, ethnic studies, and women's studies. She has published in *College English*, *African American Review*, *Research in African Literatures*, *Twentieth Century Literature*, and *MELUS*. Her book *Binding Cultures: Black Women Writers in Africa and the Diaspora* examines women's roles in the transmission of culture on both sides of the Atlantic. Presently she is working on a book exploring the relationship of ethnicity and alternative healing in cross-cultural women's writings.

Credits

Deborah Barnes, "Movin' on Up: The Madness of Migration in Toni Morrison's *Jazz*," used by permission of the author.

Susan Bowers, "Beloved and The New Apocalypse," *Journal of Ethnic Studies*, 18 (Spring 1990): 59–77. Reprinted by permission of the *Journal of Ethnic Studies*.

David Cowart, "Faulkner and Joyce in Morrison's *Song of Solomon*," *American Literature*, 62 (March 1990): 87–100. Reprinted by permission of *American Literature*.

Diane Gillespie and Missy Dehn Kubitschek, "Who Cares? Women-Centered Psychology in *Sula*," *BALF*, 24 (Spring 1990): 21–48. Used by permission of the authors.

Ed Guerrero, "Tracking 'The Look' in the Novels of Toni Morrison," *BALF*, 24 (Winter 1990): 761–73. Used by permission of the author.

David Lawrence, "Fleshly Ghosts and Ghostly Flesh: The Word and The Body in *Beloved*," *Studies in American Fiction*, 19 (Autumn 1991): 189–201. Reprinted by permission of *Studies in American Fiction*.

Lauren Lepow, "Paradise Lost and Found: Dualism and Edenic Myth in Toni Morrison's *Tar Baby*," *Contemporary Literature*, 23 (1987): 363–77. Reprinted by permission of The University of Wisconsin Press.

Barbara Williams Lewis, "The Functions of Jazz in Toni Morrison's *Jazz*," used by permission of the author.

Katherine J. Mayberry, "The Problem of Narrative in Toni Morrison's *Jazz*," used by permission of the author.

Ann-Janine Morey, "Margaret Atwood and Toni Morrison, Reflections on Postmodernism and the Study of Religion and Literature," *Journal of the American Academy of Religion*, 60/3 (1992): 493–513. Reprinted by permission of the *Journal of the American Academy of Religion*.

Sandra Pouchet Paquet, "The Ancestor as Foundation in *Their Eyes Were Watching God* and *Tar Baby*," *Callaloo*, 13 (1990): 499–515. Reprinted by permission of The Johns Hopkins University Press.

Timothy B. Powell, "Toni Morrison: The Struggle to Depict the Black Figure on the White Page," *BALF*, 24 (Winter 1990): 747–60. Used by permission of the author.

Ashraf H.A. Rushdy, " 'Rememory': Primal Scenes and Constructions in Toni Morrison's Novels," *Contemporary Literature*, 31 (1990): 300–23. Reprinted by permission of The University of Wisconsin Press.

Index